```
966.903 Oha
Ohadike.
The Ekumeku movement.
```

The Lorette Wilmot Library
Nazareth College of Rochester

WITHDRAWN

The Ekumeku Movement

THE EKUMEKU MOVEMENT

Western Igbo Resistance to the British Conquest of Nigeria, 1883-1914

Don C. Ohadike

Ohio University Press
Athens

© Copyright 1991 by Don C. Ohadike
Printed in the United States of America
All rights reserved

Ohio University Press books are printed on acid-free paper ∞

Library of Congress Cataloguing-in-Publication Data

Ohadike, Don C.
  The Ekumeku movement : Western Igbo resistance to the British conquest of Nigeria, 1883-1914/ Don C. Ohadike.
    p.   ca.
  Includes bibliographical references and index.
  ISBN 0-8214-0985-9   ISBN 0-8214-0992-1 (pbk)
  1. Nigeria—History—1851-1899. 2. Nigeria—History—1900-1960. 3. Nigeria—Relations—Great Britain. 4. Great Britain—Relations—Nigeria. 5. Igbo (African people)—Politics and government.
I. Title.
DT515.7.O36   1991
966.9'03—dc20   90-23998
                                                                                     CIP

Dedication

To the people of ANIOMA for their struggle for self-determination;
And to BUCHI EMECHETA for her contributions to ANIOMA STUDIES.

TABLE OF CONTENTS

List of Maps ix

Acknowledgments xi

Introduction. The Unfinished Story of
African Resistance Movements 1

Chapter 1. Chiefs, Slaves, and Socioeconomic
Transformations in Nineteenth-Century
Western Igboland 21

Chapter 2. British Gunboat Diplomacy and
the Conquest of Aboh: The Remote Causes
of the Ekumeku War 45

Chapter 3. Missionaries, Traders, and
the Conquest of Asaba: The Immediate
Causes of the Ekumeku War 61

Chapter 4. The Rise of the Ekumeku 81

Chapter 5. The Return of the Ekumeku, 1902-1903 97

Chpater 6. The Ekumeku War, 1904-1905 113

Chapter 7. The Last of the Ekumeku 129

Chapter 8. The Ika and Ukwuani
Resistance Movements 147

Conclusion 167

Appendix 1 175

Appendix 2 183

Appendix 3 187

Abbreviations 190

Bibliography 191

Index 201

LIST OF MAPS

Map 1. Southeastern Nigeria showing the
Igbo Culture area xii

Map 2. Western Igboland 20

Map 3. Markets of Western Igboland and the
Lower Niger 32

Map 4. Asaba Hinterland showing centers of
Ekumeku Activities 80

ACKNOWLEDGMENTS

I wish to thank Elizabeth Isichie for a long period of association and encouragement, first as my teacher, and then as a professional colleague. Without her I might never have written this book. I also wish to thank Suzanne Miers and Richard Roberts for making possible my trip to the United States, and for their financial and moral support when I was writing the final drafts of this book. My year as a visiting Associate Professor at the Department of History of Stanford University in California was a major turning point in my academic career. I must therefore thank James J. Sheehan, chair of History Department, for an additional grant which enabled me to do research at the Hoover Institute of Stanford during the summer months of 1988.

My most sincere gratitude goes to Ivor Wilks and Richard Roberts who, despite their own tight schedules, willingly read an earlier draft of my manuscript and offered many valuable suggestions.

I wish to thank Hans Panofsky, the Curator of the Africana Library of Northwestern University, for his assistance and encouragement. I am grateful to John Hunwick, the Interim Director of the Program of African Studies, who appointed me a visiting scholar at Northwestern University in October 1988. I owe much gratitude to Dan Britz, Patricia Ukoli, William Pardue, Angelia Johnson and the other librarians and support staff at Northwestern without whose assistance I might not have been able to polish up the final draft of the manuscript. In particular, I wish to thank Patricia for bearing the additional burden of typing the first draft of the manuscript on an old manual typewriter.

I wish to acknowledge the support and encouragement I got from Robert L. Harris, Jr., the Director of Africana Studies and Research Center of Cornell University. He provided me with my first regular employment in the United States and gave me other incentives to intellectual and material advancements. I wish to thank Sheila Towner of the same Department for the endless patient hours she spent typing the final draft. My gratitude equally goes to all my colleagues in the department for their support

DON C. OHADIKE
Africana Studies and Research Center
Cornell University
September, 1990
Ithaca, N.Y.

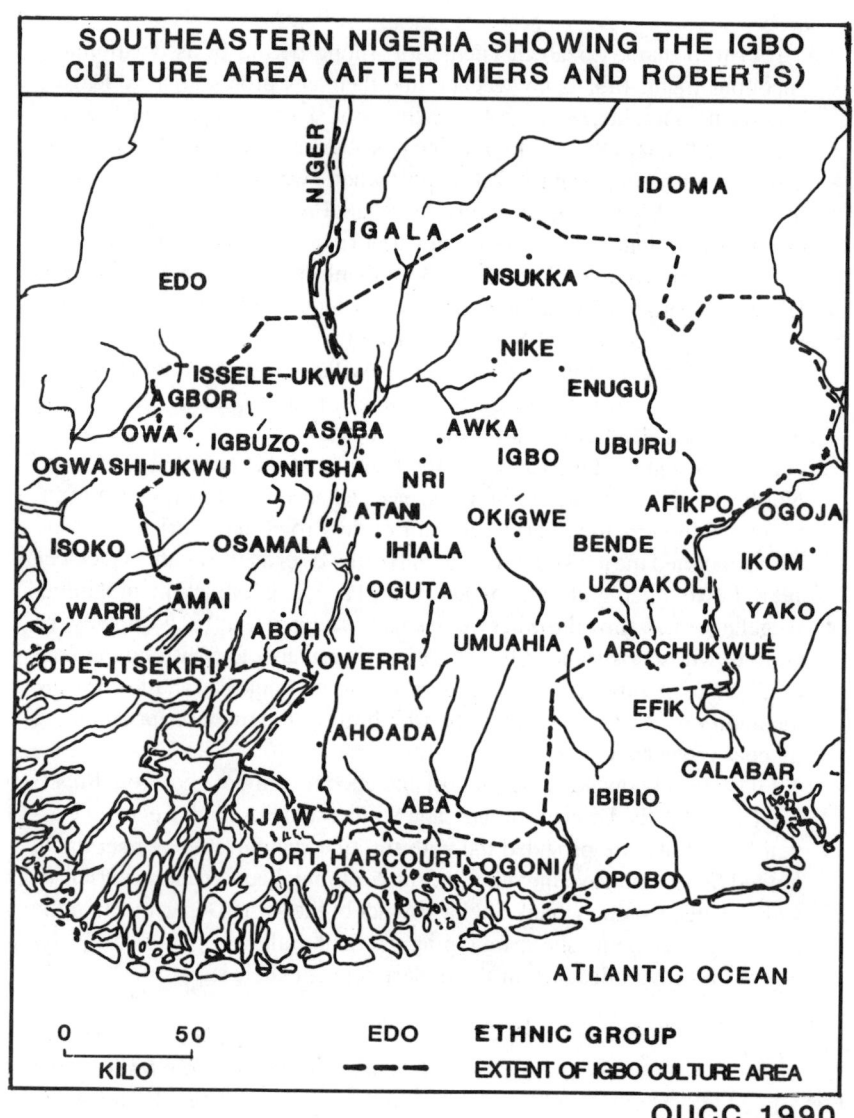

INTRODUCTION

The Unfinished Story of African Resistance Movements

THE BRITISH GOVERNMENT conquered and colonized Nigeria after a series of military operations that began with the annexation of Lagos in 1851. Until gold and diamonds were discovered in large quantities in South Africa in the 1880s and 1890s, the British regarded southern Nigeria as the most valuable part of Africa in the nineteenth century. It was the major source of palm oil and palm kernels, and the territories further inland held out promise for trade in other raw materials and British products. The Niger River was regarded as a very important gateway to the West African interior. By the last quarter of the century British policy makers could not resist the temptation of acquiring such a valuable territory by diplomacy, if possible, or by conquest, if necessary. But this imperialist design was resisted by the various ethnic groups of Nigeria, the most determined being those organized by the Igbo people.

The Igbo (sometimes called Ibo) were one of the most numerous ethnic groups in Africa. They lived entirely in the forest belt of southeastern Nigeria, an area with one of the highest rural population densities in Black Africa. The Niger River, the most important trade route in precolonial West Africa, ran through Igboland, dividing it into two unequal parts. The vast majority of the Igbo people lived on the eastern side of the river and were sometimes referred to as Eastern Igbo to distinguish them from the Western Igbo, who lived on the right bank (see map 1).

The Igbo organized themselves in clans, and because they had no centralized institutions of government, the British had to conquer each town and village separately. This explains the countless wars of conquest or "pacification" that the British had to fight in Igboland during the period 1860 to 1914. The most documented were the wars against the Aro of Eastern Igboland and the Aniocha of Western Igboland. This book is not concerned with all the Igbo wars of resistance but with those of the Western Igbo people, which involves three resistance movements: the Ekumeku, organized by the people of Aniocha; the Owa, organized by the Ika people; and the Kwale, organized by the Ukwuani. The Aniocha, Ika, and Ukwuani were the three major cultural groups of Western Igboland; each organized a separate resistance movement, but our concern here is mainly with the people of Aniocha and their resistance.

A number of strategic and commercial factors made it almost inevitable that the British would clash with the people of Western Igboland as soon as they began to trade on the lower Niger. As early as the 1850s the British government had been sending gunboats and British-trained troops into the lower Niger as part of an imperialist design that the chiefs and the people resisted. The outcome was a series of bitter encounters that lasted for over fifty years. Like other African communities that fought Europeans with inferior weapons (mainly rifles, dane guns, flintlocks, cutlasses, spears, and bows and arrows), the people of Western Igboland were defeated and compelled to accept a most degrading position in the newly established colonial estate. Although they were defeated, their descendants still recall with pride that their forebears were brave warriors who resisted British imperialism longer and more stubbornly than most other Nigerian communities. The most famous of these confrontations have come to be known as the Ekumeku war, or the war of the Silent Ones, as the British sometimes called it.

The Western Igbo were not alone in their desire to rid themselves of foreign rule. Virtually every African society resisted European colonialism, confirming that Africans hated foreign domination. For various reasons, however, certain resistance movements have been of special interest to African nationalists, historians, and others. Among them were the uprising of Samori Turé against the French in the Western Sudan, the Maji Maji against the Germans in Tanzania, the Mau Mau against the British in Kenya, the Shona/Ndebele against the British in Rhodesia (Zimbabwe), and the Ekumeku in Southern Nigeria.

The causes and complexities of these resistance movements raise three main questions. First, were there any connections between the "primary resistance" movements and modern mass nationalism in Africa? Second, considering the inferior weapons available to Africans and, taking into account the level of political fragmentation of the continent at that time, was military confrontation a rational answer to European expansion? Third, why did some African societies put up stronger resistance than others?

There are strong indications that there were connections between the primary resistance movements and modern mass nationalism in Africa as the works of Terence O. Ranger confirm.[1] In fact, some modern African nationalists have traced their own struggles against European imperialism to the primary resistance movements of the early colonial period. For example, Julius Nyerere of Tanzania reassured the members of the United Nations General Assembly in 1956 that the Tanzanian mass-nationalist agitations of the 1940s and 1950s were fundamentally a continuation of the uprisings of the earlier generations, which had started when the indigenous Africans refused to recognize the white man's claim "to govern and civilize the black." They rose in "great rebellion," Nyerere added, "not through fear of a terrorist movement or a superstitious oath, but in response to a natural call, a call of the spirit, ringing in the hearts of all men, and of all times, educated or uneducated, to rebel against foreign domination."[2]

On the other hand, Robert I. Rotberg has warned that any attempt to establish such connections is "seldom helpful."[3] Indeed, if one wishes to establish some connections between the primary and secondary protests, one might be tempted to ask if the current political and religious upheavals in parts of Africa are not a continuation of the early and later protests against colonial rule. For if one must resist foreign domination, one must equally resist ethnic or religious domination. In Nigeria, for example, British rule enabled some ethnic groups and the adherents of certain religions to continue to enjoy political hegemony, a circumstance that has sparked numerous protests since independence.

Turning to the second question, most scholars agree that no African society, past or present, would be willing to allow real power to slip from its hands into those of foreigners without a struggle. But a few like Roland Oliver and John D. Fage argue that since Europeans were better armed, and since there was no unity among the African ruling elite, "nothing was to be gained by resistance, and much by negotiation."[4] Norman Leys, who shares this view, describes the hopelessness of African resistance in a dramatic manner. Making reference to some Kenyan communities, he sees

> naked spearmen fall in swathes before machine-guns, without inflicting a single casualty in return. Meanwhile the troops burn all the huts and collect all the live-stock within reach. Resistance once at an end, the leaders of the rebellion are surrendered for punishment.[5]

Roland Robinson resorts to a highly conceptual theory of collaboration to explain the futility of African resistance. He claims that Europeans could not have conquered and ruled their non-European empires without indigenous collaborators, and that what Europeans had to offer—trade, capital, technology, military or diplomatic aid—was so attractive that "if the ruling elite chose resistance, there was usually a counter-elite to opt for collaboration" since the indigenous elite did not always form "a united interest group."[6] Sometimes imperialists imported large numbers of colonists to act as the preferred collaborators in order to rely less on indigenous collaborators; such was the case in Algeria, Kenya, and Zimbabwe.[7] Robinson goes on to explain that at times European imperialists showed a preference for coercion as a substitute for collaboration, as illustrated by the military element in French imperialism. In short, collaboration resulted in the incorporation of non-European societies into the Western capitalist system inasmuch as their refusing to collaborate, by resisting, necessitated greater imperial intervention. European imperialism, therefore, was "as much and often more a function of Afro-Asian politics than of European politics and economics."[8]

What the foregoing argument suggests is that what looked to African societies like an open door was in fact closed, that their resistance was a senseless act, and that they were already doomed by the time they were confronted by European expansion. Their subjugation thus resulted from their inability to form a unified body of noncollaborators, a result of their military weakness. Robinson cites as support for his assertion the fact that Africans and Asians gained their independence only when European imperialists ran out of indigenous collaborators.

This thesis has been attacked by eminent scholars and the debate need not be continued here. However, it should be mentioned that the theory is attractive in the sense that it draws our attention to the role of certain indigenous people in the whole process of colonial conquest and rule. Sometimes described as modernizers, collaborators were willing partners in European imperialism. The most common among them were Christian missionaries and converts, the educated elite, emirs, abas, obis, warrant chiefs, and the African recruits of the colonial armed forces. Indigenous collaborators were never lacking in Africa. During the Atlantic slave-trade era they acted as slave-trading chiefs, merchants, and slave-raiders, and since the 1960s such collaborators, including the chief executives of multinational corporations, and some heads of puppet regimes in Africa, have acted as the agents of neo-colonialism.

Nonetheless, most scholars are convinced that African societies acted rationally when they decided to resist European rule. Terence Ranger has pointed out that not all resistances were doomed to total failure and crushing suppression. Some of them, he writes, "preserved liberties, wrung concession or preserved pride," and in these and other ways "made their own important contributions to the creation of the environment in which later politics developed."[9] A. B. Davidson has likewise reminded us that "resistance left its mark on the most important internal process of development of the African people; in the course of resistance tendencies to change developed more quickly" and some amount of wider political consciousness was forged at this time.[10]

Perhaps no other writer has driven the message home more than Frantz Fanon. In his *Wretched of the Earth* Fanon admonishes all oppressed people of the Third World to shake off foreign domination by force since colonial domination is established by violence and is perpetuated by force. Fanon contends that since colonialism strips the colonized of his culture and his manhood, it is only the use of violence that frees him "from his inferiority complex, his despair and inaction; it makes him fearless and restores his self-respect."[11] In Fanon's view, violence is a means of achieving freedom, a cleansing and unifying force, binding the oppressed together as a whole against the colonizer's violence.[12] Thus, what Roland Robinson sees as a closed door is to Frantz Fanon an open one; what is a senseless act of resistance to Norman Leys is to Fanon a means of regaining self-respect, freedom and unity; and while Oliver and Fage imagine that much could be gained by negotiation, Fanon remains convinced that "the colonialist understands nothing but force," that "the colonial regime owes its legitimacy to force," and that "between oppressors and oppressed everything can be solved by force."[13]

The third question, why some African resistances were stronger than the others, should be considered in light of the fact that one cannot equate the size of a resisting society with the strength of its resistance. Instead, the case in Africa was that certain small-scale societies offered stiff resistance while some large kingdoms and empires did not.

The Sokoto Caliphate and the Benin kingdom, for example, are prime examples of large African formations that offered very little resistance. By the time the British imperialists moved into northern Nigeria to incorporate it into the British empire, Sokoto was by far the largest and, perhaps, the most respected of all the empires of the grassland region of West Africa.[14] But the British overran it almost without a fight. In 1900 Frederick Lugard hoisted the British flag in Lokoja and declared Northern Nigeria a British protectorate. This declaration angered the rulers of Sokoto but they did not mobilize the masses against the intruders. Between 1901 and 1902 the British conquered Kontagora, Bauchi, Yola, and the other Muslim emirates. These were vassals of Sokoto, but the Caliph raised no troops to defend them. Early in 1903, Lugard entered Kano and put it under British control. Two months later Sokoto itself was attacked and subdued.[15] The Caliph's soldiers began to desert within thirty minutes of the commencement of battle, and the Caliph himself, accompanied by the majority of his soldiers, turned his back to the battlefield and fled toward the east.[16] The British installed a successor, Atahiru II, as the new Caliph, and went after Atahiru I. Three months later at Burmi the fleeing Atahiru I and his men put up a substantial resistance but were defeated during a battle that lasted from eleven in the morning until six in the evening; Atahiru I himself was killed. This seven-hour battle has been described as "the longest battle in the British conquest of the Sokoto Caliphate."[17]

The British conquest of Benin illustrates a situation in which a paramount ruler, who had lost real authority in his capital, tried to retain the independence of his kingdom by avoiding a military confrontation with the British, but was led into war by the reckless activities of ambitious subordinate chiefs. The last independent Oba of Benin, Ovonramwen, fully recognized the military strength of the British and in the 1890s was worried by his own encirclement. He managed, however, to postpone the inevitable until some Benin chiefs organized the killing of a number of British officials.[18] "When the King heard this," an eyewitness reported, "he got vexed and made a big palaver with all the chiefs and told them he was going to leave the city so that if the whitemen bring another war they could fight for themselves; but they begged him so much that he did not go anywhere. The people who killed the whitemen were turned back to the bush to fight the war that the whitemen would bring."[19]

Early in February 1897, some 1,500 British fighting men marched on Benin and after a battle that lasted two weeks, entered the city. The Oba had remained in his palace during this period until a rocket landed in one of the courtyards. He at once left the city, accompanied by his chiefs, his relatives, and a large proportion of the population, thereby bringing to an end one of the most powerful kingdoms of the forest belt of West Africa. Several months later the Oba reentered Benin, not to fight, but to submit himself to British justice. He was deposed, tried, and exiled to Calabar.[20]

Unlike the rulers of Sokoto and Benin, some small-scale societies of diverse ethnicity in Tanzania, Kenya, Zimbabwe, the Jos Plateau of Nigeria, and elsewhere put up very strong resistance to European political domination and economic exploitation. In Tanzania the Hehe fought the Germans from 1891 until 1898.[21] Then in 1905 the Maji Maji war broke out when the populations of southeastern Tanzania could no longer tolerate oppressive German exploitation. The Maji Maji, according to Arnold J. Temu, opposed not only the Europeans and their oppressive colonial administrative pressure, but also economic imperialism. Thus, even though the uprising was on the surface a reaction to German imperialism, it was also directed against traders who had established themselves in southeastern Tanzania, exploiting the peasants and laborers. The major targets of the attack were Indian, Swahili, and Arab traders.[22] Like the Ekumeku, the Maji Maji played a crucial role in unifying the people against a common enemy, a unity clearly lacking in the Sokoto and Benin resistances.

The reasons behind the relative struggle — or lack of it — of various uprisings against European rule are complex. Some scholars have drawn our attention to the influence of religion. Terence Ranger and John Iliffe have demonstrated that charismatic religious leaderships helped to achieve far-flung coalitions against Europeans.[23] In the case of the Maji Maji the priests were the charismatic leaders who succeeded in imposing new regulations and prohibitions upon their followers. To accept membership in the movement, writes Ranger, was to agree to enter a new society under new laws and loyalties; the reward included immunity from bullets and resurrection after death to enter a golden age.[24] Maji was a sacred water which, once taken, provided the initiate with a new life, freeing him from "existing beliefs and superstitions." The distributors of the maji were the leaders of the movement. Temu writes that news of this magic water began to spread in 1904 and people flocked to the home of the prophetic leader, Kinjikitile Ngwale, to taste of it. Many who drank the water could not resist the urge to fight and in 1905 they rose with spears and shields, determined to drive the Germans (and the Arabs, Indians, and Swahili) out of Tanzania.[25]

East and Central Africa witnessed many risings led by prophets or medicine men, and common in all was these leaders' success in arousing mass enthusiasm and their appeal to a wider unity than had been achieved in the past. The resisters, Ranger writes, were not afraid to challenge the authority of secular leaders.[26] Such widespread risings, according to Iliffe, often spread to areas lying beyond the center of the initial outbreak to produce two negative results. First, the established authorities in the new areas felt threatened, and second, the further the outbreak spread, the sooner it lost its revolutionary appeal.[27]

Even among the large states religion played a role in the resistance, though sometimes in a negative way. In the Sokoto Caliphate, the indigenous population decided that rather than fight, they would undertake the *hijra* — emigration away from the infidels. The decision was religion-based; Islam forbade Muslims to submit to unbelievers, and

INTRODUCTION

the leaders had to choose between resistance or emigration. In 1903 they chose *hijra*. In the case of Benin, when the Oba realized that the invasion of his capital was inevitable, he resorted to human sacrifice as a means of repelling the British away from his kingdom. When the British force occupied the city, Ryder explains, few living beings were found; instead, "the remains of human sacrifice abounded—a tragic testimony to the means by which the desperate monarch had sought to avert the destruction of his kingdom."[28]

There is nothing in the traditions or written records to suggest that the Ekumeku movement was inspired by prophets or medicine men. We are told, however, that each Ekumeku warrior was armed with charms which he believed would protect him from bullets and bad luck.[29] Sometimes medicine men prepared certain charms to protect the various towns, while others buried at selected places strong charms which, it was believed, would instantly kill British soldiers when they stepped on them.[30] Magic was an integral part of Igbo warfare and, as Adiele E. Afigbo has pointed out, the Igbo warriors of the first two decades of this century relied on magic as they defended their communities against better-armed British forces.[31] Nonetheless, nowhere in Igboland did prophets or medicine men inspire the spirit of resistance or rebellion against the British.

As this brief survey of some African resistance movements shows, among African societies that rejected European domination, the strength of each group's resistance depended, not on its size, but on the extent to which the ruling elite cooperated among themselves (e.g., by pooling their military resources), the degree to which the society was inspired by some religious beliefs or charismatic figures, and the type of military strategy the society adopted.

The Maji Maji, the Mau Mau, and the Ekumeku adopted guerrilla tactics and offered strong resistance. Sokoto, Nupe, and Ilorin confronted the British in the open fields and were instantly defeated with machine guns and other precision weapons. Samori Turé adopted hit-and-run tactics and was able to keep the French forces busy in the battlefields for over ten years. Yves Person attributes Samori Turé's success to his tactical abilities and charismatic nature, as well as his ability to achieve a measure of technological parity with the imperialists.[32] Robert Rotberg states that African resistance varied "according to the nature of the alien thrust, the indigenous perception of the potency of that thrust, the structure of the society being defended, the political abilities of the leaders, and each side's differential access to modern instruments of combat.[33] These views are consistent with those of Gerald J. Bender, who notes that the strength of insurgencies differs because their circumstances are never the same. He insists that

> the nature and attraction of the cause, the manpower and money available to both sides, the motivation to fight, the type of terrain, the ethnic differences, the levels of technology, the availability to insurgents of contiguous border sanctuaries, the degree of legitimacy of the government, and the grievances and desires of the civilian population are only some of the factors which vary among as well as within insurgency situations.[34]

Almost an infinite number of resistance and protest movements were organized against European rule throughout Africa. It is therefore almost impossible to work out an accurate pattern of African resistance. Initially some societies resisted while others refused to rise. But after colonial rule had been established, some societies decided to rebel (rebellion being defined by Rotberg as "the militant expression of discontent at this later stage")[35] while some that resisted now turned collaborators. The Ngoni of Tanzania, for example, had developed strong military traditions during the precolonial period, but refused to resist the Germans at the onset of colonial conquest, only to rebel later when they became fully aware of the disruptiveness of European rule.[36] There were also some societies that resisted and were crushed, only to rebel again and again during the colonial period. Such was the nature of resistance movements among the various ethnic groups in the Plateau State of Nigeria.[37] Afigbo writes that because of the fragmented nature of some societies like the Igbo, the British had to fight every territory separately, which "took more time and more energy and was very irritating."[38]

Mention should be made of the peculiar character of resistance movements in Mozambique and Angola, where opposition to European domination lasted for many centuries. To take the Mozambican case, for instance, the research of Allen and Barbara Isaacman shows that certain communities in the area developed a strong tradition of resistance to Portuguese overlordship from very early times and did not relent in their struggles until their land was finally liberated barely two decades ago.³⁹ It is therefore difficult to make the fine distinctions between primary and secondary resistances, or even between revolutions and liberation movements in Mozambique.

While the Western Igbo society was one that put up a strong resistance to British rule, this book is not necessarily concerned with the uprising's strength but rather with the way it fits into the general pattern of African resistance. Though it is important to consider how the ruling elite—the chiefs—raised a strong military force, what is more significant are the specific economic and political grievances that provoked and sustained the resistance, the brutality with which it was suppressed, and the crisis which British rule generated for this community. The eloquence of the humanitarians and the progressive imperialists notwithstanding, the story of British imperialism in Western Igboland confirms that the purpose of owning a colony was to transform it into a source of cheap raw materials and cheap labor and to develop it as a market for industrial products. Sometimes a colony was also used as a military base. To maintain its hold on a colony, the colonizing power had to crush all native resistance "with sufficient severity" in order to let the resisters realize that "the government means business."⁴⁰

As the various battles of the Ekumeku showed, the British fighting men used heavy armaments, such as shrapnel, maxim guns, and rockets, against rural farms who fought mostly with rifles, dane guns, cutlasses, and bows and arrows. These battles were often accompanied by the destruction of homes, farmlands, and storehouses. The Ekumeku uprisings were full-scale wars that colonial government officials disguised under the name of "patrols" or "wars of pacification."

But what was this "Ekumeku?" What was its origin? And how did it function? Ekumeku was the name of a military organization that the Aniocha community of Western Igboland founded during the last decade of the nineteenth century to resist the British military penetration of Western Igboland. It was also the military arm of a secret Igbo society known as *Otu Ochichi*, the ruling party. Both the Ekumeku and *Otu Ochichi* were led by the top or "red-cap" chiefs, *ndi eze*, with the second-class chiefs, *ndi nkpalo*, acting as subordinate officers. The warriors were mostly the untitled men and youths, *ikolobia*.

The formation of the Ekumeku movement symbolized a radical

departure from traditional Igbo military traditions. It was the first recorded instance when a large number of Igbo towns combined their military forces to battle a common enemy, and the first known occasion when the Igbo consciously agreed to fight a large-scale war. Before this period, most Igbo wars were fought between neighboring towns, and deliberate efforts were made to keep the number of casualties as low as possible. During such wars a few heads were taken as trophies, and captives were either sold into slavery or exchanged after protracted negotiations between the belligerents.

The Ekumeku was not, however, a military unit per se, with a unified command and a hierarchy of officers. Instead, it was an organization to which numerous independent Western Igbo communities belonged. In times of need, these communities were required to send warriors who would fight a particular battle and then return to their home towns after completing their assignments. Troops from each town were commanded by their own leaders and were forbidden to take instructions from other men.

The decision to keep the various detachments of the Ekumeku independent of the others was a reflection of the political structures of the Igbo people. They were organized in small republics and chiefdoms and never in history had any community succeeded in imposing itself on another. Thus, even though the Western Igbo people were determined to halt British penetration of their area, they were equally anxious to safeguard the fragmentary nature of their political institutions.

The actions of the Ekumeku were well conducted, however. Before each engagement, Ekumeku leaders from the various towns assembled at a secret place to make specific decisions about targets and strategies. They might decide that some European trading posts or churches in certain towns would be destroyed at a given time. At the appointed hour, all such structures would simultaneously be attacked. If the Ekumeku high command believed that a person regarded as a traitor should die, warriors from a different town would enter the target settlement, proceed silently to the home of the named traitor, and shoot him; the neighbors and relatives of the man just killed, realizing that this was the decision of the Ekumeku, would remain quiet. Father Strub, a Roman Catholic priest who lived in Western Igboland during this period, described such killings as barbarous.[41]

The Ekumeku did not always kill or destroy; sometimes they achieved their objective by threat. If the intention was to make a man give up a practice which the Ekumeku regarded as offensive they would visit him secretly and deliver the necessary message. In 1903, a chief of Akwukwu who regularly attended Christian services was visited and warned that if he failed to wash from his head the water which he was supposed to have received in baptism, he would be shot.[42]

How did the Ekumeku get its name? Known in its formative stages as *Otu Ochichi*, during the course of its life it came to be referred to as the Ekumeku. An Igbo chief whose father joined the movement at Ogwahi-Ukwu in the 1890s disclosed that the word "ekumeku" is a misnomer, an Anglicized version of the Igbo word *ekwunokwu*, which means, "Be silent" or "Don't say a word."[43] According to Chief Adigwe, the members of the society acted silently against their enemies, which explains the organization's nickname, *Otu Ekwunokwu* (the Association of the Silent Ones), rather than *Otu Ochichi* (the Ruling Party), which its founders preferred. Nonetheless, as time went on, the society was simply called *ekwunokwu*, which the British shortened to *ekumeku* because they could not pronounce the Igbo word.

Another explanation of the word's origin is that it was coined from the solidarity cries, *"Anyi ekwugoa,"* or *"Ife anyi kwu ekwu,"* meaning, "We have said so," or "We have agreed."[44] The implicit agreement was that the white inhabitants should be expelled from the land. Elizabeth Isichei, on the other hand, describes *ekumeku* as an archaic Igbo word with the sense of something breathing or dispersing. According to Isiche, it was the name of a secret society which existed independently in many towns of the Western Igbo interior and among the neighboring Afenmai.[45] This description of the society is similar to the one given by Father Strub. According to his reports, the word "ekumeku" comprises three syllables, *"Kou me Kou"* (this is written in French), which means "to be dispersed, to strike and to be dispersed again." Strub supported this definition by explaining that the Ekumeku was a society whose members lived at different places but united for the purpose of a particular action only to disperse again. He also recalled the definition given to him by another native resident. This was *"Kou,"* to echo all over, "me," fragmented action, *"Kou,"* performed at different places. Strub insisted that the two meanings were complementary, and that the prefix "e" gave to this word its nominal form.[46]

As the movement lost the name given it by its founders, its new name came to conjure up certain feelings and images. According to historian Phillip Igbafe, the society's name in its indigenous meaning was onomatopoeic, conveying the idea of a whirlwind or something fast, devastating, invisible and yet forcefully real. The term carries a connotation of reality shrouded in fantasy, which throws much light on the society's general nature, its organization, and activities.[47]

The exact origin of the movement is shrouded in as much secrecy as the genesis of its name. Some observers strongly believe that the Ekumeku was formed when the various town clubs came together and decided to form a military organization strong enough to repel the British invasion. These town clubs had been in existence before the British came to Nigeria, Igbafe says, emphasizing that the origin of the Ekumeku "lies deep in the people's past."[48] He explains that during the precolonial era most of the towns in the Asaba district had companies, clubs, or societies that were made up of the bold, brave, and sturdy men (*ikolobia*) who were the objects of local pride during the times of inter-town strife. Some of these men, states Igbafe, were renowned for their prowess and had become heroes of a sort. Some of the town clubs pursued specific objectives, like the Ogana society, organized solely to oppose a trader from Sierra Leone, Isaac Thomas Palmer, who was leading the officials of the British Royal Niger Company into the Asaba hinterland, suggesting that some of these clubs had their origins in the days of the Royal Niger Company (1886-99).[49] Although it was traditional for Western Igbo people, like their Eastern Igbo brothers and sisters, to organize their youths into wrestling clubs, dancing clubs, and vigilante groups, among others, the coming together of the various town clubs to form a unified military force was an innovation stimulated in response to British military imperialism.

The most famous of the precolonial town clubs that formed the nucleus of the Ekumeku movement were the Otu Ochichi of Igbuzo, the Odoziobodo and the Idimobodo of Onicha-Olona and Ezi, the Ogana and Onumba of Ogwashi-Ukwu, and the Akpala and Amuma of Ubulu-Ukwu. In addition to these, most of the uncommitted able-bodied age-groups in all the towns came under the banner of the Ekumeku.[50] A specific and perhaps the most important group that joined the movement was the restless young men who previously killed and looted for personal gains. Some of them were hunters, warriors, and social bandits who roamed the forests and sometimes kidnapped people whom they sold to strategically located buyers. These young men took advantage of inter-town disputes, regardless of whether they concerned their own towns, to loot and capture. The thought of falling into the hands of such men in the bush acted as a deterrent to any slave who might be contemplating escape. Such men were particularly numerous at Ogwashi-Ukwu, and in peacetime, they contented themselves with midnight stealing of goats from neighboring towns, which made them particularly infamous. These men formed the necessary links between the various Ekumeku clubs in the Western Igbo towns.[51]

While the origins and membership of the group may be uncertain, other aspects of it have been more clearly documented. It would appear that the Ekumeku were the first warriors in southern Nigeria to fight in silence. The fact that they came to be widely known as the Silent Ones confirms that they adopted silence as a military strategy. A British colonial administrator who encountered the Ekumeku wrote:

> They realized that blood-curdling yells are not a necessary accompaniment, but a waste of breath, and have neither the effect of making a gun shoot straight nor of making the white man turn tail. . . . This habit of fighting in silence (then unknown in Southern Nigeria) may have led to their being christened "The Silent Ones" but that they can talk nineteen to the dozen when they think talking will pay, I can vouch for.[52]

One British government official described the Ekumeku warriors as "splendid bush fighters," and another called them "an enemy who is never visible except when occasionally seen darting across a path and whose position can only be determined by the smoke from his gun hanging round the dense undergrowth." Father Strub described the society as "a secret-cum-guerrilla force."[53]

Perhaps the Ekumeku were among the first Nigerians to realize the importance of guerrilla tactics and silence when fighting a better-armed adversary. They acted silently, not only against the British, but also against their indigenous detractors; at various times, some Western Igbo people turned informants to the British or missionaries, revealing plans and identifying the Ekumeku leaders. In punishing those they regarded as traitors, the Ekumeku tried to conduct themselves in a manner that would prevent panic among the people.

At the time the Ekumeku was being formed, its major point of contention internally was the unity of its command. It took many years of negotiation to acquire the assent of all the leaders to cooperate in the group's activities. Finally, the chiefs agreed to give their unanimous support for the liberation of the district, provided it was not to the detriment of the autonomy of each town. Although from 1883 each of the towns had engaged in small-scale military operations against the British, it was in 1898 that they fought their first battle under the banner of the Ekumeku.

Once the decision had been made during the 1890s to launch the Ekumeku, Igbuzo was chosen as its first headquarters. The decision was based on three factors: Igbuzo's proximity to Asaba, the busiest center of European missionary and imperial activities in Western Igboland; the strong role of the chiefs of Igbuzo in the formation of the movement; and the fact that Igbuzo was the most militant Western Igbo town at the time.[54]

One fascinating aspect of the Ekumeku is its effectiveness. The discipline instilled in its members, the tenacity of its military wing, the speed with which its activities spread to the various towns, its logistics, its scientific methods of preparing for defense and attack, and its hit-and-run tactics were innovations that were not equalled anywhere else in Nigeria. The conflicting views about its origins notwithstanding, the movement was clearly an expression of the Western Igbo people's nationalism, the objective of which was to rid the area of all foreign influences. While the society's origins might lie in the people's past, its launching in the 1890s had the expulsion of the white populace as its supreme aspiration. As Father Strub noted, "When the chiefs became tired of seeing the white men settle down in their land . . . they decided to drive them away with the help of an army made up of all the societies of the Ekumeku.[55]

The story of the Ekumeku will be related here in three parts. The first will describe Western Igbo society and its transformations; the British incursion will be examined next; and, finally, the major military actions themselves will be described. It is important to mention at this point that the uprisings in the Kwale and Agbor districts of Western Igboland were equally strong and widespread but not connected to the Ekumeku movement, exemplifying the fact that the inability to achieve a wider coalition against the European military thrust was one of the weaknesses of African resistance movements. The Ekumeku war itself is an important event in the history of the Igbo people and if adequately studied, will increase our perceptions of small-scale societies, especially in regard to their military strength and kinship organization. It should be borne in mind, however, that the focus of this book is not necessarily on the military encounters themselves but on the disruptions, transformations, and crises generated by British conquest and rule.

NOTES TO INTRODUCTION

1. Terence O. Ranger, "Connections Between Primary Resistance Movements and Modern Mass Nationalism in East and Central Africa," parts 1 and 2, *Journal of African History,* 9, nos. 3 and 4 (1968): 437-53 and 631-64.

2. Julius Nyerere, from a speech delivered at the United Nations General Assembly in 1956. Quoted in *Records of the Maji Maji Rising,* ed. G. C. K. Gwassa and John Iliffe, part 1 (Nairobi, 1969), 29.

3. Robert I. Rotberg, "Introduction," *Protest and Power and Black Africa,* ed. Robert I. Rotberg and Ali A. Mazrui (Oxford, 1970), xvii.

4. Roland Oliver and John D. Fage, *A Short History of Africa* (Harmondsworth, U.K., 1962), 302.

5. Norman Leys, *Kenya,* 4th ed. (London, 1973), 342.

6. Roland Robinson, "Non-European Foundations of European Imperialism: Sketch for a Theory of Collaboration," in *Imperialism: The Robinson and Gallagher Controversy,* ed. William Roger Louis (London, 1976), 132-33.

7. Ibid., 133.

8. Ibid., 147.

9. Ranger, "Connections," 441.

10. A. B. Davidson, "African Resistance and Rebellion Against the Imposition of Colonial Rule," in *Emerging Themes in African History,* ed. T. O. Ranger (Dar es Salam, 1968), 178.

11. Frantz Fanon, *The Wretched of the Earth,* trans. Constance Farrington (New York, 1977), 94.

12. Ibid., 93.

13. Ibid, 84, 72.

14. See Murray Last, *The Sokoto Caliphate* (London, 1967).

15. Charles Orr, *The Making of Northern Nigeria,* 2d ed. (London, 1965), 82, 127.

16. Obaro Ikime, *The Fall of Nigeria: The British Conquest* (London, 1977), 207-8.
17. Ibid., 208.
18. For a new account of this event, see Robert Home, *City of Blood Revisited: A New Look at the Benin Expedition of 1897* (London, 1982).
19. As quoted in Alan F. Ryder, *Benin and the Europeans, 1485-1897* (London, 1969), 289.
20. Ibid., 290-96.
21. Arnold J. Temu, "Tanzanian Societies and Colonial Invasion, 1875-1907," in *Tanzania Under Colonial Rule*, ed. H. Y. Kaniki (London, 1979), 90-120.
22. Ibid., 117.
23. Ranger, "Connections," 448-50; Iliffe, "The Organization of the Maji-Maji Rebellion," *Journal of African History*, 8, no. 3 (1967): 495-512.
24. Ranger, "Connections," 450.
25. Temu, "Tanzanian Societies," 118.
26. Ranger, "Connections," 451-52.
27. Iliffe, "The Organization of the Maji-Maji," 512.
28. Ryder, *Benin and the Europeans*, 290.
29. Sylverus Onochie, interview on March 23, 1978, at Ubulu-Ukwu.
30. Odafe Ikenweaju, interview on December 26, 1974, at Akwukwu.
31. Adiele E. Afigbo, "Patterns of Igbo Resistance to British Conquest," *Tarikh* 4, no. 3 (1973): 20.
32. Yves Person, "Samori and Resistance to the French," in *Protest and Power*, ed. R. Rotberg and A. Mazrui, 111-12. See also A. S. Kanya-Forstner, *The Conquest of the Western Sudan: A Study in French Military Imperialism* (Cambridge, U.K., 1969), 98-270.
33. Rotberg, "Introduction," *Protest and Power*, xvii.
34. Gerald J. Bender, "The Limits of Counterinsurgency," *Comparative Politics* 4 (1972): 354.
35. Rotberg, "Introduction," *Protest and Power*, xvii.
36. Temu, "Tanzanian Societies," 111.
37. Elizabeth Isichei, "Colonialism Resisted," in *Studies in the History of the Plateau State, Nigeria*, ed. Isichei (London, 1972), 206-23.
38. Afigbo, "Patterns," 23.
39. Allen Isaacman in collaboration with Barbara Isaacman, *The Tradition of Resistance in Mozambique: The Zambesi Valley, 1850-1921* (Berkeley, 1976). See also Allen Isaacman and Barbara Isaacman, *Mozambique: From Colonialism to Revolution, 1950-1982* (Aldershot, Hampshire, U.K., 1983).
40. PRO, CO520/3/320/2519, Ralph Moor to Colonial Office, December 29, 1900.
41. SMA (Society of African Missions Archives, Rome), R. Strub, "Le Vicariat Apostolique de la Nigeria Occidentale depuis sa foundation jusqu'à nos jours (1929)," entry no. 15794, 18/80404, fol. 13.
42. PRO, CO520/24/20839, W. E. B. Coupland-Crawford, divisional

commissioner, Central Division, to the government of Southern Nigeria, June 13, 1904.

43. Chief Adigwe, interview on August 5, 1974, at Ogwashi-Ukwu.

44. Vincent A. Modi, interview on December 10, 1982, at Ubulu-Ukwu.

45. Elizabeth Isichei, *The Ibo People and the Europeans* (London, 1973), 139.

46. SMA, Strub, fol. 13.

47. Philip Igbafe, "Western Igbo Society and Its Resistance to British Rule: The Ekumeku Movement, 1898-1911," *Journal of African History* 12, no. 3 (1973):442.

48. What Igbafe does not point out, however, is just how ancient this military tradition was. By the precolonial period, does Igbafe mean the few years before the actual imposition of colonial rule in Southern Nigeria, or the period as far back as the days of the Benin wars of expansion into Western Igboland (as A. E. Afigbo is tempted to interpret Igbafe)? See Afigbo, "Patterns," 18-19.

49. Igbafe, 443.

50. Ibid.

51. Olu Ohadike, interview on December 9, 1982, at Igbuzo.

52. PRO, CO520/54/02032, The Operations in the Agbor District, Southern Nigeria, June-August, 1906 consequent upon the murder of Mr. O. S. Crewe-Read.

53. PRO, CO520/93/18685, draft comment (signed), R. S. W. to Mr. Strachey, Colonial Office, June 18, 1910. PRO, CO52/24, Captain Hogg to Officer Commanding Southern Nigeria Regiment, March 14, 1904. On their "invisibility," see PRO, CO52/24, Captain Hogg to Officer Commanding Southern Nigeria Regiment, March 14, 1904. Strub's description is in SMA, Strub, fol. 13.

54. Father Carlo Zappa described Igbuzo as "the most arrogant because it was the strongest of the towns around Asaba." See SMA 14/80302/15982, Zappa to Superior, January 26, 1898. This view is equally shared by J. C. Anene, who writes on p. 240 of his *Southern Nigeria in Transition,* "The most formidable opposition to the spread of missionary work was centered at Ibusa [Igbuzo], which was apparently the strongest of the Ika [Western Igbo] towns and was feared by the others." Also, the CMS agents, W. J. John, Rev. Julius Spencer, and Rev. Edward Phillips, described the various wars which the people of Igbuzo fought simultaneously against Asaba, Oko, and Ogwashi-Ukwu, among others. See, for instance, CMS CA3/04, W. J. John to Rev. S. Perry, Onitsha, November 1879 and CMS CA3/031, from the annual letters of Rev. Edward Phillips, September 10, 1879. These contemporary European reports corroborated oral traditions gathering from many Western Igbo towns concerning precolonial Igbo warfare. The praise names of the Igbuzo were *isu na mbogu* (warriors) and *isu fu ogu ju nni* (fighters).

55. SMA, Strub, fol. 13.

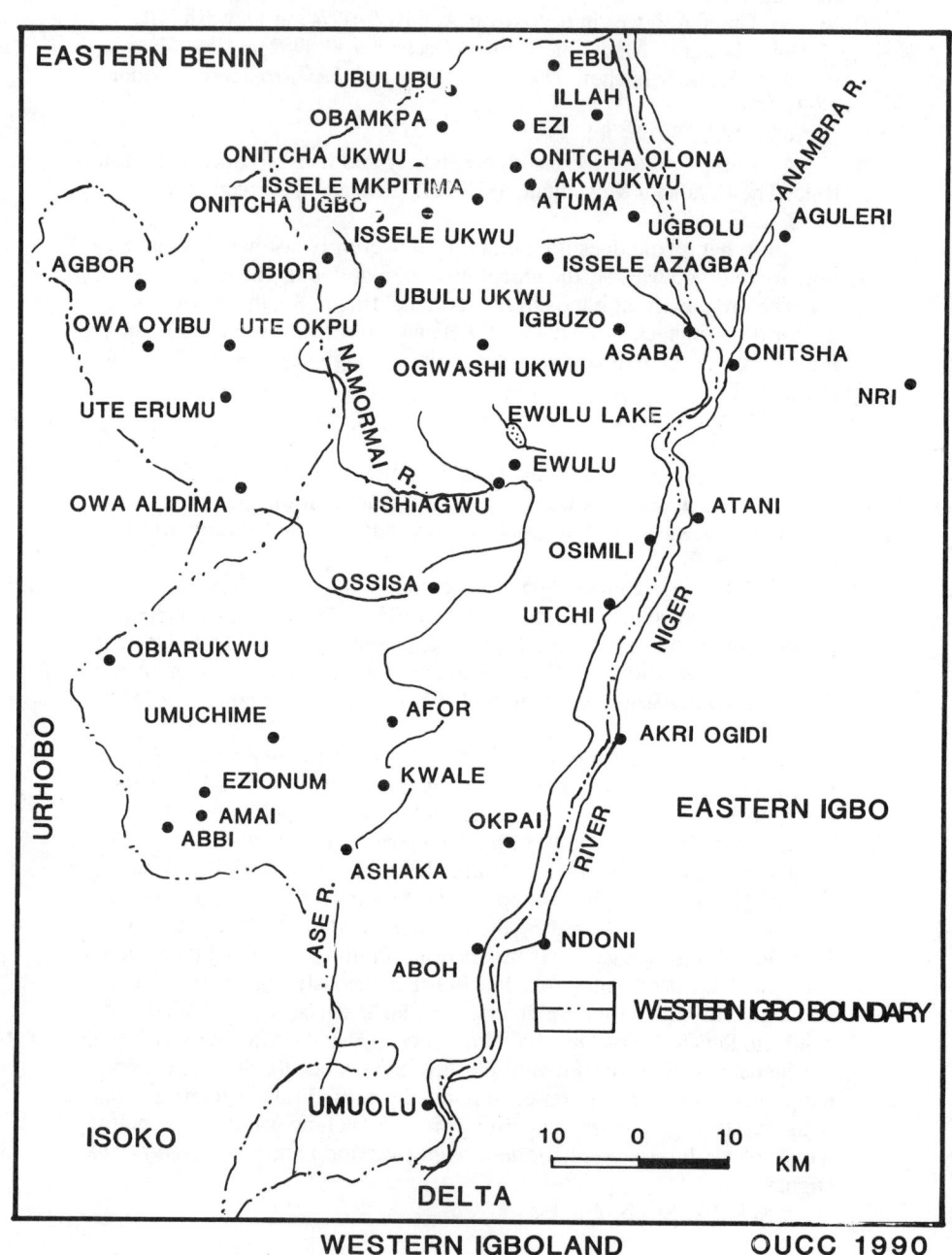

WESTERN IGBOLAND OUCC 1990

CHAPTER ONE

Chiefs, Slaves, and Socioeconomic Transformations in Nineteenth-Century Western Igboland

WESTERN IGBOLAND, situated in the southern region of Nigeria, north of the Niger delta, and west of the river, was divided into three cultural districts: Aniocha (centered around the city of Asaba), Ukwuani (centered around Kwale and Aboh), and Ika (centered around the town of Agbor). The British conquerors of Nigeria later designated these three cultural divisions the Asaba, Kwale, and Agbor districts, and the Ekumeku movement was organized by the people of the Asaba region.

Western Igboland represented an overspill of population from Eastern Igboland. Emigration from that territory is believed to have begun in the eighth century A.D., stimulated by soil deterioration and over-population in the Awka-Orlu area, east of Onitsha. This area, sometimes called Isuama, is believed to be the cradle of the Igbo, the place where *Chukwu* (the Creator) made the gift of yams to the Igbo people. A sophisticated civilization flourished there, and an elaborate commercial relationship was established between the Igbo people of Isuama and the outside world. The search for fertile lands, raw materials, and commerce impelled many Igbo from this area to disperse among their neighbors.[1] Some moved south into the Niger delta, some east into the Cross River estuary, and others crossed the Niger to occupy sites on the opposite bank of the river, where they were known as Western Igbo or Anioma people.

On arrival there, they organized themselves along strict Igbo kinship lines. The smallest unit of social organization was the family. A number of families formed the lineage, *umunna,* and a collection of lineages formed a village or town. At the head of a lineage was an *onyisi umunna,* sometimes called a *diokpa* or *okpala,* the oldest man in the lineage. Matters affecting the lineage were discussed at the meetings of the elders with the assistance of the adult male members of the lineage. In inter-lineage disputes, elders from the affected lineages met to discuss solutions, the oldest man in the gathering presiding.

The authority of the head of the lineage derived from three sources. First, he was recognized as the oldest living representative of the founding fathers of the lineage. Second, he was the custodian of ancestral lands; no man, no matter his status, could have access to a piece of lineage land without the diokpa's permission. Third, he was the keeper of his lineage *ofo,* an object which linked the community with the departed members of the lineage and their ancestral lands. Anyone who swore falsely on lineage *ofo* could be sure that there would be unpleasant consequences. As the *ofo* of one lineage was not recognized by another lineage it meant that the members of one lineage could not be protected by nor subjected to the authority of another lineage. In addition, since all relationships were traced to the ancestors, outsiders, such as slaves, were not accorded any recognition in the lineage organization because they had no claims whatsoever to the protection of the lineage *ofo.*

Even though the council of elders acted as the final court of appeal in judicial matters, administrative and executive matters were in the hands of the age-grade and title associations, which cut across the lineages. In Asaba, for instance, the senior age-grade, known as *oturaza,* dealt with all habitual criminals. Thus, while the *diokpa* of a lineage could punish a thief, a man whose constant indulgence in such criminal pastimes brought shame to his lineage could be handed over to the *oturaza,* who had the discretion to bind him hand-and-foot and cast him into the Niger to drown.[2] On the other hand, if the *oturaza* imposed a fine on a man and the fine was not promptly paid, the *oturaza* could descend upon the offender's lineage and demand payment. If payment was not almost immediately forthcoming, the *oturaza* would plunder the lineage and carry away as much booty as they could so as to compel a prompt payment.[3]

In Agbor, if a person was found guilty of murder, the Obi (head chief) in council with the elders would grant him a certain number of days during which to hang himself or leave the town. If he ignored this directive and overstayed his days of grace, he was forcibly hanged in public by an age-grade known as *ikoro* (young men between the ages of eighteen and thirty-six), which was vested with the responsibility of performing such executions.[4] The age-grades also acted as the communal labor force, and in times of war, they formed the fighting force.

This basic political and social organization of the Western Igbo people was later modified as a result of the arrival of a large number of immigrants. The transformations that took place in Benin in the sixteenth and seventeenth centuries caused large-scale population movements into Western Igboland. In addition, some Edo-speaking people, fleeing from political and religious persecution, came in as refugees and were soon joined by a number of Benin warriors and hired Yoruba mercenaries of the Oba of Benin. And finally there came some Igbo-speaking people who had settled either in Benin City proper as craftsmen, ritual specialists, or traders, or in the Edo-Igbo borderland and who had emulated certain Edo customs; these now fled toward the Niger as the Obas of Benin tried to subdue or incorporate them into the Benin kingdom. Among these were the founding fathers of the Umuezechima clan.[5]

The rise of the Atlantic slave trade in the sixteenth and seventeenth centuries stimulated the arrival of adventurers from Benin, Igalaland, Ijoland, and Ishanland (Esaland), anxious to participate in the new industry. As Kenneth O. Dike has rightly observed, the lure of the great commercial highway of the Niger valley itself must have stimulated another migration within the hinterland, and the hardy and adventurous people from the Benin area once again established themselves at places on the river bank favorable to trade.⁶ The settlements at Aboh and Onitsha were founded, and Asaba expanded, at this time.

The growth of Asaba illustrates the way in which newcomers were welcomed and incorporated into existing Western Igbo communities. Asaba traditions recall that the first settlers in Asaba were the descendants of Ezeanyanwu. Nothing is known about his provenance but his name suggests that he originally came from Eastern Igboland. He may have been one of those Igbo men who crossed the Niger into Western Igboland in the earlier centuries in search of fertile lands, meat, and elephant tusks.

This wave of settlers was followed by the descendants of Nnebisi. Nnebisi is believed to be the child of a union between an Igala man named Ikenga and an Igbo woman from Nteje near Awka. Strictly speaking, therefore, Nnebisi was not pure Igbo, as Asaba was a patrilineal community. Other immigrants were from Esanland. Oral traditions state that the Umunkwo quarter of the Umuezei lineage of Asaba was founded by Nkwo, who had come from an Esan town. Nkwo, it is said, married Onyebuchi, a daughter of Ezenei, and it was from this union that the present-day people of Umunkwo sprang. However, because Nkwo was a stranger and Onyebuchi a female, the people of Umunkwo could not produce a *diokpa* in Asaba, and not even in Umuezei. Like the people of Umunkwo, the occupants of the Ogbe-Ochele quarters of Asaba descended from another immigrant from Esanland. The founders of the Idumojei and Uuokwubata lineages came from Osamala and Igalaland, respectively. Finally, the Ogbeilo extended family of the Umuonaje lineage was founded by immigrants from Ijoland.⁷ Thus the people of Asaba were a broad mix.

Strangers, provided they were not slaves who had been captured, kidnapped, or purchased, were welcomed throughout Western Igboland, where they were incorporated as free men and women into the society. The arrival of large numbers of strangers through the centuries caused the people of Western Igboland to develop certain characteristics not often found in other parts of Southern Nigeria. For instance, they were able to combine elements of the Igbo kinship system with the Edo (Benin), Igala, and Yoruba monarchical structures to build small-scale, autonomous chiefdoms and republics. Unlike the Igbo east of the Niger, but like the Edo and the Yoruba, they preferred to settle in urban centers where they combined the Edo kingship system (under the rule of a paramount chief called *Obi*) with the Igbo title system (sometimes called the *ozo* or *eze* system) to produce political structures that were neither Igbo nor Edo. It is important to note that the *eze* title system belonged to the Umunri kingship system and that this institution was widespread in the areas near the Niger.[8] The institution of obiship, on the other hand, originated from Benin and was widespread in adjacent areas. It was a strong feature of those communities that claimed Benin origin and, because of the sword of office, *ada,* which their paramount chiefs carried, Ikenna Nzimiro has styled them the "ada kings."[9]

By the end of the eighteenth century, however, the major waves of migration into Western Igboland had come to an end and most lands had been effectively occupied. New immigrants were constrained to seek refuge in already existing settlements, where they were made to conform to the cultural etiquette of their hosts.[10] Besides, this was the peak period of the Atlantic slave trade, when the horrors generated by the traffic might have convinced many West African communities, especially those living side-by-side with hostile and slave-raiding empire builders, that concentrated settlements offered them better protection than diffused ones.[11]

The year 1750 was particularly important for the people of Western Igboland. This was the year which brought to a final close all Benin pretensions to imperial claims in Western Igboland. In that year the soldiers of Benin, who had made an attempt to subdue the Obi of Ubulu-Ukwu, were defeated in a battle at Igbuzo and were rolled back to Benin. Saddled with civil wars, succession disputes, and the rebellion of their vassal states, the Obas of Benin were never again able to send troops into Western Igboland.[12] Thus, until the British began to make their appearance in Southern Nigeria in the nineteenth century, the Western Igbo people were left alone to develop those special traits we now call Anioma or Western Igbo culture.

ECONOMIC PROSPERITY IN THE ERA OF THE ATLANTIC SLAVE TRADE, 1650-1850

The two hundred years beginning in about 1650 represented a period of economic prosperity for Western Igbo people. It was a prosperous age for those communities who traded in slaves and for those who produced yams, maize, cotton, and palm oil for export. Western Igbo people participated in all the different phases of the precolonial European trade, and before the rise of the Atlantic slave trade this area had been integrated into an interregional trade involving all sorts of commodities. As early as A.D. 1500, a trading pattern had been well established in the area now known as southeastern Nigeria, in which fish and salt of the delta area were exchanged for yams and other foodstuffs from the lower Niger. An early Portuguese explorer, Duarte Pacheco Pereira, reported in the sixteenth century that the canoes he encountered at the mouth of the Rio Real were "large enough to hold 80 men. These come down the river from a hundred leagues and more and convey yams . . . and many slaves, cows and sheep."[13] When the Atlantic slave trade became the dominant industry in the seventeenth century, Western Igbo people entered it, buying and selling slaves and at the same time producing large quantities of the foodstuffs that went into the provisioning trade.

Provisioning was itself a significant economic activity. Until recently, most discussions about the export slave trade have neglected the provisioning trade that went side-by-side with it. "Provisioning" refers to the trade in yams, palm oil, maize, and other foodstuffs normally taken by European ships' captains for the sustenance of crews and slaves when ships were anchored on the coast and during the middle passage.[14] Slaves and crewmen had to be fed during the long periods that the ships spent at the coastal ports collecting their cargos, and also during the middle passage. Thus many communities indirectly participated in the slave trade and made a good living out of it by producing the food for provisioning. Kingsley Ogedengbe has drawn our attention to the fact that the overseas slave trade brought about great changes in Africa in the trade in food items, and could conceivably have made provisioning as profitable as the slave trade itself.[15]

This view is shared by David Northrup, who has demonstrated that the population of the delta communities vastly expanded during the era of the Atlantic slave trade, which contributed to their inability to provide for all their own food requirements. According to Northrup, three major factors were responsible for this phenomenon. First, the population of the coastal entrepots increased rapidly during this period, thereby increasing the strains on delta soil which, in any case, was "too saline and/or swampy to grow all of their food." Second, these coastal communities neglected fishing, farming, and eventually salt-making because of their preference for trading. Finally, as the slave trade grew, so did the demand for provisions. Yams, maize, and palm oil were required to feed both slaves and ships' crews. Northrup estimates that at least 400,000 yams annually entered this trade from the Bight of Biafra at the beginning of the eighteenth century, and increased to 1.2 million at the end of the century.[16]

This estimate is reliable, for explorers Richard and John Lander observed during their Niger expedition of 1830 that most of the yams which the people of Brass imported from Aboh were sold to European slave ships. The canoe in which the brothers were taken from Aboh to Brass contained over two thousand yams which, they reported, were intended for sale to a Spanish slave ship on the Brass River.[17] Laird and Oldfield also described the trade of the lower Niger, in which yams and foodstuffs from the hinterlands were exchanged for salt and a number of European manufactured goods from the delta.[18] On the basis of these and other reports, Northrup has concluded that "one finds confirmation in the middle of the nineteenth century of trade in the same items that Pereira noted at the beginning of the sixteenth: food crops (especially yams) and livestock in exchange for salt."[19]

Of all the communities in the region between Lokoja and the Niger delta, the Western Igbo people were the best favored for the production and transportation of yams to the coastal ports. A bulky commodity, yams were not suitable for long-distance trade except where cheap means of transport were available. Thus, even though the areas around the Niger-Benue confluence produced large quantities of yams, any profit likely to accrue from selling them at the coast would have been nullified by the extra transport cost. A journey by canoe from the delta to Idah took over eight days, a distance of about three hundred miles. Partly because of political constraints and partly because of the expense involved, only small quantities of yams were actually sent down from the confluence to the coast. In addition, only a few people could have succeeded in raising the capital necessary for this form of long-distance trade for, as Chieka C. Ifemesia has noted, such a venture "demanded considerable capital investment in canoes and cargos to make it an economic proposition."[20]

While the people of the Niger-Benue confluence could not effectively participate in the provisioning trade because of transport problems, neither could the Eastern Igbo people in and about the area adjoining the Niger River, which suffered from very serious ecological and sociological problems. This area was seriously deficient in agricultural production. The land of the Ogbaru people (south of Onitsha) was generally flooded for more than half the year, so that it failed to attract large populations.[21] Even today Ogbaruland forms part of the least populated and least developed district of Igboland. Thus, based partly on ecological factors and partly on cultural preference, the Ogbaru took more to fishing and trading, to the relative neglect of farming.[22]

When considering the upland region east of Ogbaruland, called Isuama (the Nri-Awka and Orlu areas), one is confronted with a paradox. The area carried one of the heaviest population densities in sub-Saharan Africa and yet its soils were in a very advanced stage of depletion. Richard Henderson writes that these lands are today in a condition of serious soil deterioration."[23] Farming was so unrewarding in the earlier centuries that many people in the Nri-Awka and Orlu areas took to trading, craft manufacture, itineration, or outright emigration.[24] From ancient times these people relied on their neighbors for some of their food requirements. The result was that a trading system developed in which Isuama received yams that were ferried across the Niger for sale.

It is clear, then, that the Western Igbo people were better placed than their neighbors to produce and trade yams and other goods down the river into the Niger delta. Western Igboland had very fertile soils that rarely flooded, except for a few areas around Okpai and Aboh. Rainfall was plentiful and reliable. The vegetation cover was very thick, with trees suitable for the lumber industry, and in general the area was very important for the production of food crops, especially yams, and by the twentieth century, cassava as well.

Food and slave trading on the Niger, in which large numbers of captives were ferried down the river from distant lands, was well established even before the rise of the Atlantic slave trade, if we are to believe the account of the explorer Pereira.[25] E. J. Alagoa has also noted that, "By the beginning of the sixteenth century this north-south trade was already far advanced, and carried on with huge canoes on a large scale over long distances." He adds, "It was on this trade that the overseas trade hitched."[26] David Northrup has also observed that by time of "the arrival of the Portuguese the region was already a veteran of long-distance trade both up the Niger and Westward to the Gold Coast, and in the case of the inter-coastal trade it was the Europeans who had to make the adaptation to existing African patterns."[27]

Pereira did not disclose the ethnic origin of the men who owned the large canoes he found at the mouth of the Rio Real in the sixteenth century. However, oral traditions reveal that before the rise of the Aboh to prominence in the eighteenth century, the people of Akri were the dominant power on the lower stretches of the Niger, between Asaba and the delta.[28] These people have been described as the children of the Niger, *umu oshimili*, who supposedly could not be drowned in the river.[29] They had settlements on both sides of the Niger and must have developed the lower Niger trade. They were later defeated in a battle by the Aboh, who proceeded to expand the Niger trade in response to the growing European trade on the Atlantic coast.

Aboh chiefs and merchants maintained a large fleet of war and trading canoes that plied the Niger, bringing slaves and foodstuffs downriver to be exchanged for European manufactured goods. The Aboh were the most notable middlemen on the lower Niger, acting as intermediaries between the Igala and the Niger delta traders. Although they developed strong military traditions, they did not raid for slaves. Ossai, the obi of Aboh, reportedly said in 1841, "When other chiefs quarrel with me and make war, I take all I can as slaves."[30] Obi Ossai's statement only emphasizes the obvious, however, because most war captives were automatically enslaved. The chiefs of Aboh derived much of their respect and power from the fact that they protected the outlying settlements from the menace of the Ijo from Patani and below, who had developed the practice of raiding the villages on the Niger and its tributaries.[31] Only the Aboh were sufficiently powerful on the water to prevent these raids, and as the price of protection the villages had to acknowledge the Obi's overlordship.[32] If the chiefs of Aboh played the role of protectors, it hardly seems that at the same time they would raid their people for slaves.

In certain respects, however, who dominated the lower Niger trade was not as important as who produced the yams that went into the external trade. For, unlike slave raiding and slave trading, yam production was a peaceful vocation requiring neither large capital investments nor elaborate state structures to maintain. This may well explain the reason for the relative peace that reigned in Western Igboland even during the turbulent years of the export slave trade. Throughout the period 1650 to 1850 there was a constant demand for outsiders to produce yams and other crops, to paddle the trading canoes, and to act as domestic servants. During this period slaves were acquired to augment household labor and, despite their relatively large numbers, they did not cause any major changes in the relationship of dependency nor did their presence alter the kinship structures of the society. Effective political control in society remained with the elders and the age-grades, not with slave owners. Slaves were regarded as kinless dependents whose duties did not differ very significantly from those of the members of the host society even though they were also regarded as property that could be sold if the need arose.

PALM OIL, SLAVES, AND THE EMERGENCE OF A CLASS OF SLAVE-OWNING CHIEFS

The society of Western Igboland experienced rapid social and economic transformations during the second half of the nineteenth century as a result of the palm-oil trade. Two of the most notable changes of this period were the sudden expansion of domestic slavery and the rise of a new class of slave owners who elbowed out the elders and age-grades as the effective rulers of the society. These were the men who launched the Ekumeku and the other resistance movements when the British tried to interfere with domestic politics and economics.

There was nothing new about the palm-oil trade from the lower Niger; the only difference was that up to 1800 Europeans preferred exporting slaves to exporting vegetable oils. The peoples of southern Nigeria had produced and traded oil for countless ages; David Northrup writes that "the export of palm oil may be traced to the early sixteenth-century Portuguese who purchased palm oil from the Niger Delta for sale at Elmina on the Gold Coast."[33] This trade grew over time, almost imperceptibly at first, but increasing gradually during the last years of the eighteenth century and the first decades of the nineteenth. By the second half of the nineteenth century, not just a few hundred, but up to 40,000 tons of palm oil were being shipped from West Africa to the United Kingdom alone each year.[34]

It is almost impossible to conceive of the amount of labor that was required to produce this amount of palm oil in addition to the palm kernels, foodstuffs, and other commodities that had to be produced at the same time. The preparation and transportation of palm oil and palm kernels were grueling, dangerous, and time-consuming tasks. As Susan Martin has explained, the harvesting of the ripe fruit was masculine work, usually reserved for the agile young men, for it was extremely dangerous. The palm climber was supported with a pair of ropes as he climbed the tree and, since the palm could grow to a height of up to sixty feet, a fall could be fatal.[35] Once the fruit bunches had been harvested in the dense forest they were carried home where the individual fruits from the spikey bunches were carefully picked to avoid pricking, which could be very painful. Harvesting a palm fruit bunch, carrying it home, and extracting all its fruits was more than a day's task for one person.

To realize the necessary oil, the fruits had to be boiled and pounded in a large mortar or a hollowed-out tree stump until they were reduced to a mass of fibers and nuts within which the dark-red oil would begin to appear. The whole mass was then squeezed, washed, and squeezed again and again until all traces of oil were extracted from the fibers.[36] It could take a full day for a family of six to produce four gallons of oil by this process. Since this family had to provide its own food and other necessities of life, it might take a whole week to produce this small amount of oil, which fetched only six pence in Umuahia in the 1920s.[37] Evidence from all parts of Africa confirms that the most dangerous and arduous tasks were reserved for slaves, except where they could not be found. Among the people of Western Igboland, it was almost a taboo for a free-born man to climb the palm tree or process palm oil except for cooking purposes.

On the demand side, it might be asked why British traders who had been doing business on the coast for some three centuries should now move into the hinterlands to ask for such large amounts of palm oil. Alan McPhee has explained that the rapid increase in the demand for the oil in the United Kingdom was a result of three factors. First, there was an increased demand in Europe for fats and oils of all sorts. Second, there was an increased demand for soap for washing and for candles for lighting, both by-products of vegetable oils. Third, lubricants were needed for the new machinery of the factories and the railroads that proliferated during the Industrial Revolution.[38] In addition, this

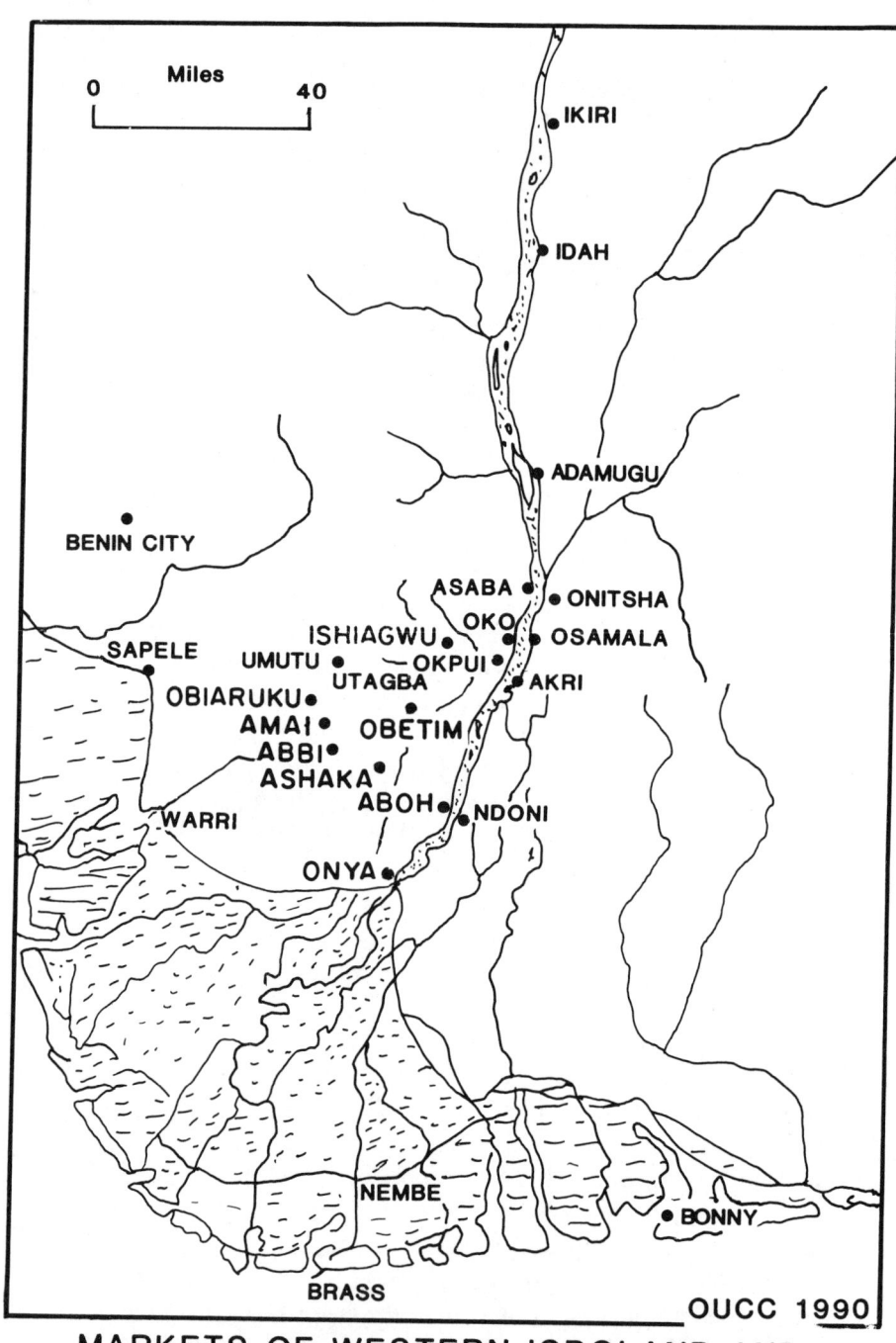

MARKETS OF WESTERN IGBOLAND AND
THE LOWER NIGER (AFTER OGEDENGBE)

increase in the demand for palm oil and kernel coincided with the age of steamships. European traders, who hitherto had stayed on the coast, were now able to ascend the Niger to buy directly from the inland producers. Between 1857 and 1879 European traders established over forty trading posts between Aboh and Lokoja, each spaced at approximately twenty-mile intervals.[39] Trading posts were also established in Oguta, Old Calabar, Bonny, Opobo, and in virtually every delta city-state. The rapid proliferation of European trading posts in these places clearly illustrates the sudden increase in activity surrounding the demand and supply of the product.

Perhaps the single most important factor in the whole demand-and-supply mechanism was the high price that European traders were prepared to offer for oil and kernels; when the demand drove the price up, many Western Igbo people responded by expanding their production. Since the amount of labor at the disposal of each household was limited in the short run, a corollary to the whole palm-oil cycle was that some enterprising local producers turned to the use of slave labor to augment their production.

Unlike the warrior aristocracies of the savanna region of West Africa, which relied primarily on warfare to secure slaves, and only secondarily on purchase, Western Igbo producers secured their slaves only by purchase.[40] Igbo homelands were situated on one of the most important slave-trading routes in Africa—the Niger River. On an island in the river between Asaba and Onitcha was a famous market where traders from Aboh and the Niger delta met once each week to exchange slaves, yams, livestock, salt, cloth, metalware, and other goods with traders from Idah and Lokoja upstream.[41] This island was traditionally regarded as belonging to Asaba, the point where the influence of Aboh and Idah (the two military powers on the lower Niger) converged, a circumstance which guaranteed Asaba's safety and neutrality in the event of any war on the river.[42] Many Igbo people regularly came to this island market to buy slaves, salt, and other commodities (see map 3).

After 1840 there was a dramatic drop in the price of slaves on the lower Niger, which coincided with the period when the demand for palm oil was expanding rapidly. The slave trade was diminishing for a number of reasons. First, the presence of the British naval patrols on the coast of southern Nigeria discouraged slave export. Second, an over-supply existed; the regions that supplied slaves to the lower Niger communities continued to do so with ever-increasing efficiency even after the closure of the overseas markets. In the addition, the Islamic reform movements launched from Sokoto in 1804 soon spread to other parts of the grassland belt of Nigeria, generating wars on an unprecedented scale and yielding thousands of captives.[43] Each day hundreds of slaves were ferried down the Niger for sale, while thousands more were displayed in the Kano, Zaria, Bida, and Lokoja markets.[44] Thus, by the second half of the nineteenth century the slave markets of Northern Nigeria and the lower Niger had been glutted. Those Western Igbo producers who wished to increase their output of palm oil and foodstuffs took advantage of the steep drop in the price of slaves to expand their slave holding. Some, like Obi Ossai, kept over three hundred slaves; his son, Chukwuma, had over two hundred, and his brother Aje, had a hundred.[45] In 1841, MacGregor Laird reported that he visited the plantation of an Aboh woman who owned over two hundred slaves whom she kept to collect palm oil and cultivate yams.[46]

It should be noted that the slaves acquired by Western Ibo people at this time were not all employed in the production of palm oil. Many worked on the yam crop, which had been commercialized since the days of the provisioning trade. While the demand for yams to sustain slaves and ships' crews had decreased as the external slave trade was brought to a halt, the internal demand for this commodity continued to expand throughout the century. One factor was the growing population of the Niger delta communities because of the rapid proliferation of the trading houses.[47] Another stimulus to the yam trade was the palm-oil trade itself, as farming was often abandoned in favor of the much more lucrative palm-oil production. In addition, Onitsha had been transformed into the largest commercial center of southeastern Nigeria. The teeming population that gathered there for commercial (and later, administrative and intellectual) purposes had to be fed. Another stimulus was the permanent closure of the overseas slave trade from Nigeria (and the rest of Africa); this brought a resumption in the growth of the population, which had stagnated over the previous centuries.[48] Obviously, the larger the population, the greater the demand for food to feed it. Thus, apart from the labor required to produce palm oil and palm kernels for export, there was an increasing demand for labor to produce yams and other food crops for the internal market.

Whether they devoted their entire energies to harvesting palm produce alone, or combined it with the cultivation of yams, a number of enterprising inhabitants of Western Igboland profited from the economic prosperity of this period. Many of these entrepreneurs invested their wealth in slaves and titles for economic and political reasons. The most important title among the Western Igbo people, especially in the communities that launched the Ekumeku movement, was the title of eze. The taking of this title was very expensive, demanding elaborate feasting, the offering of animal sacrifices, and the paying of very high initiation fees. Admission was not by birth but by hard work manifested in wealth. Prior to the nineteenth century only a few male members of the community succeeded in completing the rituals connected with taking this title. The prosperity that accompanied the yam and palm-oil trade in the nineteenth century, however, gave to many men the wherewithal to complete the initiation. Both oral and written sources confirm a marked expansion of the corporate titles among the lower Niger Igbo people in the nineteenth century. In Asaba, for instance, the number of eze men rose from about half a dozen at the beginning of the century to over three hundred in 1888.[49] At Igbuzo, their number jumped from four to two hundred during the same period, and at Onitsha, the inferior chiefs, *ndichie okwa,* increased their number from the traditional sixteen to seventy.[50] A Christian missionary agent resident in Asaba in the 1870s was so fascinated by the large number of chiefs he found there that he described the town as a land where "Every man is a king, or nearly so."[51] Those he regarded as nearly kings were the holders of the inferior title known as *alo.* These men were not chiefs but because they had purchased several junior titles like the *nkpisi* and *alo,* they sometimes paraded themselves as chiefs when an *eze* was not around.

All in all, the holders of the *eze* title were the wealthiest and the most politically active members of the society in the nineteenth century. Although elders continued to preside over minor lineage disputes, *eze* men soon emerged as the final decision makers in important political matters. They represented their respective towns in such matters as slavery, European trade, Christianity, and treaty making. European traders and missionaries could not establish themselves in any town without their permission. They also reserved the right to decide when trade had to be closed down or reopened, and the amount of tolls, tributes, or customs that European traders had to pay. These tributes were sometimes wrongly described as "dash," or presents, and, as we shall see in the next chapter, they were a major source of friction between Western Igbo chiefs and the Europeans.

Every man coveted the *eze* title because it guaranteed its holder a seat in the governing council of his town and entitled him to certain portions of livestock slaughtered in his lineage and portions of all fees paid by new initiates into the title association. Most importantly, the title exempted its holder from all manual labor. His red cap, decorated with eagle feathers, and his staff of office, or *otonsi,* were immediately recognized anywhere he went. He was greeted with the salutation, *"igwe"* (His Highness), and anyone who troubled him or failed to give him the respect he deserved was made to pay a heavy fine. To cause an *eze* man bodily harm was to risk being sold into slavery. In short, these chiefs constituted the non-laboring, ruling class.

It is important to note the strong connections between the palm-oil trade, slave ownership, title taking, and class formation among the people of Western Igboland during the nineteenth century. Unlike the first generation of cocoa farmers in Yorubaland and in southern Ghana, the first palm oil producers of Western Igboland did not have to plant palm seedlings, nurture them, and wait many years for the trees to mature. Since the trees grew semi-wild in the forest and on abandoned farmlands, they were ready to supply palm oil once the Europeans showed a willingness to buy it, a fact Obi Ossai pointed out to the members of the Niger expedition of 1841.[52] The high prices Europeans were ready to offer for the oil acted as an added incentive to produce. Most importantly, the labor problem was immediately solved by employing slaves who could be bought cheaply in the Niger markets because of the closure of the overseas outlets for African slaves and the expansion of the internal supply. Most Western Igbo men became slave owners almost overnight, and as soon as they accumulated enough wealth, they invested part of it in the corporate titles, thus becoming chiefs and members of the ruling elite.

The development of the palm-oil trade took a different course in the Igbo heartland, where the population was dense, ranging between two hundred and three hundred people per square mile. Because the area was already becoming over-crowded, it had limited capacity to admit outsiders—as slaves or otherwise—on a large scale. Thus its people had to continue to rely on household or family labor. As Susan Martin has shown, inhabitants in the Ngwa district responded to the palm-oil trade by intensifying the exploitation of female and child labor and by giving up some amount of leisure. Women and children carried the heavy fruit bunches from the bush to the village, tended the fires and carried the water necessary for processing the oil, squeezed the mass of fibers to extract the oil, and cracked the nuts for their kernel. The men, on the other hand, farmed the yams and other food crops and intervened in palm-oil production only by undertaking the most dangerous and tedious tasks of cutting down the ripe fruits and pounding the nuts in the mortar.[53] Although these communities as a whole produced large amounts of oil and kernels, the contribution of each household was not substantial.

Thus, the communities of southeastern Nigeria that profited most from the nineteenth-century palm-oil business were those which gave up farming entirely for trade, or those whose low population densities enabled them to hold large numbers of slaves. Typical among these communities were Old Calabar, Bonny, Opobo, Oguta, Aboh, Osamala, Asaba, Ode-Itsekiri, and Ebrohime. Each of these received such a large influx of outsiders that the number of strangers sometimes dwarfed and even frightened the host communities. In Old Calabar, for instance, the free-born were kept in perpetual fear of slave revolts, especially since the days when the slaves banded themselves in a covenant of blood (hence the name the Bloodmen) and tried to form their own branch of the Ekpe society.[54] This was a secret society to which the members of the ruling elite and wealthy merchants belonged. In the Niger delta the host communities were kept in perpetual fear of what has been described as "the Igbo peril," as the society became literally inundated by outsiders.[55]

But the economic strength of these communities lay in the exploitation of slave labor on a large scale. Although every free-born member of the community was allowed to buy slaves, most slaves were owned by the chiefs and the principal merchants. Men were chiefs because they could exploit the labor of a large number of dependents; as in other parts of Africa, a man could not sit alone and become a chief.[56] Thus while the slaves were at least an implied threat, they were at the same time a very real source of power. It was a necessary paradox, and in the absence of a standing army and a sophisticated state machinery, one of the problems facing any small-scale society wishing to hold large numbers of slaves is that of control. To cope with the sudden influx of strangers, the chiefs of Western Igboland adjusted the ideologies that regulated the treatment of slaves, manipulating these ideologies as circumstances warranted.[57] The greater the number of slaves in the society, the greater the need to maintain a balance between harshness and extremism. Slaves had to be sufficiently terrified to enlist their cooperation but not to provoke their rebellion. Thus, in the nineteenth century Western Igbo chiefs adopted segregation and discipline as forms of slave control.

One of the more terrifying tactics was the use of human sacrifice — or at least, rumors of it. There is evidence to confirm that the Christian missionaries exaggerated their so-called eyewitness accounts of human sacrifice among the lower Niger Igbo. Bishop Samuel Crowther, himself a freed slave turned missionary, reported that Obi Igweli, an *eze* title holder at Asaba, sacrificed a slave to thank the gods for his partial recovery from a serious illness.[58] Contemporary accounts suggest, however, that only chiefs had the privilege to perform human sacrifice and that the custom was tied to the installation and burial of chiefs. It should be noted that many European trained missionaries and explorers were quick to report on certain African customs they hardly understood. As we shall presently see, most of these reports were exaggerated because they were intended to justify European conquest of Africa. Although this book contains some references to human sacrifice, the purpose is not to resurrect the so-called African barbarism, but to place the conflicts between the Igbo people and the Europeans in their proper historical context.

In any case, partly to effect the necessary discipline and partly because of their large numbers, Western Igbo slaves were not allowed to live in the homes of their owners. Instead they were kept in special slave villages known as *ugwule,* where they were allowed to lead their own lives undisturbed, except when required to work for their masters. It was in the best interest of masters to treat the slaves humanely and in fact custom demanded it. Slaves, for their part, realized that good behavior had its rewards. Every slave owed his entire existence to his owner. He owned no separate farm and was made to realize that his own happiness depended on the success of his master. Unlike the Niger delta people, Western Igbo chiefs did not insist on the rapid acculturation of their slaves.⁵⁹ And because slaves descended from some unknown ancestors who, in any case, were not co-founders of the clan, the clan, they were not allowed to organize themselves in lineages. Slaves had neither councils of elders (*ndisi umunna*) nor councils of chiefs (*ndi-nzele*), as they were not allowed to purchase even the lowest titles or form any cross-cutting associations.

Any child born in a slave village belonged to the owner of the baby's mother. It is inaccurate to speak of marriage between slaves because there was no one to receive the customary bride wealth, a kind of dowry that sealed marriages. Any financial transaction that entailed the transfer of rights over slaves was regarded as purchase. Therefore a master who wished to reward a faithful, hard-working male slave could purchase a female slave for him. Both slaves lived as "husband and wife" and labored together for their master, who also reserved the right to treat them and any children that might result from this "marriage" as chattel. In practice, however, the master would not part with any of them because, as Miers and Kopytoff would put it, the family grouping would have moved from "total marginality towards greater and greater incorporation" into the host society.⁶⁰

Marriage between a slave and a free person was taboo. Any sexual relationship that took place between a free and a slave individual was known as *alu,* abomination, and should an offspring result, the child was declared a slave. Under no circumstance could a union between a free person and a slave produce a free person. In some African societies where manumission was practiced, a female slave could be set free in order to accord her offspring the status of a free person, but the Western Igbo people had no such custom.⁶¹

The slave village, the *ugwule,* was a social unit established and controlled by the slave owners. Deprived of any cross-cutting institutions and confined to the different slave villages, Western Igbo slaves remained politically weak and could not rebel against their masters. These slaves were purchased, not as prestige items, but as tools of production, even though we can probably accurately infer that a chief who owned one hundred slaves enjoyed greater prestige than one with only ten.

The nineteenth century was on the whole a prosperous period for Western Igbo chiefs, who succeeded in establishing strong relations of domination over a large number of slaves and others from whom they extracted surplus-labor. The Ekumeku war broke out at the end of that century when the British, obsessed with what they saw as a civilizing mission, began to interfere with that prosperity. In its early stages, the Ekumeku uprising was a revolt of the slave owners against the British emancipation ideals, together with the unwelcome involvement of the Christian missionaries with local customs and politics, and in its later stages, it was a resistance against British rule and its attendant administrative irresponsibility.

NOTES TO CHAPTER ONE

1. For accounts of the early history of the Igbo people, see A. E. Afigbo, "On the Threshold of Igbo History: A Review of Thurstan Shaw's Igbo-Ukwu," *The Conch* 3, no. 2 (1971): 205-218; Thurstan Shaw, *Igbo-Ukwu: An Account of Archaeological Discoveries in Eastern Nigeria* (Evanston, 1970), 271-185; Michael A. Onwuejeogwu, "Nri Activities and Their Relationship to Igbo Civilization," *The Journal of Odinani Museum* 1, no. 1 (1972): 41.

2. NAI, CSO/26 No. 30927, H. Vaux, "Intelligence Report on the Asaba Clan" (1936), 4.

3. Ibid.

4. NAI, CSO/26/4 No. 3038X, J. M. Simpson, "Intelligence Report on the Agbor, Oligie and Emuhu Clans, Agbor District, Asaba Division" (1939), 11.

5. Don C. Ohadike, "The Rise of Benin Kingdom and the Settlement of Edo-speaking People in the Igbo Culture area," *Ivie: Nigerian Journal of Arts and Culture* 1, no. 3 (1986): 25-31.

6. Kenneth O. Dike, *Trade and Politics in the Niger Delta* (Oxford, 1956), 25.

7. Don C. Ohadike and Rick N. Shain, eds., *Western Igbo,* Jos Oral History and Literature Texts 6 (Jos, 1988), i-ii.

8. M. D. Jeffreys, "The Divine Umundri Kings," *Africa Magazine* 3, no. 8 (1935): 346-54. Northcote Thomas, *Anthropological Report on the Ibo-Speaking People of Nigeria, Part IV: Law and Custom of the Ibo of Asaba District* (New York, 1914), 54.

9. Ikenna Nzimiro. *Studies in the Ibo Political System* (London, 1972), 8.

10. Ohadike, "The Rise of Benin," 25-31.

11. On the slave trade, see Philip D. Curtin, *The Atlantic Slave Trade: A Census* (Madison, 1969), 116; Anthony G. Hopkins, *An Economic History of West Africa* (London, 1973), 101-3; Paul Lovejoy, "The Volume of the Atlantic Slave Trade: A Synthesis," *Journal of African History,* 23, no. 4 (1982): 473- 501. On political reactions to the slave trade, see Robin Horton, "Stateless Societies in the History of West Africa," in *History of West Africa,* ed. J. F. A. Ade Ade Ajayi and Michael Crowder (Cambridge, 1971), 1:97-98.

12. Ohadike, "The Rise of Benin," 28-30.

13. Duarte Pacheco Pereira, *Esmeralde de situ orbis.* Trans. and ed. George H. T. Kimble (London, 1973), 123.

14. See, for instance, Leo Wiener, *Africa and the Discovery of America,* (New York, 1972), 1:231. See also David Northrup, *Trade Without Rulers: Pre-colonial Economic Development in South Eastern Nigeria* (Oxford, 1980), 28.

15. Kingsley Oladipo Ogedengbe, "The Aboh Kingdom of the Lower Niger, c. 1650-1900" (Ph.D. diss., University of Wisconsin, 1971), 293.

16. Northrup, *Trade,* 177-80.

17. Richard and John Lander, *Journal of an Expedition to Explore the Course and Termination of the Niger,* (New York, 1858), 2:254, 237.

18. MacGregor Laird and R. A. K. Oldfield, *Narrative of an Expedition into the Interior of Africa by the River Niger* (London, 1857).

19. Northrup, *Trade,* 28.

20. Chieka C. Ifemesia, "British Enterprise on the Niger, 1830- 1869" (Ph.D. thesis, University of London, 1959), 261.

21. Richard N. Henderson, *The King in Every Man* (New Haven and London, 1972), 36.

22. Ngozi E. Ojiakor, "A Cultural History of Ogbaru Community of the Lower Niger," Research Project, Department of History, University of Jos, 1982.

23. Henderson, *The King in Every Man,* 36.

24. Onwuejeogwu, "Nri Activities," 41; for another view on Igbo population, see Simon Ottenberg, "Ibo Receptivity to Change" in *Continuity and Change in African Cultures,* ed. William R. Bascom and Melville J. Herskovits (Chicago, 1959), 134-35 and 140.

25. Pereira, *Esmeraldo de situ orbis,* 123.

26. E. J. Alagoa, "Long-distance Trade and States in the Niger Delta," *Journal of African History* 11 (1920): 322.

27. Northrup, *Trade,* 22.

28. Chief Godwin Chukwuma, interview on December 20, 1982, at Okpai Olichi.

29. Henderson, *The King in Every Man,* 51-52.

30. W. Allan and T. R. H. Thomson, *A Narrative of the Expedition to the River Niger in 1841,* (London, 1848), 1:218.

31. Local Government Archives, Benin City, file no. 26769. Captain E. A. Miller, "Aboh Intelligence Report," (1931).

32. NAI, CSO/26/3, No. 26769, Vol. 1. G. B. Williams, "Intelligence Report on the Ibo-Speaking Clans of the Kwale Division, Warri Province," (1931).

33. Northrup, *Trade,* 29.

34. Hopkins, *An Economic History of West Africa,* 128.

35. Susan M. Martin, *Palm Oil and Protest: An Economic History of the Ngwa Region, South-eastern Nigeria 1880-1980* (Cambridge, U.K., 1988), 33.

36. Ibid., 44.

37. S. N. Nwabara, *Iboland: A Century of Contact with Britain, 1860-1960* (London, 1977), 184.

38. Alan McPhee, *The Economic Revolution in British West Africa* (New York, 1978), 30-31.

39. CMS, G3/A3/1889/66, Observations of Bishop Crowther, 1879.

40. On obtaining slaves, see Richard Roberts, *Warriors, Merchants, and Slaves: The State and the Economy in the Middle Niger Valley, 1700-1914* (Stanford, 1987); Paul Lovejoy, *Transformations in Slavery: A History of Slavery in Africa* (Cambridge, U.K., 1983).

41. MacGregor Laird and R. A. K. Oldfield, *Narrative of an Exploration into the Interior of Africa* (London, 1971), 164-67.

42. NAI, CSO/26, No. 30927, H. Vaux, "Intelligence Report on the Asaba Clan," (1936).

43. Mahdi Adamu, "The Delivery of Slaves from the Central Sudan to the Bight of Benin in the Eighteenth and Nineteenth Centuries," in *The Uncommon Market*, ed. Henry A. Gemery and Jan S. Hogendorn (New York, 1979), 171-72.

44. William B. Baikie, "Notes of a Journey from Bida in Nupe to Kano in Hausa Performed in 1862," *Journal of the Royal Geographical Society*, 37 (1867): 92-107.

45. Kingsley Nwachukwu-Ogedengbe, "Slavery in Nineteenth-Century Aboh," in *Slavery in Africa*, ed. Suzanne Miers and Igor Kopytoff, (Madison, 1977), 141.

46. Laird and Oldfield, *Narrative*, 100.

47. Dike, *Trade and Politics*, 97-127.

48. Joseph E. Inikori, "Historical Problems in the Assessment of the Impact of the Atlantic Slave Trade in African Populations," paper presented for the international colloquium on the Tricentenary of the Code Noir, Dakar, 1986, 25-41.

49. Elizabeth Isichei, *A History of the Igbo People* (London, 1976), 100. See also CMS, CA3/A3/1888/48, reports by Henry Johnson, May 21, 1988.

50. For the Igbuzo statistics, see PRO, FO2/179, *Daily Graphic*, February 7, 1898; for Onitsha, see Peter R. McKenzie, *Inter-Religious Encounters in West Africa* (Leister, 1976), 74.

51. CMS, CA3/031, from the annual letters of Edward Phillips, August 31, 1880.

52. Alan and Thomson, *Narrative*, 221.

53. Martin, *Palm Oil and Protest*, 31-34.

54. Monday Efiong Noah, *Old Calabar: The City States and the European, 1800-1885* (Uyo, 1980), 110.

55. For "the Igbo peril" see Adiele E. Afigbo, "Igboland before 1800," in *Groundwork of Nigerian History*, ed. Obaro Ikime (Ibadan, 1980), 86.

56. Miers and Kopytoff, *Slavery in Africa*, 14.

57. Paul E. Lovejoy, ed., *The Ideology of Slavery in Africa* (London, 1981), 21-27.

58. *Church Missionary Intelligencer,* 1879, 238-42.

59. For the acculturation of slaves in the Niger delta, see Robin Horton, "From Fishing Village to City State: A Social History of New Calabar," in Mary Douglas and Phyllis M. Kaberry, eds., *Man in Africa* (London, 1969), 38-64.

60. Miers and Kopytoff, *Slavery in Africa,* 19.

61. Lovejoy, *Transformations in Slavery,* 2:6-8. Miers and Kopytoff, *Slavery in Africa,* 29-39. On the relationships between free and unfree persons in Igboland see Don C. Ohadike, "The Decline of Slavery Among the Igbo People," in *The End of Slavery in Africa*, ed. Suzanne Miers and Richard Roberts (Madison, 1988), 437-61.

CHAPTER TWO

British Gunboat Diplomacy and the Conquest of Aboh: The Remote Causes of the Ekumeku War

THE AVENUES FOR a potential conquest of Western Igboland were opened by explorers, traders, and missionaries, whose presence marked the beginning of British designs upon the territory. Aboh, the most important Niger Igbo town in the early nineteenth century, was the first to welcome the British; it was also the first town to be overwhelmed by British economic competition and colonial violence. The events that led to the conquest of Aboh and the eventual rise of the Ekumeku movement can be traced to the period when the British, who had been leading the African slave trade, decided to abolish it because it was no longer consistent with their economic interests.[1] As they had dominated the trade, so did they spearhead the movement which eventually discredited it. In 1771 the British Parliament declared that any slave who was in or had been brought to England was automatically free. In 1806 an act of the British Parliament made it illegal for British subjects to engage in the slave trade.

In 1833 another act abolished slavery throughout the British Empire. At the same time other European countries passed laws forbidding their citizens from engaging in the trade, as did the United States.

Nevertheless, it was soon obvious that the mere declaration that the slave trade was illegal was not enough to stop it so long as Europeans and Americans still bought slaves in the Americas. To enforce its declarations the British Government signed a series of treaties with the other slave-trading countries which gave ships of the British Royal Navy the right to stop and search other ships and, if slaves were found on board, to liberate them and punish the ships' captains.

Discussions were also begun in certain quarters with a view toward working out alternative means of abolishing the slave trade. Some argued that perhaps a more effective means of stopping the trade would be by opening up the interior of Africa for trade, for Christianity, and for what was described as "good government." Thomas F. Buxton, one of the leading humanitarians of this period, said of Africa:

> We must elevate the minds of her people and call forth the resources of her soil. . . . Let missionaries and schoolmasters, the plough and the spade go together and agriculture will flourish; the avenues to legitimate commerce will be opened; confidence between man and man will be inspired; whilst civilization will advance as the natural effect, and Christianity operate as the proximate cause of this happy change.[2]

Even before Buxton made this idealistic declaration in 1839, several societies had been formed in Europe for the purpose of promoting scientific knowledge and "opening up" the African interior. Between 1788 and 1830 the African Association despatched a number of expeditions into the interior. In 1795 the explorer Mungo Park reached Segu on the Niger, but drowned at Bussa during a subsequent expedition.[3] In 1825 Hugh Clapperton reached the Niger at Bussa, then visited Kano and Sokoto, where he attempted to negotiate a treaty with the Sultan to stop the slave trade in his Sultanate. The refusal of the Sultan to entertain such an arrangement dismayed Clapperton but did not discourage the British from sending further expeditions to trace the course of the Niger.

In 1830, Richard Lander, accompanied by his brother, John, followed the course of the Niger from Bussa to the sea. The two men had a safe canoe ride downstream from Bussa but were captured at Asaba by Aboh men who presented them to their paramount chief, who sold them to King Boy, an African trader on the Brass River.[4] This trader had hoped to make a profit from his purchase but was disappointed when he presented the explorers to Captain Lake, a Liverpool merchant trading on the coast, who sailed away with them without at least refunding him his investment. It may be that Captain Lake deliberately refused to pay the Brass trader because the British Parliament had made it illegal for any British citizen to engage in any transactions that could be described as slave dealing.[5] This assumption is supported by an event that took place in Onitsha some years later, when Bishop Samuel Crowther pleaded for the release of a slave who was to be offered up as sacrifice. The chiefs asked him to buy the slave and with the proceeds a bullock would be purchased and sacrificed instead. Crowther refused to save the life of this unfortunate victim because, he said, he would not want to be involved in any transactions that could be described as slave dealing.[6] Fortunately, the slave was eventually released, despite these machinations.

The Lander brothers were warmly welcomed in England, as they had solved the long-standing mystery about the mouth of the Niger. Arrangements were subsequently made to send expeditions up the Niger to establish trading contacts with the people of the interior. In 1832, an expedition up the Niger was sponsored by MacGregor Laird, but it ended in disaster. Out of the forty-eight Europeans who made up the party, thirty-eight died from tropical diseases.[7]

In 1841, another expedition was sent up the Niger, its purpose to establish a trading post, a Christian mission station, and a model farm at Lokoja. This expedition was sponsored by the British government and was inspired by the ideals of Thomas Buxton as enunciated in his book, *The African Slave Trade and Its Remedy*. Like the expedition of 1832-34, this one also ended in disaster. Out of the 145 Europeans who accompanied it, 48 died from disease.[8] It was partly because of these mortalities that the African interior came to be described as the "whiteman's grave."

These disasters proved only a temporary setback to the attempts to establish trading and missionary contacts with the peoples of the lower Niger. In 1854 another expedition, sponsored jointly by the British government and MacGregor Laird, went up the Niger and was deemed successful; this time none of the party died, thanks to the use of quinine to fight the malaria that had previously proven so deadly.[9] The way to the interior was opened, and each succeeding year another expedition ventured up the great river.

Most discussions about the Niger expeditions have neglected the underlying economic motives and have emphasized such themes as the quest for scientific knowledge, the love of adventure, and the desire by the humanitarians of Europe to stop the slave trade. To claim that the explorations were motivated primarily by noneconomic factors is to misunderstand the entire history of European enterprise in West Africa. As Philip Curtin has pointed out, Western Europeans had tapped the wealth of West Africa both at the continent's northern and western shores for centuries. They were also fully aware that such goods as hides and skins, timber, ivory, and gold were available in the interior. Since the days of Prince Henry the Navigator, when Europeans first began to trade on the African shores, the Europeans had expressed a desire for direct access to the producing areas in the hinterland as well as a desire to cut out the African middlemen traders.[10]

During the late eighteenth and early nineteenth centuries direct access to the African interior became even more important because the Industrial Revolution was expanding the European market in both raw materials and manufactured products. Trade in tropical woods, palm nuts, ground nuts, gum Arabic and coffee was growing. There was also further hope for increasing trade in gold, iron ore, and cotton. British manufacturers were becoming increasingly concerned about their dependence on the United States for most of their cotton, and attention was now directed toward Africa as an alternative source of supply.[11] Convinced that cotton and other items indigenous to the tropics could be produced cheaply in Africa, the British drew up an ambitious program for converting the continent into a major source of raw materials.

If the background of those who sponsored the Niger expeditions is considered, it becomes clear that economic considerations outweighed humanitarian ones in the opening of the African frontier. The men who founded the African Association were businessmen—men like its president, Sir Joseph Bank, along with Sir Andrew Stewart, and the Earl of Moira.[12] The explorers themselves expressed views that betrayed the economic motives of their endeavors. Mungo

Park clearly stated that he had "a passionate desire to examine the products of the country so little known," and hoped he would succeed in rendering them more familiar to his countrymen, which might facilitate the opening "to their ambition and industry new sources of wealth, and new channels of commerce."[13] William Baikie endeavored to keep an accurate record of the "various commercial products fit for European markets to be obtained at present from the countries bordering on the Niger."[14]

Kenneth O. Dike contends that although diverse non-economic forces helped to stimulate the initial interest in African exploration, it was the economic change taking place in Europe at the time that made it possible for diverse interest groups to unite their efforts for the realization of a common objective.[15] Alexander Nzemeka has questioned whether the advancement of scientific knowledge was worth the great risk and danger which the African climate held for Europeans.[16] Even though the Europe of Mungo Park's days never lacked adventurers, men who were "willing to defy the dangers and uncertainties of the unknown in the Dark Continent,"[17] an indisputably major motive of the Niger expeditions was economic.

Whatever were the real and imagined motives of the Niger expeditions, their historical significance for this study lies in the fact that they set the stage for the subsequent British penetration and conquest of Western Igboland. For no sooner had the Lander brothers returned to England with the news about their discovery than the British began to rush into the mouth of the Niger as if to suffocate her. Most of the subsequent expeditions up the Niger were undertaken by missionaries and traders, sometimes accompanied by government officials. Their common aspirations were to promote trade, especially in palm oil, and to plant the seeds of European cultural and political imperialism in the area.

BRITISH VIOLENCE AND THE DECLINE OF ABOAH

The Niger Expedition of 1857 resulted in the establishment of British trading posts at Aboh, Onitsha, and Lokoja, and because of the increasing European demand for palm oil many more trading posts were established on the lower Niger during subsequent years. In addition, an expanding African demand for guns, textiles, hardware, iron bars, gin, salt, and tobacco spurred establishment of these entrepôts along the great river. The 1860s and the early 1870s were particularly favorable for British and Igbo traders on the Niger. However, after 1875 these apparently "smooth and painless" beginnings came to a sad end when the palm-oil trade went into a long period of economic depression. The prices that palm oil had attracted in Europe fell so sharply that the British traders on the Niger decided to reexamine their methods of securing their cargos. First, they began to offer lower and lower prices for palm oil, and second, they began to resist paying the usual tributes and protection fees to the Niger chiefs. Events surrounding the Aboh highlight the type of crisis that the palm-oil trade generated among some African communities; analysis of these events contradicts the view expressed by Anthony G. Hopkins and David Northrup that the transition from the slave trade to legitimate commerce was achieved with little difficulty because those regions which traded in slaves also produced and exported oil down to the mid-1800s.[18] As we shall see, there was indeed much difficulty related to this transition.

The fame of the town of Aboh rested on the fact that it was the major commercial intermediary between the Niger delta states and the upriver communities.[19] Aboh trading canoes were found not only in such delta states as Akassa, Brass, Kalabari, Bonny, and Opobo, but also in such upriver markets as Asaba, Onitsha, Idah, and Lokoja. By 1830, when the Lander brothers were brought to Aboh as captives, Aboh still dominated the trade of the lower Niger from Asaba downstream. Only north of Asaba was the authority of the Obi challenged by the powerful Attah Igala. By this date the traders of Brass were still paying tribute to the Obi of Aboh for permission to ply the Niger.[20]

During the second half of the nineteenth century, however, there were clear indications that Aboh was declining both militarily and economically. The circumstances responsible for this decline were directly related to British trade competition and gunboat diplomacy on the Niger. Kingsley Ogedengbe has observed that "In spite of European ambitions on the Niger in the 1830s, the traditional pattern of trade remained inviolate. The state system about which the Niger trade revolved remained powerful and flourished economically."[21] But, Ogedengbe explains, the system of direct trade which the Europeans initiated overturned the old pattern of commerce and undermined the foundations of the traditional power structure of the Niger valley kingdoms, which had been based on the monopoly of trade.

In accounting for the decline of Aboh, Ogedengbe is careful not to blame European competition entirely; the state of anarchy that accompanied the death of Obi Ossai has to be considered. Obi Ossai's demise proved doubly tragic for Aboh: "First, it removed a powerful influence at a crucial period of Aboh's history and second, it gave rise to a protracted succession dispute whose repercussions were felt in the entire Niger valley."[22] The succession dispute centered around two personalities, Aje, the son of Obi Ossai, and Olise, a descendant of a previous Obi of Aboh. For over ten years the supporters of the two claimants fought one another while the throne remained vacant. In the end, Olise was confirmed in the office while Aje, who appeared to be "much favored to be elected king of Aboh" was rejected. The effect of such a prolonged succession dispute, Ogedengbe says, was that "the prestige and office of the Obi was shaken, and central power was well-nigh obliterated."[23]

That the central power of Aboh had been shaken is supported by Crowther's contemporary observation that "every headman is a master in his own quarter," and by Baikie's report that many towns that were vassals of Aboh "have ceased to pay tribute, and have become independent."[24] Further evidence that Aboh no longer enjoyed its past influence is derived from the fact that by the second half of the century Brass men visited Aboh without paying the usual tolls.

What these facts show is evidence of Aboh's decline, not the cause of that decline. Aboh could no longer enjoy her past glories, not solely because of protracted succession disputes, even though they lasted ten years; the activities of British traders and British gunboats on the Niger added impetus to that decline. British traders established themselves in the traditional markets of Aboh upstream and down, while on a number of occasions the British gunboats attacked both Aboh and these markets. Such attacks curtailed the military glories which Aboh had enjoyed since 1650, and weakened the economic base of the kingdom.

By the 1840s the overseas trade in slaves had been drastically reduced on the Bights of Benin and Biafra due to the activities of the British navy. As the palm-oil trade grew, some communities were able to export both slaves and oil together. By the 1850s, the slave trade from the Niger delta had virtually stopped, having been replaced by the palm-oil economy. There is enough evidence in the records to show that Aboh made several attempts to give up the old trade for the new. The representatives of the British government had arranged with Obi Ossai in 1841 that if he gave up dealing in slaves he would be sent regular vessels for legitimate trade. The Obi assured the Europeans that he was willing to stop the slave trade if a better commodity would be substituted. In addition to this pledge the Obi entered a treaty arrangement with the leaders of this expedition, in which he promised that "the slave-trade shall be utterly abolished in the Aboh country," that European traders would not be molested, and that British vessels would be allowed to navigate the Niger free of tolls.[25]

After this brief meeting, however, the Europeans departed and for many years the Obi awaited the white men and the fulfillment of their promise; neither was forthcoming. As Bishop Crowther expressed in dramatic terms, "Hope grew fainter and weaker, until at last hope died out. The old man [the Obi] said, 'The white men have forgotten their promise too' and at last he died himself."[26]

It was only in 1857 that the British established a trading post at Aboh. The post was, however, small and could not fulfill the longstanding promise, nor could it hope to compensate for the loss of the profits of the slave trade. In 1860, barely three years after the trading post had been erected, the people of Aboh attacked and plundered it. In reprisal, a British gunboat bombarded the city.[27]

Nonetheless, trade was resumed, but the next few years were very unfavorable for the chiefs and merchants of Aboh, who were completely deprived of their monopoly rights as British trading boats bypassed them and traded directly with the people living upstream. The chiefs and merchants of Aboh who, in any case, had not really observed the clauses of the treaty of 1841, renounced it and reverted to slave trading. Aje, one of the successors of Obi Ossai, denied knowledge of such a treaty even though he was a signatory to that document (see Appendix 1). The relationships between Aboh and the British remained strained until 1883, when three British gunboats bombarded Aboh. This bombardment was not in any way connected with the slave trade, but with certain minor issues which in more humane times would have probably been settled amicably.

One of the issues involved taking gifts. When the British first arrived on the Niger they developed a practice which Bishop Crowther described as a "system of giving gratuitous presents to the native chiefs on the banks of the Niger as a token of friendship to pacify them." These "presents" came not only from the employees of the trading firms, but also from the imperial agents and missionaries. The chiefs regarded them as custom duties or tributes but a few British agents pretended they were gifts, and sometimes tried to avoid paying them. The chiefs, who knew that these were not gifts, insisted that the tributes should be collected, the amounts demanded being proportionate to the volume of trade. According to Crowther, on a number of occasions the chiefs "actually scorned and refused them as not enough," and closed down trade.[28]

Evidence from other parts of southern Nigeria confirms that before the British traders penetrated the Niger valley the chiefs of the various states collected tolls, duties, or tributes from passing traders in return for protection and other services along different segments of the river. Men from Brass paid tributes to the Obi of Aboh if they wished to trade in Aboh territory, and Aboh traders paid tributes to the Attah of Igala if they wished to trade in the territories beyond Asaba.[29] In the Ngwa district in Igboland, east of the Niger, the members of the *Okonko* society, who maintained and policed the trade routes, collected tolls from those who used them.[30] Arthur G. Leonard, who encountered these people, observed that it was common for the members of this society to sit by the trade routes and "demand toll from all passing with goods for trade. . . . If this is refused, they plunder the goods, and in many cases, seize the owners, or drive them away."[31]

When the British traders first arrived, they paid these tributes because they expected the local chiefs to protect them. However, in the 1870s, when British gunboats began to ply the Niger more frequently, and as British imperialist attitudes began to grow more and more intolerant, the traders began to refuse to pay. "Hitherto," observed Felix Ekechi, "the local rulers had had the upper hand in palavers between them and the *Oyibo,* foreigners. By 1879 British military intervention had tilted the balance in favor of the European traders and missionaries," and they began to treat the chiefs with contempt.[32]

Bishop Crowther, who hated the idea of Europeans paying any form of tributes to African chiefs, supported this refusal. He argued that even though the chiefs received lavish presents, they had not reciprocated as expected of them by providing adequate protection to British subjects and their property. He claimed that the chiefs looked at the practice "as a mere gratuity from the inexhaustible stores of the *fools* [his emphasis] who have more than they know what to do with." He then recommended that "the system of giving presents without insisting upon something in return" should stop.[33] The chiefs, on the other hand, contended that their effort to maintain peace was hindered by the tendency of European traders to meddle with local politics and engage in such trade malpractices as price-fixing. Since European traders were not willing to meet the cost of their own protection, the chiefs relaxed security and some private citizens, like Andrew and Ambeefa of Onitsha, took advantage of the situation to molest Europeans and to organize widespread robberies in Aboh, Alenso, Osamala, and Onitsha.[34]

African merchants in the Niger delta and at Aboh, who had been disturbed when European traders began to bypass them to trade with the people further upstream, sent letters to the British Foreign Office in London complaining that British traders were depriving them of their means of livelihood.[35] Realizing that the British government had no sympathy with their plight, some communities resorted to open violence, and between 1860 and 1879 armed Africans harassed some British trading posts and vessels.[36] Obviously, such actions and the retaliatory responses they often provoked generated much mistrust and violence on the lower Niger.

Anthony G. Hopkins blames the strained relationships of this period on trade difficulties, contending that the decline in West African trade began in the 1870s, giving rise to a period of disaffection between the Africans and their European trading partners; by the late 1870s British traders had begun to complain to their home government about the attitude of Africans toward them.[37] This observation is accurate, for we are told that in 1877 the general agent of the West African Company Limited sent a document to the British Foreign Office in which he complained of "several outrages that have been committed by the chiefs of Oko and Osumari (Osamala) on our Agents and property located in these places for the purpose of pursuing legitimate commerce." He begged the Foreign Office to give his petition a "grave consideration and take such measures as would prevent their occurrence at any future period." He reported that the people of the lower Niger had, on several occasions, stopped trade in order to extort presents from the white traders, and that the agents of some trading firms had been "barbarously handled . . . and grossly insulted." After a catalogue of allegations against the chiefs and the people, the general agent warned that the lives of the employees of the trading companies on the lower Niger were not safe and that, "If immediate decisive steps are not taken against these people . . . they will in the next place break through our property as their greed and covetousness are beyond all comprehension."[38]

Indeed, by 1879 the British government had become not only more sympathetic to the cries of British traders, but also more prepared to give them military assistance. This was demonstrated all too clearly in October 1879 when the general manager of the West African Company, David McIntoch, complained about the hostility of some citizens of Onitsha and the British War Office responded by authorizing Captain Burr of the warship *Pioneer* to bombard the town. Captain Burr described the encounter which began on October 26, 1879:

> I immediately landed with our small arm-party under Sub-Lieutenant Luke and opened fire. . . . I opened fire on the upper part of the beach town, Onitsha proper being three miles inland with an estimated population of 10,000, with our ship's guns, and the small-arm men burned that part of the town down. Towards evening I caused shell and rockets to be thrown into every part of it.
>
> The following morning it was reported that the natives had concentrated in the bush in the rear of the town, and were about to attack the factories in force. I ordered everybody belonging to us and all friendly-disposed people to repair on board the different vessels, and then opened fire with shell and rockets continuously through the day, not only into the lower town, but also into the bush beyond.
>
> On the 28th, after very mature consideration, I came to the conclusion that I could not leave Onitsha with credit to the flag after what had taken place . . . without bombarding and marching on Onitsha inland.[39]

After bombarding Onitsha, Captain Burr led his men into the town and "destroyed every object" they could find. Among these were "some very solid houses," the king's palace, casks of palm oil, and crops.

The resistance which the warriors of Onitsha organized soon melted before the superior British firearms.

The British regarded the destruction of Onitsha as a mere example and vowed to deal even more severely with any other Niger community that molested British traders. They argued that since the chiefs were unable to punish or control their subjects, it was appropriate that British "moral force" should be demonstrated so that acts of violence might never again be directed against British subjects. This policy was demonstrated in 1883 when, on the charge that some Aboh citizens had attacked a British trader, three British warships, *Alecto, Flirt,* and *Sterling,* stood in mid-river and shelled and destroyed Aboh. After shelling the town, a landing party put ashore and the people of Aboh responded by mounting a stiff resistance during which hundreds of them were killed.[40]

Despite the bombardment of 1883, Aboh managed to survive and even showed signs of recovery, a resurgence that would soon come face-to-face with the activities of the Royal Niger Company. By the time the Royal Niger Company appeared, the need for protection from the marauding bands of Ijos had ceased, and there was no longer any opportunity of enforcing discipline within the obiship. In consequence, "services to the Obi and Aboh began little by little to be neglected."[41] With the local power structure in disarray, the opportunity presented itself for the Royal Niger Company to set up its court, and it soon became the supreme power on the river. Aboh merchants could not cope with the aggressive commercial practices of the company, and gradually all went into bankruptcy. All subsequent accounts of this ancient city and its chiefs were filled with sad reminiscences concerning their decline. In 1890, Claude MacDonald wrote:

> The king of Aboh, who was an Ibo, and who at one time was a man of considerable power and influence, now rules over at the most some four or five villages; nearly all the Ibo villages in the district would allow that he is by descent their chief, but any attempt on his part to meddle with their affairs would result in a "war palaver."[42]

In another report MacDonald described the king as a man who "at one time was a very important personage though no longer so," and noted that in 1833 the population of Aboh was about 6,000 but by 1890, it was "probably not half that number."[43]

Certainly, the transition from the slave to the palm-oil trade was neither smooth nor painless for Aboh. In fact, the chiefs of Aboh were not the only Niger rulers to be ruined by British commercial imperialism at this time. The Attah Igala, like the Obi of Aboh, did not benefit from the new trade. Perhaps the Attah found himself in an even more pathetic position than the Obi. It is said that in dealing with the white man the Attah had hoped to "become fat" but he was to find that he had "shrunk up and become dry."[44] Like Aboh, the town of Idah, the Attah's ancestral homeland, was bombarded by British gunboats in 1883. These military attacks were extremely provocative, and gradually, the Niger communities began to consider means of driving the British out of their territories. The Ekumeku wars were the natural culmination of the political disturbances of the 1870s and 1880s.

NOTES TO CHAPTER TWO

1. British slave traders transported to the Americas more slaves than all the other European and American traders put together. See Philip D. Curtin, *The Atlantic Slave Trade: A Census* (Madison, 1969), 211. There is an extensive literature on British abolition. See, for instance, Eric Williams, *Capitalism and Slavery* (London, 1975); Roger Anstey, *The Atlantic Slave Trade and British Abolition, 1760-1816* (London, 1975); Suzanne Miers, *Britain and the Ending of the Slave Trade* (London, 1975).

2. Thomas F. Buxton, *The African Slave Trade and Its Remedy* (London, 1840), 282.

3. On Mungo Park's expedition, see Christopher Lloyd, *The Search for the Niger* (London, 1937), 57.

4. Ibid., 119-23.

5. It should be noted that British authorities later redeemed King Boy's debt.

6. Peter R. McKenzie, *Inter-Religious Encounters in West Africa*, (Leicester, 1976), 40-41.

7. MacGregor Laird and R. A. K. Oldfield, *Narrative of an Expedition into the Interior of Africa in 1832, 1833 and 1834* (London, 1891), vol. 1, passim.

8. For a complete account see William Allen and Thomas R. N. Thom-

son, *A Narrative of the Expedition to the River Niger in 1841* 2 vols. (London, 1884).

9. William B. Baikie, *Narrative of an Exploring Voyage up the Rivers Kwora and Binue in 1854* (London, 1856), passim.

10. Philip D. Curtin, *The Image of Africa: British Ideas and Action, 1780-1850* (Madison, 1964), 2:434.

11. Ibid., 435.

12. Richard Lander and John Lander, *Journal of an Expedition to Explore the Course and Termination of the Niger* (New York, 1953), 1:xxvi-xxvii.

13. Mungo Park, *Travels in the Interior of Africa* (New York, 1971), 2.

14. Quoted in Alexander D. Nzemeka, *British Imperialism and African Responses: The Niger Valley, 1851-1905* (Paderborn, 1982), 38.

15. Kenneth O. Dike, *Trade and Politics in the Niger Delta, 1830-1885* (Oxford, 1962), 14.

16. Nzemeka, *British Imperialism*, 39.

17. Ibid., 39.

18. Anthony G. Hopkins, *An Economic History of West Africa* (London, 1973), 128-29. David Northrup, *Trade Without Rulers* (Oxford, 1980), 182.

19. Chieka, C. Ifemesia, *South-eastern Nigeria in the Nineteenth Century: An Introductory Analysis* (New York, 1978), 36.

20. Laird and Oldfield, *Narrative*, 1: 97.

21. Kinglsley Nwachukwu-Ogedengbe, "The Aboh Kingdom of the Lower Niger, c. 1650-1900," (Ph.D. diss., University of Wisconsin, 1971), 339.

22. Ibid.

23. Ibid., 341.

24. Samuel Crowther and John Christopher Taylor, *The Gospel on the Banks of the Niger* (London, 1863), 19; Baikie, *Narrative*, 1:50.

25. Allen and Thomson, *Narrative*, 1:221. For the full text of the treaty, see Appendix 1.

26. *Church Missionary Intelligencer*, 1857, 193.

27. Local Government Archives, Benin City, File No. 26769. E. A. Miller, Aboh Intelligence Report, April 1931.

28. CMS/CA3/04/736, from the journals of Bishop Crowther, February 11, 1886.

29. Allan and Thomson, *Narrative*, 237; Ogedengbe, "The Aboh Kingdom," 313-14.

30. John N. Oriji, "A Re-assessment of the Organization and Benefits of the Slave and Palm Produce Trade Amongst the Ngwa-Igbo, *Canadian Journal of African Studies*, 16, 3 (1982): 537.

31. As quoted in ibid., 537.

32. Felix Ekechi, "Traders, Missionaries and the Bombardment of Onitsha, 1879-1880," *The Conch*, 5, nos. 1 and 2 (1973): 61.

33. CMS, CA3/04/736, from the journals of Bishop Crowther, February 11, 1886. 34. Ekechi, "The Bombardment of Onitsha," 66-67.

35. John E. Flint, *Sir George Goldie and the Making of Nigeria* (Oxford, 1960), 28.
36. Dike, *Trade and Politics,* 171-81.
37. Hopkins, *An Economic History,* 154-55.
38. PRO, FO84/1487 of August 3, 1877, from the General Agent of the West African Company to the Foreign Office, London.
39. Ekechi, "The Bombardment of Onitsha," 66-70.
40. Local Government Archives, Benin City, File No. 26769, E. A. Miller, Intelligence Report on Aboh. Casualty reports for this and other military actions throughout this book are at best sketchy and at worst nonexistent.
41. Ibid.
42. PRO, FO84/2019, Claude McDonald, "Report on the Administration of the Niger Company's Territories," received at Foreign Office, January 9, 1890, chap. 1.
43. PRO, FO84/2019, military notes of MacDonald, July to November, 1889.
44. Ibid., report from MacDonald, chap. 1.

CHAPTER THREE

Missionaries, Traders, and the Conquest of Asaba: The Immediate Causes of the Ekumeku War

CHRISTIAN MISSIONARIES PLAYED an important role in the British conquest of Western Igboland. As the first foreigners to venture inland in fairly large numbers, their accounts of what they found helped stimulate British imperial ambitions in the region. As early as 1862, when British policy makers were still "reluctant" to build an African empire, Rev. John Christopher Taylor of the British Church Missionary Society had informed some Onitsha converts that the British government would protect them against certain customary Igbo restrictions when it formally took over the Niger territories.[1] The involvement of Christian missionaries in the politics of the colonial conquest of Nigeria has never been disputed. "From the start," writes Emmanuel A. Ayandele, "missionary propaganda . . . was not just a religious invasion. In effect, it was associated with a political invasion as well. In the background was the secular arm of Britain to be invoked when practicable." In Yorubaland, Ayandele contends, missionaries prepared the way for the "governor, exploiter and teacher."[2] And in Western Igboland they prepared the way for the violent annexation of territories. In fact, the available evidence shows that the fiercest military encounters occurred in those parts of Western Igboland, such as Asaba, Issele-Ukwu, and Illah, where missionaries were established, whereas the areas missionaries avoided, like the Agbor district, remained relatively quiet for some time.

In the Asaba district of Aniocha the general conduct of Christian missionaries often provoked indigenous resistance, which then drew in British military intervention. It is not surprising, therefore, that long before British colonial administrators moved into Western Igboland to hoist the British flag, they had brought in troops to protect the lives and property of missionaries. Even after the establishment of colonial rule in Western Igboland, British officials occasionally restrained missionaries from visiting or establishing themselves in some areas because of the fear that their presence might provoke an uprising. Under the circumstances, it is not difficult to conclude that the Ekumeku movement was partly organized to resist the spread of Christianity. As will be shown, the missionaries were implicated in all the battles of the Ekumeku, and along with the Christian converts were the first targets of attack whenever an uprising broke out. Since Christian missionaries played such an important role in the British conquest of Western Igboland, it is important to examine their history there. It soon becomes clear that the friendly reception the people of Western Igboland gave the missionaries when they first arrived eventually turned to resentment when the political intentions of the visitors became clear.

The first Christian missionaries to work in Western Igboland were the agents of the British Church Missionary Society (CMS). Founded in 1799, it was a combination of lay and clerical agency.[3] The society soon established a mission in Freetown, Sierra Leone, and by the mid-nineteenth century Freetown had become the center from which CMS missionaries were sent to other parts of West Africa.

The Egbas of southwestern Nigeria were among the first converts to return to their homeland to teach the gospel. They made such an impression that settlers there whose original homes were in other parts of Africa entreated the society to send more missionaries. Among such settlers were a hundred liberated Igbo who petitioned the bishop of Sierra Leone, stating that "they had long pondered over the effort made on behalf of the Yorubas, and that they could no longer refrain from an earnest petition that Missionaries might also be sent to their country."4 Their petition was considered and as a result Rev. E. James and three other Igbo were sent out to visit Fernando Po, an island off the coast of Nigeria, to collect information about the possibility of extending Christianity into Igboland. This initial attempt was not particularly successful; it did not lead to the collection of the desired information, nor did it pave the way for the Christian penetration of Igboland.

In 1841 another attempt to bring Christianity to Igboland was made, and its results would prove much broader and longer-lasting. This was part of an expedition which was not only "conjointly commercial and missionary in its object," but also part of a grand design to launch British imperial expansion into Africa.5 Christian missionaries were involved in this expedition because the realities of nineteenth-century British imperialism in Africa made it necessary for missionaries to work hand-in-hand with British traders and soldiers.

The three names most commonly associated with the 1841 expedition were James F. Schon, a German, Samuel Ajayi Crowther, a freed Yoruba slave who would rise to the rank of bishop in the Christian Missionary Service, and Simon Jonas, an Igbo ex-slave from Sierra Leone who acted as an interpreter. On arrival at Aboh, Schon and Crowther established contact with Obi Ossai, who assured the visitors that he would allow the traders and missionaries to establish themselves in his chiefdom. Obi Ossai was so impressed with this visit, and especially by Simon Jonas's ability to render verses from the Holy Bible into the Igbo language, that he requested him to remain behind and teach the gospel while the rest of the expedition went up to Lokoja. "You must stop with me," said Obi Ossai, "you must teach me and my people. The white people can go up the river without you; they may leave you here until they return, or until other people come."6

Schon and Crowther could not object to such a friendly request. They therefore instructed Jonas to remain behind and make preparations for the establishment of mission stations at Aboh and the neighboring Igbo settlements on the Niger. Jonas moved about with freedom and preached the Gospel, but his stay was cut short when the expedition returned earlier than had been planned because the party was wracked by disease, a fate that also quashed a second expedition in 1854. It was only during the 1857 expedition that the CMS built a mission post at Onitasha. This mission was headed by Rev. John Christopher Taylor, an Igbo man born in Sierra Leone.[7] Missionary enterprise in Igboland is generally regarded as having started in 1857 since the 1841 and 1854 expeditions did not lead to the establishment of Christian missions. From 1857 onwards Onitsha became the headquarters of the CMS Niger Mission.

THE ASABA MISSION

After establishing the Onitsha mission in 1857, the agents of the CMS occasionally traveled to a number of towns on the lower Niger, hoping to open up centers there, too. In September 1873 Rev. John Buck visited Asaba for this purpose but achieved nothing substantial by this visit. Soon after that Rev. M. Romaine went to Asaba and was assisted by Obi Igweli to secure a piece of land for a proposed mission post.[8] Rev. Romaine paid the agreed price, ten pieces of grey cotton fabric valued at £5, to Obi Igweli, who was described as "a chief of the first rank of Asaba."[9] Soon after this bargain had been struck Rev. Romaine left for Sierra Leone and Rev. Edward K. Phillips was asked to take over the station.

The building the Church Missionary Society later erected at Asaba on the piece of land they bought from Obi Igweli became the first Christian missionary establishment in Western Igboland. Rev. Phillips, the first agent at Asaba, became the first Christian missionary to work in Western Igboland. At the end of the first year of ministration at Asaba, Crowther reported that a few persons were "timidly coming forward to hear the word of God on the Lord's day, but fear of domestic persecution, and of being laughed at, kept them back from making an open confession of Christianity."[10] Crowther also lamented that the chiefs who promised to send their children to school had not done so, though the children themselves were very anxious to attend. Nonetheless, a small congregation, averaging thirty, assembled each Sunday, nine of whom were candidates for baptism, and by the end of the first year seven boys had been enrolled in the mission school. The congregation of converts grew slowly and by 1879 the missionaries were pleased to see a gathering of what they described as "some fifty or eighty humble worshippers, who, a few years ago had no knowledge of their maker."[11]

Whatever success the Church Missionary Society might have achieved, it was evident from the beginning that it would meet with strong opposition from the people of Asaba. Initially, the Christians were attracted by the friendliness of the city's inhabitants. The people of Asaba were generally peaceful and hospitable, facts which induced Crowther to describe them as "sociable and tractable."[12] He was equally aware, however, that Asaba was a difficult field for evangelization. In 1875 Crowther noted that the people of that place would not abandon their customs, and that the town was "one of the places where the Satan's seat is."[13] After thirteen years of continuous missionary activity at Asaba, the CMS could boast of no more than a handful of free-born converts. These first converts were drawn principally from three groups that had no status whatsoever in the traditional society of the town—strangers, outcasts, and slaves.[14] The strangers were mainly the soldiers and laborers of the Royal Niger Company, who in 1888 attended services regularly. The outcasts were those who had been accused of some crime, or those who were believed guilty of some shameful act. The bulk of the first converts of the CMS at Asaba, however, was drawn from the slave population.

Whatever might have been the source of the converts, the CMS missionaries continued to strive for success in Asaba. They arranged their work under "three principal heads," namely, "Sunday duties, School work and Visiting and Intinerating." Some youths were attracted to the settlement's industrial center, where cotton, bricks, and furniture were produced.[15]

The relationship between the chiefs of Asaba and the Church Missionary Society fluctuated between indifference and open hostility. The chiefs objected to the Christians' interference with local customs and their tendency to incite the slaves into rebellion by preaching against human sacrifice. The missionaries also preached the equality of all people before God, not a message welcomed by the leaders in a society that accepted slavery. The dispute over human sacrifice was very heated and was championed by Bishop Crowther, who soon became engaged in a series of bitter encounters with the Muslims and traditional religionists on the Niger. At Idah, relates Peter R. McKenzie, Crowther disputed with the Attah over certain "central points of traditional doctrine, such as the perennial one about the provision of attendants for a king or chief just died in the unseen world."[16] In the Niger delta

Crowther quarreled with chiefs over the practice of offering up prisoners-of-war in sacrifices. He also challenged the practice of venerating the sacred lizards or iguanas, sharks, and pythons, as well as the worship of visible and imaginary objects. Throughout Crowther's career on the Niger, points out McKenzie, he stuck to the policy of confrontation with non-Christians. To Crowther it was "a conflict between light and darkness." He therefore could not be restrained from saying unpleasant things about the local people no matter how much they might be offended.[17]

Inter-religious confrontations are a normal phenomenon in any situation where different religions or creeds are made to interract for the first time. Nevertheless, the historical significance of the confrontations that took place at Asaba lies in the fact that they marked a decisive turning point in Anglo-Nigerian relationships on the Niger and in the delta. Before 1888 the Christians were under constant attack by the traditional religionists and were not assisted by the representatives of the British imperial government. The bombardments of Onitsha in 1879 and Aboh in 1883 were ostensibly intended to protect British traders and were not intended to assist Christian missionaries, who had to rely on the good will of the local chiefs for their protection. Sometimes this protection was not forthcoming. For example, in 1868 the people of Onitsha openly molested the Christians even when British gunboats were anchored nearby. According to Crowther, "In the presence of the Gunboats, trade was stopped, the Christians were persecuted, and prevented from going to church." Shortly after the gunboats had sailed away the Christians were fined thirty bags of cowries valued at about £30.[18] Also at Onitsha the property of the CMS was attacked by the traditional religionists for the Christians' refusal to throw away the twin babies of one of the converts.[19] At Obosi, following a misunderstanding with some British traders, the traditional religionists threatened to eat any Christian they might catch.[20]

The missionaries sent many reports back to Europe concerning the hostile manner in which they were treated by the people of Asaba and in neighboring towns. In 1878, for example, John Buck wrote that "the state of things in the middle part of the Niger is becoming more and more alarming." He warned that the lives of the Christians were in "jeopardy every hour," and complained about what he called "the difficulties, trials, and oppositions" they were experiencing with the local populations among whom they lived. He claimed that black missionary agents were often beaten and at times killed: "Late Mr. Joshua Smith was killed by Ogene's son of Onitsha . . . the Rev. S. Perrey was severely beaten when he went to rescue Mrs. John who was equally guiltless and done nothing to provoke them." He concluded, "This dreadful contagion is not only seizing large towns, but small villages also. Alenso now is far from being what it was years gone by."[21]

Bishop Crowther had one other reason to be angry with the chiefs of Asaba. It involved the tendency among them to regard all European traders, imperial agents, and missionaries as one, and in the event of a disagreement with one party, to antagonize the rest. In 1879 the chiefs of Asaba had cause to close down trade, denying all Europeans permission to purchase provisions for their sustenance because, as Crowther put it, "they would not give presents according to their wishes"; the bishop protested "the injustice of including the mission agents with the merchants." Obi Igweli received his protest with close attention and "acknowledged the wrong" but explained that "as one party of civilized people was forbidden, the other should be included also."[22]

However, after the conquest of Asaba the tables were turned decisively against the traditional religionists. The Christians were thenceforth given official military backing each time their lives were threatened. As we shall presently see, some of the Ekumeku disurbances started when government troops rushed to the rescue of the missionaries. The policy of giving official protection to Christians and of physically attacking local communities on purely religious and noncommercial reasons was initiated by the Royal Niger Company, and Asaba was made the scapegoat.

The officials of the Royal Niger Company justified their actions by contending that the chiefs had broken certain clauses of the protection treaties, which stipulated among other things that "Christians, of whatever nation or country . . . shall be left in the free enjoyment and exercise of the Christian religion, and shall not be hindered or molested in their endeavors to teach the same to all persons whatever willing and desirous to be taught"; further, the chiefs would use all the means in their power to put a stop to human sacrifice, as "the custom is displeasing to the Queen and people of Great Britain."[23] As we have seen, Onitsha and Aboh were bombarded by British gunboats because the people of these places molested British traders and stole their goods; yet these same gunboats ignored the plight of Christian missionaries who were under constant attack by the traditional religionists. These same attacks must also be viewed as politically motivated, for in the traditional context both ritual and political powers derived from the same source. The chiefs and ritual specialists rightly judged that their power and influence over their people would diminish in the same proportion as the influence of the Christians increased. The officials of the Royal Niger Company, ignoring such reasoning, proceeded to destroy Asaba under the pretext of stopping human sacrifice and protecting the Christians.

THE ROYAL NIGER COMPANY AND THE CONQUEST OF ASABA

The British expeditions of the 1840s and 1850s resulted in the establishment of a trading post at Lokoja in 1857, and Dr. William Belfour Baikie, the leader of the successful Niger expedition of 1854, was appointed British representative there. The position, which he held until he retired about 1864, was similar to that of a British consular agent.[24] But Lokoja did not hold out great prospects for trade and in 1869 the British closed their consulate in that town.

This closure did not discourage the British trading firms that had established themselves there. These were the West African Company of Manchester, Holland Jacques and Company, Alexander Pinnock and Company, and Miller Brothers of Glasgow. In addition, a few African merchants from Lagos and Sierra Leone traded in the area. What discouraged these traders (both British and African) was not necessarily the declining volume of trade, but the arrival of two French trading firms. A trade that was barely large enough for four British firms could hardly sustain the arrival of two French ones in addition to the Lagos and Sierra Leone merchants.[25] The period 1875 to 1884 was marked by severe competition and none of the trading firms, either European or African, seemed to be doing well until an ambitious army officer who had traveled widely in Africa came on the scene. George Goldie Taubman's primary ambitions were to frustrate French activities on the Niger, to "replace the monopoly of the African traders with that of the British, and above all, to color the map red."[26]

Taubman, who became popularly known simply as Goldie, has been described as a man endowed with a "rare business ability that was combined with political and diplomatic skill of a high order."[27] In him were personified all the attributes of the new British economic imperialism. He came to be involved in the Niger trade through his family connections; Holland Jacques and Company, the smallest of the four British firms trading on the Niger, was the worst hit by the cutthroat competition of the period, and its secretary appealed to the Taubman family for assistance. They responded by buying out the entire assets of Holland Jacques. Goldie was put in control of the company and was specifically asked to put the business in order.

From the beginning Goldie's firm assumed an aggressive policy toward all its rivals. Goldie himself rightly judged that none of the British firms was doing particularly well. He therefore planned to amalgamate them into a powerful combine. According to biographer John Flint, in Goldie's eyes, "over-competition was the disease, and monopoly the only cure."[28] In 1882 Goldie's company became known as the National African Company, and it soon eliminated some of the weaker firms and bought out the rest, including the two French firms. Thus, on the eve of the Berlin Conference of 1884-85, instead of six, there was only one powerful European firm trading on the Niger. These moves by Goldie, coupled with the treaties he claimed to have signed with the local chiefs, enabled Britain to lay claim to the Niger and the Benue valleys at the Berlin Conference.

The National African Company was granted a royal charter in 1886, partly "in recognition of its services in the interior," and partly because of Britain's clumsy and inconsistent policy toward colonialism. The British government was at first reluctant to grant the charter, but when Goldie threatened to sell the treaties he claimed to have concluded with African chiefs, the British government reluctantly granted the request.[29] Thus, on July 10, 1886, the National African Company became the Royal Niger Company, Chartered and Limited. This charter vested in the company a wide range of authority over the Lower Niger Protectorate, a strip of land on both sides of the Niger River running from the coast to undefined points in the interior.

Having received the charter, the Royal Niger Company saw itself as the only recognized government in the entire Niger territory. All "native authorities" were at once considered dissolved and in a dramatic turnaround, the leading members of each Niger community were required to sign a treaty of protection and trade with the agents of the company, at the same time surrendering their sovereignty. If a community failed to send its representatives, a treaty was signed on its behalf by some unknown and uncomprehending persons whose X marks were subsequently used to prove that the community accepted the authority of the Royal Niger Company. A close look at the treaties of the company strongly suggests that most of them were forged. (see Appendices 2 and 3).[30]

The government that the officials of the company subsequently established on the lower Niger was arbitrary, dictatorial, and repressive. Its high-handedness caused great discontent, not only among Africans, but also among other European traders and agents of the British government. Officials of the company were said to have shot and killed one hundred Brass men and women "annually and without cause" other than for alleged smuggling.[31] Soon the whole Niger territory became tense with wars and rumors of war.

The company's strength came not only from bits of paper — a charter and a group of suspect treaties; it also had sufficient resources with which to carry out its program of aggression. It was authorized by the British government to raise a military force officered by Englishmen, which became the notorious constabulary force of the Royal Niger Company, formed primarily with a view toward promoting and maintaining British economic imperialism in the interior. By the end of the century this force was incorporated into the Royal West African Frontier Force, but in 1888 it consisted of "5 English Officers, 2 Native Officers, 2 Sergeant Majors, 15 Sergeants, 16 Corporals and 380 privates."[32] Some of these men were stationed at Asaba, the administrative headquarters of the Protectorate. The rest were deployed at various points on the lower Niger between Akassa and Lokoja. Other members of the force were posted aboard the two marine vessels, *Masaba* and *Emily Waters.* In addition to these, there were the S. S. *Kano,* S. S. *Bussa,* and S. S. *Niger,* each of which was capable of carrying over 300 troops, a fact that enabled the various detachments "to be moved about as circumstances might require."[33]

The recruitment of the constabulary forces is noteworthy. Like the several hundred employees of the company, the soldiers and policemen were foreigners to the lower Niger. Out of every eight soldiers, five were Fanti from modern Ghana, two were Hausa from northern Nigeria, and one Yoruba from western Nigeria. The Hausa were said to be "bold and plucky but in bush fighting . . . apt to get out of hand and think too much of loot." The Fanti were supposedly far steadier in the bush than the Hausa but lacked individual pluck even though they fought well in a body.[34] One thing all these mercenaries had in common was their readiness to shoot down their fellow Africans at a command from their European masters. It was with a force so recruited and so armed that the Royal Niger Company terrorized the people of Asaba.

In 1886 the representatives of the Royal Niger Company concluded a treaty with the chiefs of Asaba. Among other things, the chiefs agreed to give up slave trading and human sacrifice.[35] The officials of the company pledged, for their part, not to interfere with the customs and religion of the people of Asaba except where they threatened law and order. But the chiefs of Asaba, who did not seem to understand the implications of the treaty they signed, continued to observe all aspects of their customs and religion. They bought and sold slaves and performed human sacrifice, completely disregarding both the treaties and any pretensions of authority from the company. By 1887, relations between the two parties had becme irreparably strained, not only on political and philosophical grounds, but also on a more mundane level: the soldiers of the company stole fowls, for example, and caught the natives' goats and cows. They also molested the inhabitants by invading their farms and by stealing their property.[36]

In 1886 Sir James Marshall, a chief judge and an employee of the Royal Niger Company, was sent out to establish a regular judicial system at Asaba. On his arrival, the agents of the CMS informed him that the people of the town indulged in human sacrifice and that there was no prospect of convincing them to give up the practice. "Asaba is a very dark spot in heathendom," reported Rev. Henry Johnson. "This human sacrifice has been the shocking custom from time out of mind . . . the land is defiled with blood and is groaning for deliverance."[37] The missionaries complained that each time they preached against the practice the people of Asaba responded, "It is the custom of our ancestors and we their children will be regarded as degenerated ones if we should either swerve or depart from that which was being done from countless ages back."[38]

Sir James did not have to be urged by the Protestants to take punitive actions against Asaba. He had himself received "a rigid Catholic upbringing" and was a most ardent Romanist who, during his brief stay at Asaba, "went over to Onitsha regularly on Sundays to attend divine services" (There was no Roman Catholic church in Asaba when Sir James arrived in 1886.).[39] Even before his arrival he must have been aware of the great volume of correspondence which the European-sponsored missionaries were sending from Africa to Europe each month. Most of this correspondence, observes Peter O. Esedebe, "bristled with accounts of what they described as the wickedness and abominable customs of pagan society." Some of these letters, Esedebe further points out, were published in reputable journals mainly to stimulate missionary subscriptions but over time "they became an unwitting source of racism."[40] There is little doubt that Sir James, a staunch Catholic and an avowed imperialist who had served as a chief magistrate and judicial assessor for the Gold Coast Colony in the 1870s,[41] must have been influenced by this barrage of propaganda. If the chiefs of Asaba would not give up the sentiments and customs of centuries by moral persuasion, could they not be compelled to do so by a show of force? Sir James called a meeting of some chiefs and warned that if they failed to give up the practice, he would send the soldiers of the company against them.[42]

The chiefs of Asaba did not take Sir James's warning seriously. They wondered how they could abandon their customs merely because a European trader had asked them to do so, and as a result they dismissed the warning as no more than the usual interference of the Europeans with local politics and religion. This pattern emerged as a common component of the process of British conquest and penetration of parts of southeastern Nigeria. First British agents used the slightest excuse as an opportunity to demonstrate their strength while, as J. C. Anene has pointed out, "the indigenous groups whose independence was being threatened did not realize that the white man meant business." Thus, while the indigenous people argued that the white man "had no business in their own territories," imperial agents like Sir James Marshall and Sir Ralph Moor argued that "the natives must be made to fully understand that the Government is their master and is determined to establish in and control their country," that is, "to demonstrate the effective power of the government."[43]

CHAPTER THREE 73

In mid-April 1988, shortly after Sir James had issued his warning, news came to him that Asaba was again the scene of human sacrifices. Sir James saw in this report an act of disobedience that would justify his making an example of Asaba through a show of strength. Instructions passed from top to bottom, and two constabulary officers and 206 privates assembled on the parade ground. Also with them were a number of "Executive Officials" and twenty-five men who were simply described as "Allies."[44] On the final instruction of the commanding officer, this force left "Soldier Town" and moved toward the main town.

When news reached the town that the constabulary soldiers were coming in force, the warriors of Asaba declared war. They armed themselves with cutlasses, dane guns, and bows and arrows, and consulted the *dibia* (medicine men). The invaders were met with fierce resistance. Gunfire sounded all day, and as darkness fell, the men of Asaba retreated into the hilly forests of the neighboring Okpanam and Igbuzo. The grim struggle lasted four days and, as Father Carlo Zappa, a Roman Catholic priest stationed at Lokoja, recalled, "It took all the energies of the military forces of the company to conquer the *petite chefs* of the town."[45]

Asaba lost many men in the attack.[46] Some of the chiefs were captured by the soldiers and taken to the barracks where they remained as prisoners. Among the captives was a chief who had sacrificed a slave to honor his dead brother. A message was sent to the people in the bush, informing them that their town would remain occupied until another man who had offered a human sacrifice at his brother's funeral was handed over to the soldiers.[47] Asaba remained occupied for several more days, after which the soldiers returned to the barracks; there is nothing in the records to show whether or not the wanted man came forward.

While Asaba was still occupied, Rev. Hugh S. Macaulay, a CMS agent stationed in the town, wrote a letter to his grandfather describing the scene; the grandfather was Bishop Samuel Crowther, then in Lagos. The letter is dated April 16, 1988:

> I simply write this to inform you that war has broken out at Asaba between the constabulary and the Natives of Asaba, owing to the unwillingness of the people to give up their human sacrifice. Sir James had called a meeting and told them that

if they don't give it up, they will have to do it by force of arms. Two kings [chiefs] died lately and though they promised they would not offer human sacrifice at their burial, yet they did so. Consequently, all last week fire was opened on the town and half of Asaba is now destroyed. One man is now in irons at the Barracks who offered human sacrifice to bury his brother, a king. The other man is demanded by the Constabulary and if he is not brought in a day or two, fire will be opened on the other half of Asaba. Our work is completely stopped for the present, the church people and school children are all scattered, . . .[48]

In failing to comply with the wishes of the *oyibo* (foreigners) to stop human sacrifice, and in confronting the constabulary forces, did the people of Asaba hope to overcome the invaders? It is doubtful. Already familiar with the military might of the white man, they were perhaps equally aware of their own military weakness. Thus, when they decided to resist the constabulary forces on that historic April day, their action, like that of Brass men a decade later, was the result of frustration and desperation. They realized that the real issue was one of economic and political survival. Their major economic institutions, like those of the Delta States, had come to depend very much on slave labor. A slave was a profitable asset that could be made to produce palm oil or yams; the destruction or forced surrendering of property (and slaves were property) is economic murder. The use to which tangible assets can be put depends on a wide range of cultural, social and economic factors, and the situation along the banks of the Niger was no different. "The question of use," point out Miers and Kopytoff, "is never purely an economic matter, but is governed by the total social and political economy of each society."[49] The Asabans were merely using their assets, and were threatened by the loss of those assets.

In addition, the people of Asaba knew it was dangerous to take instructions from strangers. Economically, they realized that the society was becoming rapidly stratified; the most important vehicles for social mobility remained slave ownership and slave sacrifice to mark the installation of a chief or to signify the departure of a successful man into the land of his ancestors. If the chiefs followed British instructions and gave up human sacrifice, would not the next step be the abolition of slave ownership itself? In a society where slaves con-

CHAPTER THREE 75

stituted a large proportion of the population, how could these potentially dangerous elements be held in check except by some form of social control such as the fear of being sacrificed or executed? These circumstances, well understood by the chiefs of Asaba, fired their determination to resist any attempt by the Europeans to usurp their independence of thought and action.

If the battle of 1888 was not the first major war of the people of Asaba, it was certainly their last. Thenceforth, they were made to feel the inconveniences of an army of occupation as they "were constantly molested and earned no rest both at night and day until the soldiers . . . moved from Asaba."[50] Every Sunday, and in fact every day of the week, slave owners watched with disgust as their slaves trooped to the Christian churches and industrial centers where they were taught to sing, to read and write, and to recite verses from the Bible. The slaves became very active and sometimes violated local customs in the name of Christianity. They also began to "spy" for the missionaries, exposing many activities of the town. As a result, observes Clara Onianwa, the people of Asaba nicknamed all Christians *ndi na ka anyi uka,* or simply, *ndi uka,* that is, "those that spy on us" or "those who backbite us."[51] And because the bulk of the first converts of the CMS at Asaba was drawn from the slave population, the church earned the appellation, *uka-ugwule,* that is, "the assemblies of slaves." These sentiments toward the missionaries and their churches, coupled with the bitter feelings which the conquest of Asaba provoked, caused the free-born to sever completely their relationships with the CMS.

It should not be construed that the Royal Niger Company abolished the slave trade or domestic slavery in Asaba after the subjugation of the chiefs. What the company did was simply to compel the slave owners to give up the more heinous forms of cruelties against slaves. In fact, far from abolishing slavery, officials of the company shut their eyes to it. According to a Roman Catholic source, as late as 1888, and despite the declaration of British protectorate over the Niger territories, fifty slaves were still being sold on the sand bank in Asaba each day and many more in "the other great markets," while at Aboh, Major McDonald observed about one hundred being sold in a single day in 1890.[52] Even Sir James Marshall, who personally ordered the conquest of Asaba, adhered to the policy that domestic slavery should not be interfered with. While he was in the Gold Coast he described slaves as "part and parcel" of the families to which they belonged, "to which they are so much attached as their children are."[53] The issue for the Asabans was not loss of slaves, but loss of power.

The slaves of Asaba were disappointed with the limited reform the British insisted on. They had hoped that the decree against human sacrifice would be followed by another, abolishing the legal status of slavery, but when this did not happen, they began slowly to withdraw from the Christians. The missionaries then went from one slave village to another exhorting them to return to the church, but the slaves did not respond favorably.[54] In 1891 Rev. Julius Spencer noted with a feeling of utter disgust that

> It is now obvious that nearly the whole of the slaves who began to attend Church at that time, did so merely to please the *oyibo* who delivered them from death: for, up to the present moment, very few have shown the least signs of a determination to give up themselves to the Lord.[55]

All in all, the slave-owning chiefs of Asaba had been subdued and burdened with two sets of strangers: the agents of the Royal Niger Company and their constabulary soldiers on the one hand, and the agents of the Church Missionary Society on the other. The chiefs' dream of a greater trade turned into a nightmare. Their autonomy was overturned as their interests were subordinated to those of the Royal Niger Company. Slaves were now becoming difficult to control, as the laws and customs of Asaba increasingly came under attack by the Christians. With the deployment of the men of the West African Frontier Force to Asaba in 1900, the town was automatically converted into a British dependency and saddled with a Native Court Council and a judicial personnel composed mainly of the colonial officials and Warrant Chiefs. The rule of its own chiefs was at an end.

NOTES TO CHAPTER THREE

1. CMS, CA3/037, Journal of Rev. John Christopher Taylor, November 10, 1862, "Report on the Political and Spiritual State of Onitsha," 1864.
2. Emmanuel A. Ayandele, *The Missionary Impact on Modern Nigeria, 1864-1914: A Political and Social Analysis* (New York, 1966), 8, 29.
3. Kenneth O. Dike, *Origin of the Niger Mission, 1814-1819* (Ibadan, 1962), 3-9. See also Elizabeth Isichei, *The Ibo People and the Europeans* (London, 1973), 91.
4. *Church Missionary Intelligencer,* 1853, 253.
5. *Church Missionary Intelligencer,* 1857, 194. On the "grand design," see Chieka C. Ifemesia, "British Enterprise on the Niger, 1830-1869" (Ph.D. thesis, University of London, 1959), 278.
6. *Journals of Rev. James Frederick Schon and Mr. Samuel Crowther: Expedition up the Niger in 1842* (London, 1842), 2d ed. with a new introduction by J. F. Ade Ajayi (London, 1970), 60.
7. Rev. Samuel Crowther and John Christopher Taylor, *The Gospel on the Banks of the Niger* (London, 1863).
8. CMS, CA3/09 from the journal extracts of John Buck from September 1873 to September 1874.
9. CMS, CA/04/1875, from the annual reports of Bishop Crowther, 1875.
10. CMS, CA3/04/76, report on Crowther's visit to the Niger mission, 1870.
11. *Church Missionary Intelligencer,* 1879, 230.
12. CMS, G3/A3/1882/131, November 5, 1887, Crowther to Lang.
13. CMS, CA3/04, from the annual reports of Bishop Crowther, 1875.
14. CMS, CA3/04/744/761, from the reports of Bishop Crowther, 1876.
15. *Church Missionary Intelligencer,* 1879, 230.
16. Peter R. McKenzie, *Inter-Religious Encounters in West Africa* (Leicester, U.K., 1976), 52.
17. Ibid., 92-93, 15.
18. CMS, CA3/04/736, from Crowther's journal, February 11, 1868.
19. McKenzie, *Inter-Religious Encounters,* 61.
20. CMS, G3/A3/1887/131, Crowther to Lang, November 5, 1887.
21. CMS, G3/04, John Buck to Crowther, December 23, 1878.
22. CMS, CA3/04, Crowther's report on annual visits to the Niger mission, February 14, 1879.
23. See Appendices 1, 2, 3.
24. Paul Mbaeyi, *British Military and Naval Forces in West African History, 1807-1875* (New York, 1973), 173.
25. F0403/234. No. 120, Ralph Moor to Foreign Office, received November 27, 1896.
26. Godfrey N. Uzoigwe, *Britain and the Conquest of Africa: The Age of Salisbury* (New York, 1978), 80.

27. Arthur Norton Cook, *British Enterprise in Nigeria* (London, 1964), 81.
28. Flint, *Sir George Goldie,* 29.
29. Ibid., 82.
30. See Appendices 2 and 3 for the treaties of the Royal Niger Company.
31. F0403/217, Confidential File no 6668, Sir J. Kirk to Marquess of Salisbury, received August 30, 1895.
32. F084/2019, "Military Notes on the Countries of West Africa Visited by Major MacDonald," July to November, 1889.
33. Ibid.
34. Ibid.
35. For treaties of the Royal Niger Company, see, for instance, F02/4/N/03462, See also Appendices 2 and 3.
36. Isichei, *The Ibo People and the Europeans,* 118-19.
37. CMS, G3/A3/1888/48, from the reports of Henry Johnson, Archdeacon of the Upper Niger, January 6, 1888.
38. CMS, CA3/031, from the annual letters of Rev. Edward Phillips, October 1875.
39. CMS, G3/A31/1888/48, from the reports of Henry Johnson, January 6, 1888.
40. Peter O. Esedebe, *Pan-Africanism* (Enugu, 1980), 23-24.
41. Paul E. Lovejoy, *Transformations in Slavery,* (Cambridge, U.K., 1983), 253.
42. CMS, G3/A3/1888/50, Hugh S. Macaulay to Crowther, April 16, 1888.
43. J. C. Anene, *Southern Nigeria in Transition 1885-1906* (Cambridge, U.K., 1966), quoted 220 and 221; C0520/2, Moor to Colonial Office, May 28, 1901.
44. F084/2019, military notes of Major MacDonald, chapter 9.
45. SMA, 14/80302/15829, Father Zappa to Superior, October 4, 1888.
46. Casualty statistics for this and other military confrontations described throughout this book are often unavailable. Such figures often went unrecorded in the written records and have not survived in the oral ones.
47. CMS, G3/A3/1888/50, High S. Macaulay to Crowther, April 16, 1888.
48. Ibid.
49. Suzanne Miers and Igor Kopytoff, *Slavery in Africa* (Madison, 1977), 21.
50. Isichei, *The Ibo People and the Europeans,* 119.
51. Clara Nkechi Onianwa, "The Coming of Christianity to Asaba," Research Project, Department of History, University of Jos, 1980), 45.
52. SMA, *Bulletin de la Congregation,* 1, no. 8, (February 1888) 464.
53. Lovejoy, *Transformations,* 253.
54. CMS, G3/A3/1892/77, Johnson to Lang, July 5, 1888.
55. CMS, G3/A3/1892/52, Rev. Julius Spencer reporting from Asaba, December 1891.

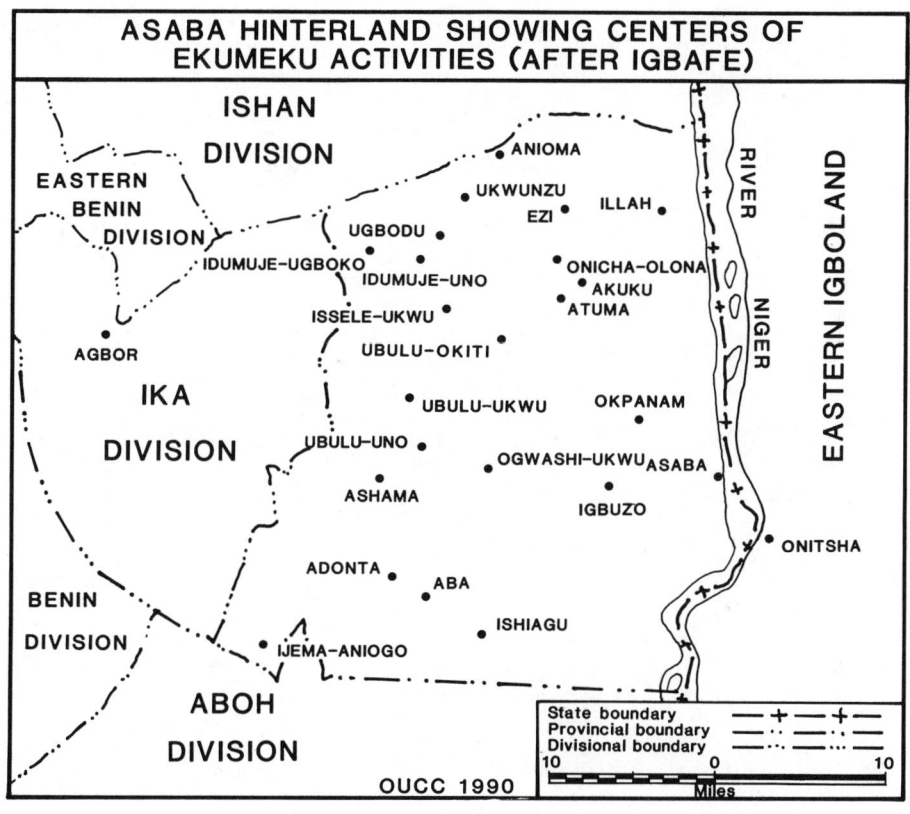

CHAPTER FOUR

The Rise of the Ekumeku

ONE OF THE problems facing peasant communities wishing to rid themselves of repression, fear, or injustice is that of forming a viable coalition against the enemy. "Peasants often harbor a deep sense of injustice," observes Eric Wolf, "but this sense of injustice must be given shape and expression in organization before it can became active on the political scene."[1] To channel peasant discontent into a strong political action, an individual has to speak to the group, communicate the right message, and provide the oppressed people with the necessary guidance and leadership. Evidence from many parts of Africa confirm that strong leadership and a deep sense of patriotism often emerged when a community was threatened by external forces. Sometimes resistance was organized around specific groups of local power holders, or around charismatic figures, or even around strong religious beliefs. As we have seen, the Tanzanian peasantry endured German, Arab, and Swahili injustices until 1905 when Kinjikitile Ngwale, the priest of a religious cult, offered them the magic water, *maji*.[2] In Sierra Leone, it was the paramount chief, Bai Bureh, who moved the peasants to a violent political action.[3] And in Algeria, the oppressed and dispossessed peasants were mobilized against French imperialism by the secular and religious leaders. There was a strong appeal to Islam in which the emir appeared "as the instrument of God gathering the community of the faithful in a holy war against Christianity."[4]

In the 1880s and 1890s the Western Igbo were initially plagued by the problem of a lack of unity and leadership. The communities were fragmented; the powers of the local chiefs and religious cults were small and restricted to the villages and clans. If any coalition could be formed, only the local chiefs, who had become somewhat militant in their dealings with the Europeans, could initiate the formation of a coalition against the enemy. There was a high level of discontent; what was lacking was mobilization, and this came in stages.

The major irritant to Western Igbo people as a whole was the British conquest of Asaba, which, as we have seen, had led to bloodshed in 1888. Although at this time neither British traders nor missionaries had established themselves in any meaningful numbers in the interior, the inland people believed that sooner or later settlement would occur, bringing repression, war, and destruction to them as it had to Asaba. The two communities most threatened by British imperial presence were Igbuzo and Okpanam, the closest neighbors of Asaba. They would therefore be the first to declare war against the Royal Niger Company.

In August 1888, barely four months after the war of Asaba, certain agents of the Royal Niger Company who were exploring the forest on the western side of Asaba for rubber were ambushed by armed Igbuzo men.[5] Although these agents fought their way through, it was evident that adventures into the hinterland would be resisted. During the next few years the people of Igbuzo and Okpanam engaged the Royal Niger Company in a series of small scale battles during which the native Africans suffered great reverses. They soon realized that the whites represented a formidable military power they could not overcome unless they pooled their resources.

The first signs of a determined effort to contain the threat posed by the British military encroachment were manifested in Igbuzo, where the local chiefs began to organize and transform the youth clubs into companies of young warriors, *otu aya*. Such a company numbered between twenty and fifty men, sometimes more, and was named after its patron. In 1895 almost fifty such companies had been formed in Igbuzo, the most popular being Otu Elikwu, Otu Ofogu, Otu Chidi, Otu Umejei, and Otu Uwechua.[6] The patrons of these companies went further to form a coalition of warrior chiefs, called the *Otu Ochichi*, which met periodically to discuss matters relating to the British military penetration of southern Nigeria and the undermining of ancient customs and traditional belief systems by the teachings of the Christian missionaries. Patrons sometimes enabled their followers to secure firearms, charms, and military training.

By 1896 the members of the Otu Ochichi society of Igbuzo had begun to send emissaries to the chiefs of the neighboring towns, urging them to join in the common struggle. Some chiefs responded favorably but the vast majority hesitated until 1897, when news reached Western Igboland that the British had destroyed Benin City and chased off the Oba and his titled chiefs. The conquest of Benin increased the Western Igbo chiefs' concern about their own encirclement. Onitsha had been destroyed in 1879, Aboh and Idah in 1883, Asaba in 1888, Nana's Ebrohime in 1894, Brass in 1895, and now Benin in 1897. Would the next places not be Igbuzo, Ogwashi-Ukwu, Ubulu-Ukwu, and Onicha-Olona? Convinced that there was no other way out of this predicament, most Western Igbo chiefs became determined to fight the British; tempers could no longer be held down as the slightest act of provocation threatened to spark a general war. This was exactly what happened in 1898, when war broke out over what had appeared to be a minor religious dispute between the Roman Catholics and the traditional religionists of Issele-Ukwu.

The available evidence confirms that the first shot was instigated by the activities of the Roman Catholics in Issele-Ukwu. The circumstances of their establishment in Asaba and their subsequent spread into the neighboring districts were central to the outbreak of hostilities. For one thing, the mere timing of their arrival, during a period when tempers ran very high, created a great sense of mistrust toward them.[7] Second, the zeal and determination of the Catholic fathers easily surpassed that of the Anglican priests, which further alarmed the indigenous population. It is not clear in the records whether or not other missionaries visited Issele-Ukwu soon after Rev. Julius Spencer's visit of 1878.[8] We do know that in 1893 Father Carlo Zappa of the Roman Catholic mission traveled from his new headquarters at Asaba to Issele-Ukwu. He had contemplated opening a mission post there and had sent word to the Obi requesting his permission to visit his chiefdom. When the necessary permission came, Father Zappa, accompanied by guides and carriers, left Asaba on May 15, 1893. They made brief stops at Okpanam, Issele-Asaba, Anifekide, and Ubulu-Okiti, and arrived at Issele-Ukwu the following morning.[9]

Father Zappa was not received with the same enthusiasm that met Rev. Julius Spencer fifteen years earlier. The Catholic priest was simply welcomed by the Obi's messengers, who took him to an influential personality, Mokwenye, an intimate friend of Obi Egbuna. Father Zappa also had an interview with Chidi, the Obi's mother, before he was allowed to see the Obi. During his interview with the Obi, Father Zappa explained the object of his visit. The discussion that followed was cordial, although packed with emotion. While the recent conquest of Asaba by the British was a topic of concern, the major point of contention, of course, was the question of human sacrifice. The Catholic priest seized the opportunity of his visit to preach against the ancient custom. Father Zappa told the Obi:

> I will tell you without fear that we do not approve of what you do. You spill the blood of your slaves in front of your idols. This is evil. I must tell you that the lives of these slaves do not belong to you, and that the slaves, like you, are the children of the Great God.[10]

The Obi was stunned by the reckless utterances of the white priest. He remained silent, fighting to hold back his anger. His face was fixed to the ground and, as Father Zappa later recalled, "Not a single fold on his fore-head betrayed his feeling." After a prolonged period of tense silence, the Obi slowly exchanged words with his advisers and, looking toward Father Zappa, replied: "Listen, white man! The battle which the English waged against Asaba makes me hesitate. I know you are not a soldier and that you have brought the word of God, but that notwithstanding, the white man frightens me." The Obi paused, his eyes turned again to the ground. Finally, he resumed: "If you come into my town your eyes will see things which your heart will reject and you will be upset. You don't like the customs which we received from our ancestors. . . . This is why I hesitate."

After this brief comment, Obi Egbuma dismissed the priest, telling him that he needed time to consider the matter. Fifteen days after this visit, Father Zappa again traveled to Issele-Ukwu and the Obi received him with great cordiality. "His answers were clear and to the point," noted Father Zappa. In the end, the Obi of Issele-Ukwu gave a vast area of land to the Catholics.[11]

The reasons for the cession are complex. Obi Egbuna had been merely a boy when his father died and, during the 1878 visit of Rev. Spencer, Issele-Ukwu was under the rule of a regent.[12] The premature death of the Obi's father probably enabled his mother to exercise a very strong influence over him. Father Zappa, in his search for assistance, may well have approached the mother, Chidi, from whom he must have learned that the chief was sympathetic to his aspirations; in fact Father Zappa later attributed his success in acquiring the Obi's gift of land to the Obi's mother. "One would say that the sympathy which this woman inspired was beyond comparison," Father Zappa reported. "She revealed a magnanimity one does not often find among blacks."[13] Father Zappa claimed that Chidi, with a naive simplicity, her face covered behind her palms, had told him, "Oh whiteman, priest of God, you are great. You are too good for my eyes to look at." Father Zappa, who seemed to have been captivated by the amiability of this royal character, observed that if the Obi showed a favorable disposition toward the Catholics, they owed it all to his mother. In Chidi, Father Zappa must have found his conception of "the noble savage."

A portion of the land allocated to Father Zappa was immediately cleared and a hut built on it with wood supplied from the nearby forest. The Obi's messengers were sent to Asaba to bring some old metal sheets which served as a roof. In 1894, the Catholics added more structures to the settlement at Issele-Ukwu, so that instead of a single hut there were now several mud houses, two of which were used as a church and a place of instruction in the catechism. Father Rousselet was placed at the head of this mission.

During the next few years the Roman Catholics of Issele-Ukwu grew in strength. Among their first converts were slaves who welcomed the teaching of the Christians because it promised them better treatment. On the other hand, slave owners were disturbed by the insurrectionary creed of the Catholics because it incited the slaves to disobey their masters. Apart from the teaching of the Christians, many of the town's populace worried about the undue influence the Roman Catholic priests seemed to be wielding over Obi Egbuna. Their power over the Obi was exemplified one day when the Obi himself

himself was preparing to perform a traditional religious ceremony and Father Zappa arrived and personally demanded that the ceremony be put aside. Obi Egbuna complied with this demand, and even went further, freeing all his slaves. A few days later, he issued a decree against certain religious practices in Issele-Ukwu.[14] The stage was set for a major confrontation.

THE FIRST BATTLE OF THE EKUMEKU

The Obi of Issele-Ukwu had owned over a hundred slaves; they were his property, and in the eyes of his people, he had the right to set them free if he so desired. But what the Obi's subjects could not accept was his public declaration that certain religious practices were abolished in the chiefdom. By this decree, the paramount chief had demonstrated a flagrant and unconscionable disrespect for the customs and democratic institutions of his people. In particular, he had infringed upon the liberties of the slave-owning chiefs who, since the 1850s, had emerged as the effective ruling class in Issele-Ukwu and the neighboring towns. Under no circumstances could the Obi single-handedly abolish a traditional practice.

Certain factions in Issele-Ukwu now decided that the undermining of their society had gone far enough and could not be allowed to continue. In December 1897 these leaders rose in arms and demanded the immediate removal of the Obi.[15] A civil war broke out, dividing the town. One section, composed mainly of titled chiefs, most of whom were slave owners, demanded the expulsion of the Obi and all people harboring European sympathies. In the opposing camp were the supporters of the royal cause, composed mainly of the personal friends of the Obi, a few Christian converts, and the bulk of the slave population.

The news of the civil war in Issele-Ukwu soon spread far and wide, and the chiefs of the neighboring towns, who had been equally alarmed by the spread of European influence, and who had only recently formed or joined the Otu Ochichi, sent their warriors to assist the Issele-Ukwu rebels. Most of these warriors came from Igbuzo, which at this time was its capital. Others came form Onicha-Olona, Ezi, Illah, Ogwashi-Ukwu, Ubulu-Ukwu, and Ukwunzu. The arrival of these warriors, all of them armed with dane guns and cutlasses, greatly frightened Obi Egbuna and his supporters. Realizing that the royal cause was hopeless without external assistance and that the royal cause was also the Catholic cause, Father Zappa appealed to the authorities of the Royal Niger Company at Asaba for help.

Early in January 1898, the soldiers of the Royal Niger Company left Lokoja and entered Western Igboland. But rather than attack the Issele-Ukwu rebels and their Otu Ochichi supporters in Issele-Ukwu, they attacked Igbuzo.[16] This excellent military strategy was aimed at relieving Issele-Ukwu itself of the burden of war. As the leaders of the Niger Company forces had suspected, the Otu Ochichi warriors abandoned their locations in and about Issele-Ukwu and rushed to the rescue of Igbuzo. For six weeks the two sides were locked in a severe battle.

In mid-February the company's forces, under the command of Lieutenant Festing, made a series of raids on Igbuzo, during which most of the town was burned down and many of the chiefs were killed or captured. Seeing their capital in ruins and their cause hopeless, the Otu Ochichi warriors dispersed. William Wallace, the governor of the company, and Lieutenant Festing imposed a forced peace on Igbuzo.[17] The terms under which hostilities were concluded were:

1. The abolition of human sacrifice
2. The opening of roads to all the tribes
3. Missionaries would be allowed to reside and erect buildings in three of the Igbuzo towns
4. One king with a council of twelve would be appointed and be responsible to the government, instead of the two hundred chiefs then reigning.[18]

The subjugation of Igbuzo did not dishearten the Otu Ochichi. Rather, it shifted the center of their activities to the northern districts, and instead of coming out into the open, they turned to guerrilla tactics. An official British source stated that the Otu Ochichi began their meetings again "but not so openly." By the end of June 1898, they had fully reorganized their ranks, the report said, and by July they had begun to operate again at Issele-Ukwu, where they "decided" that Father Rousselet, the head of the Roman Catholic mission at Issele-Ukwu, "should die." The priest was accused of wielding an undue influence over the Obi of Issele-Ukwu. A company of Otu Ochichi warriors arrived from Ezi and Onicha-Olona and surrounded the mission. Father Rousselet sent to Asaba for help, but for reasons not stated in the report, these warriors left without causing any harm to the priest nor any damage to the mission buildings.[19]

Meanwhile, hostilities continued to spread into all parts of Aniocha. On August 2, 1898, a prominent leader of the Issele-Ukwu detachment of the Otu Ochichi was captured by the soldiers of the Royal Niger Company, and a few days later his compatriots made a swift move to rescue him, but two of their members were seized and taken away to the Asaba prison. Throughout August the Otu Ochichi remained very active in all the towns. It was at this time that Dunkwu (Isusu) of Onicha-Olona began his career as a powerful and uncompromising Otu Ochichi leader.

Initially, the Otu Ochichi avoided such towns as Asaba and Illah, where the Royal Niger Company troops were stationed, but Dunkwu planned an assault on Illah with one major objective, namely, to destroy the Roman Catholic mission church that had caused so much annoyance to the people. The chiefs and people of Illah had warned the Catholics that their church, which was "built in close propinquity to the big juju house," was repugnant in the eyes of the gods, and the refusal of the Catholics to remove their church from this site caused "differences between the mission and the people." In August 1898, a British report states, "a powerful chief" of Illah organized an assault on the mission house but he was overwhelmed and captured by the soldiers of the Royal Niger Company. Despite such skirmishes, the Catholics continued "to celebrate mass next door to the big juju house."[20]

On October 4, 1898, Dunkwu and his Otu Ochichi warriors moved into Illah and destroyed a portion of the Catholic mission. Perhaps this was intended merely to warn the Catholics to start packing, but rather than heed the warning, the two missionaries based at Illah, the Reverend Fathers Frigerio and Frederick, along with two sisters of the Lady of Apostles escaped to Asaba, where they reported the matter to the Royal Niger Company.[21] The company responded by sending some "inadequately armed" troops who arrived at Illah the same day.[22] The presence of this force infuriated the Otu Ochichi and the next morning they gave vent to their rage by razing the entire mission establishment. Father Zappa described the unfortunate episode: "Early on the morning of that fateful day trumpets and war *tam-tams* were heard on all sides, leaving no room for doubt as to their meaning; and the rebels poured into Illah from every side. The mission buildings were destroyed."[23] Father J. J. Hilliard claimed that the company's soldiers did not go to Illah to fight but were merely "called in to fire their guns on the town just to show what would be done if law and order were not quickly restored."[24] This might be true, but it is also possible that the Niger Company troops were brought in to reinforce the defenses at the company's establishment rather than give protection to the Catholics. This view is supported by Father Zappa's subsequent claim against the Royal Niger Company for its failure to give his mission the expected protection. The substance of this claim was derived from the belief that the mission land was leased to the Catholics by the company. "On the strength of this," pointed out Major Arthur G. Leonard, "the Father Superior interpreted this to mean a guarantee of protection." When the news of the destruction of the Catholic mission houses reached Asaba, the soldiers of the Royal Niger Company were immediately despatched to Illah and after a fierce encounter they managed to drive the Otu Ochichi out of the town.[25]

It will be remembered that after the menacing of the Issele-Ukwu mission, the Otu Ochichi warriors had left without a fight, and neither Father Rousselet nor any Christian convert at Issele-Ukwu had been harmed. But the action had disturbed the Christians at Asaba, first, because of the great number of Christians from the neighboring towns seeking refuge there and, second, because of rumors that the uprising was spreading rapidly. The Roman Catholics at Asaba, in addition, were initially concerned over the failure of Father Rousselet to arrive with the first wave of refugees. According to Father Strub, "Father Rousselet in charge of the station at Issele-Ukwu was the only person who was not present at the roll call. There was little chance of seeing him arrive, because he had a trip of 40 kilometers to do in this hostile region."[26]

The events at Illah only added to these fears, so that at the request of Father Zappa, Dr. Craster of the Royal Niger Company led a column of soldiers to search for and protect Father Rousselet. The Royal

Niger Company troops arrived safely at Issele-Ukwu and occupied the town without opposition from the indigenous warriors. They proceeded to the Catholic mission and were glad to find Father Rousselet in perfect health. The conduct of these troops was subdued during their occupation of Issele-Ukwu; they merely made a brief demonstration of their strength by marching round the town and then began to withdraw to their headquarters at Asaba.[27]

But the presence of the Royal Niger Company troops in Issele-Ukwu seemed to arouse the pride of the Otu Ochichi warriors, who had retreated to the forest but quickly organized themselves to oppose the troops on their way back to Asaba. Trees were cut down to block the road and a great fire was started in the forest, which caused the injury of several soldiers. With the road blocked, Craster and his soldiers, rather than continue to Asaba, returned to Issele-Ukwu and camped at the Catholic mission quarters. They remained barricaded in the mission establishment for many weeks where, besieged, they were threatened with starvation and eventual destruction.

The success of this operation coupled with the events at Illah seemed to give rise to exaltation among the Otu Ochichi, and they became even more anxious to force the issue with the Europeans at other locations. The Christian mission stations at Ezi, Ebu, and Ubulu-Ukwu were ransacked, their buildings burned down, and their personnel driven off. "If Issele-Ukwu mission was spared," wrote Strub, "it was because of the Otu Ochichi's very wise recognition that although they succeeded in stopping troops with fire in the bush, they could not take a chance against a guarded mission at Issele-Ukwu."[28] Meanwhile, the news of the successes at Illah and Issele-Ukwu spread far and wide. The chiefs of the various Esan communities sent their warriors to aid the struggle. Thus, with the exception of Asaba, Okpanam, Ugbodu, and Issele-Ukwu, all the Western Igbo towns in the Asaba district and parts of Esan came under the effective control of the Otu Ochichi.

Panic arose at Asaba when neither Father Rousselet nor Craster and his troops returned. Another expedition was sent to search for them but the Otu Ochichi acted swiftly, attacking and forcing the relief expedition to retreat. The Royal Niger Company sent out yet another expedition, which the Otu Ochichi also drove back. Finally, the company brought in its gunboats and bombarded all the settlements that were within reach of the gunfire. Troops landed and the Otu Ochichi warriors were drawn into a prolonged battle. In the end, they found themselves desperately short of arms and ammunition and gave up their resistance. Father Rousselet, Dr. Craster, and the soldiers of the Royal Niger Company who had been barricaded at the mission compound at Issele-Ukwu were rescued.

As part of their punishment for destroying Christian missionary establishments and for bearing arms against the authority of the Royal Niger Company, heavy fines were imposed upon all the towns that had taken part in the war. The officials of the Royal Niger Company hoped to compensate the Catholic mission for its losses from the fines so levied, but soon abandoned this plan "because they found out that the cost of collection exceeded the amount received."[29]

As will be seen, the charter of the Royal Niger Company was withdrawn at the end of that year (1899); nevertheless, Father Zappa pressed the colonial administration to compensate his mission for the damage done to his church at Illah by the resisters. The Colonial Office in London refused to entertain such a claim on the grounds that the attack on the mission should be considered an incident in a series of hostile movements which the company did all in its power to repress. The office also pointed out that if the company were to be compelled to pay compensation, it probably would be able, sooner or later, to use the same arguments against the colonial government should one of the company's factories be destroyed by the "natives." Finally, the Colonial Office argued that Roman Catholic Fathers "who establish their church close to a juju house cannot expect better treatment from savages than a Wesleyan Mission would get from—say the Spaniards—if they built their chapel next to the R. C. Cathedral."[30]

Nevertheless, although the Royal Niger Company had scored a local success over the Otu Ochichi, it was soon apparent that the Niger territories were seething with discontent and far from subdued. At the same time, it became evident that the authority of the Royal Niger Company did not extend much beyond a few miles inland from the Niger River, and that the company could not maintain law and order in the hinterland.[31]

The war between the people of Brass and the forces of the Royal Niger Company at Akassa in 1895 had sparked much discussion within official British circles concerning the position of the Royal Niger Company. Sir John Kirk's report on the Brass attack on company property was "a very strong indictment against the administration of the Niger Coast Protectorate, besides throwing light on a condition of affairs prolific of disorder and discreditable to British prestige."[32] In fact, after the Akassa raid by Brass men, the British government was constrained to pay "a very large sum of money" as compensation for losses sustained in a war that was largely provoked by the company.[33] Since the Akassa war, the feeling had been growing among British officials that the charter of the Royal Niger Company ought to be withdrawn not only to save the British administration from further embarrassments, but also to eliminate "the awkward geographical location of the administrations," one of which was a general territory under influence of the Crown and the other a narrow strip of riverbank under the aegis of the Company, with both overlapping at certain points. For instance, Brass men whose lands lay outside the Company's territories could not reach their markets on the Niger without crossing the Company's frontiers and paying duties each time they did so.[34] By 1897 it had become evident that the dual administration of these territories was the source of much conflict in the area. The situation could not continue, and "a curtailment of the Company's privileges was suggested."[35]

The Royal Niger Company was also proving itself incapable of extending British influence in the territories north of the Niger-Benue confluence. "As early as 1897," points out Godfrey N. Uzoigwe, "it had become clear to Salisbury that diplomatic action was necessary if further territories were to be added to what Britain already possessed."[36] The subsequent occupation of Bussa by the French and their moves toward Nikki and other locales in Borgu alarmed the British government. Although the Royal Niger Company had succeeded in subduing Nupe and Ilorin in 1897, it was clear that the company could not be expected to keep the French out of Sokoto and the Germans out of Adamawa unless the British government was prepared to adopt a more determined forward policy. The victories in Nupe and Ilorin notwithstanding, Foreign Office officials were determined "to get rid of the Company."[37] Even as George Taubman (Goldie) and his troops were marching on Nupe, the immediate financial effects of withdrawing the rights and functions of the chartered company were being considered at the Colonial Office. On May 27, 1897, Goldie was personally informed by Chamberlain, the colonial secretary, of the determination of the government to withdraw the Royal Niger Company's charter. The decision was not immediately implemented; it was not an easy matter to revoke a charter, since much bargaining had to take place and numerous financial, administrative, and military arrangements made to achieve a smooth transfer of power. On December 31, 1899, however, the charter of the company was officially withdrawn. By this act, the company was required to surrender the administration of the Niger territories to British imperial agents.[38] The Royal Niger Company forces would fight no more wars in Western Igboland. The battle of January to December 1898, the first battle in which the Otu Ochichi participated, was the last battle of the Royal Niger Company on the lower Niger.[39]

NOTES TO CHAPTER FOUR

1. Eric Wolf, *Peasant Wars of the Twentieth Century* (New York, 1969), xiii.

2. G. C. K. Gwassa and John Iliffe, *Records of the Maji Maji Rising*, part 1, (Nairobi, 1969), 9-11.

3. LaRay Denzer, "Sierra Leone—Bai Bureh," in *West African Resistance*, ed. Michael Crowder, (New York, 1971), 233-67.

4. Wolf, *Peasant Wars*, 218.

5. CMS, 93/A3/188/47, Johnson to Crowther, August 13, 1888.

6. Obi Esekwe, interview on July 15, 1974 at Ogboli-Igbuzo.

7. The Catholics established themselves in Asaba in 1888 after the conquest of the town by the forces of the Royal Niger Company. They were invited by Sir James Marshall, a High Court Judge and an employee of the Royal Niger Company. In a letter he wrote to Father Poirier at Lokoja inviting the Catholics, Sir James assured the priests that he would put himself at their disposal. On arrival, they were enabled to secure a suitable site for a mission overlooking the Niger. Father Zappa was later to write that Sir James showed himself to be a good Roman Catholic by insisting that the Catholic Mission benefitted from the presence of the Royal Niger Company by establishing a mission at Asaba. See SMA, 14/80302, Asaba, Zappa to Superior, October 4, 1888.

8. *Church Missionary Intelligencer*, 1879, 239.

9. The account is from SMA, Le Missions Catholiques, No. 1279, December 8, 1893, 586.

10. Ibid.

11. Ibid., 586-87.
12. *Church Missionary Intelligencer*, 1879, 239.
13. SMA, *Les Missions Catholiques,* No. 1279, December 8, 1893.
14. SMA, 3. B. 45, from the journals of some early Fathers of the Diocese of Benin City, trans. from the French by Father J. J. Hilliard, 32.
15. Ibid.
16. C0520/3/270, entry No. 3687, November 12, 1900.
17. SMA 14/8030/15984, Zappa to Superior, February 20, 1898.
18. PRO, F02/178, *The Daily Graphic,* February 7, 1898 (extract).
19. C0520/3270, entry No. 3687, November 12, 1900.
20. Ibid.
21. SMA, Strub, Folio 14. Actually, the Sisters took refuge in the company's establishment till the following morning, when they managed to escape to Asaba. See SMA, J. J. Hilliard, *Journal of Some Early Fathers of the Diocese of Benin City,* 38.
22. PRO, C0520/3/270, entry No. 3687, November 12, 1900.
23. SMA, *Annals of the Propagation of the Faith, 1899,* 163, Father Carlo Zappa writing from Asaba.
24. SMA, 3 B 45, p. 19.
25. PRO, C0520/3/265/35286 of October 12, 1900, report on claim of French Roman Catholic mission.
26. SMA, Strub, Folio 14.
27. SMA, Strub, Folio 15.
28. Ibid.
29. PRO, C0520/3/270/36867, November 26, 1900.
30. Ibid.
31. *Church Missionary Intelligencer,* 1896, 433.
32. Ibid.
33. PRO, C520/2/184 of July 3, 1900.
34. Rhodes House Library, Oxford, 710. 17s4/6 Brass Enquiry 1899. Niger Territories Confidential 221. Sir J. Kirk to Marquess of Salisbury (received August 30, 1897).
35. *Church Missionary Intelligencer,* 1896, 433.
36. Godfrey N. Uzoigwe, *Britain and the Conquest of Africa* (New York, 1978), 101.
37. John E. Flint, *Sir George Goldie and the Making of Nigeria* (Oxford, 1960), 267.
38. Ibid, 213.
39. It should be noted that by the time hostilities started in 1898 between the Royal Niger Company and the Otu Ochichi, the former had already known that its charter would be revoked. Certainly, this knowledge vexed the officials of the company (See Flint, 268: "This was a bitter disappointment and Goldie took it as a personal blow. He therefore approached the meeting in a truculent and defiant mood, determined to exploit any advantages he possessed to the full.") This disappointment might have contributed

to the ruthlessness with which the war of 1898 was prosecuted. Note also that between 1886 and 1899 the forces of the company fought more than fifty battles in Nigeria and overwhelmed such scattered places as Patani and Akassa in the Niger delta, Keffi and Wase on the Jos plateau, Ilorin and Bida in the northwest, and Gloria Ibo and Oguta in the southeast; see Anthony H. M. Kirk-Greene, "A Preliminary Note on New Sources for Nigerian Military History," *Journal of the Historical Society of Nigeria,* 3, no. 1 (1964): 135-38.

CHAPTER FIVE

The Return of the Ekumeku, 1902-1903

BY THE MID-1890S the British government had become convinced that the three British forces in the Niger area could not be relied upon to contain French and German threats, and at the same time advance British interests into new areas while repressing indigenous resistance movements in the already conquered regions.[1] In 1897, therefore, an agent of the British government, Frederick Lugard, was asked to raise a West African force for operations in the region. Lugard accepted the challenge and by the end of the following year he had formed the West African Frontier Force. Initially the force comprised two battalions consisting of eight companies of 150 men each, under the command of a lieutenant-colonel.[2] By the beginning of the twentieth century this force had expanded appreciably and was divided into regiments, each regiment responsible for the conquest of a particular colony. For instance, the Southern Nigeria Regiment of the West African Frontier Force was responsible for the consolidation of British rule in Southern Nigeria. There was also a Northern Nigeria Regiment, and a Gold Coast Regiment, among others. These designations indicate that Northern and Southern Nigeria were regarded as two distinct colonies; it was only after the amalgamation of 1914 that the two regiments were merged.

Western Igboland came under the jurisdiction of the soldiers of the Southern Nigeria Regiment. These men were better drilled, better armed, and better paid than the soldiers of the Royal Niger Company, and even though they were recruited from the Gold Coast, Yorubaland, and Northern Nigeria, as had been the soldiers of the Royal Niger Company, the majority of them were Hausa or Muslims.[3] A great number of the Hausa were former slaves who "deserted their masters and took service under the government, either as soldiers, police, transport carriers, or laborers in the Public Works Department,"[4] while the initial recruits from Yorubaland were mostly "the Ibadan Warboys," who did not "like an agricultural life after being so long engaged in warlike operations against the Ilorin."[5] Most of these men were already familiar with military operations in a tropical environment and therefore proved a very useful instrument for colonial conquest and consolidation.

As Samson C. Ukpabi has rightly observed, the British, having committed themselves to the use of force in Nigeria (and throughout West Africa), were prepared to advance the money necessary for the funding of the army, although in the long run the costs of this policy were charged to the accounts of the victim regions and were recovered either through direct taxation, through confiscation of property, or by the imposition of fines.[6] Sometimes failure to pay promptly was regarded as refusal to pay, necessitating further punitive measures. Because these territories were conquered by force of arms, the British came to consider their wealth, such as mineral deposits, as belonging to the victors. In 1913, for example, Frederick Lugard declared that all mineral rights in Southern Nigeria were "vested in the [British] Crown by right of conquest"; consequently the British government of Southern Nigeria tried to extend this principle by abolishing all provisions for sharing fees, rents, and royalties with the "natives" in whose lands these deposits were found.[7] In addition, the forced labor laws that were passed during the early colonial period, the conscription of men into the British armed forces during the First and Second World Wars, and the imposition of taxes on rural communities were all justified in Britain's view by the fact that Nigeria was acquired, not just by treaties, but by conquest.

The British government assumed the direct responsibility of administering the former Niger territories in January 1900 and thenceforth tried to make the various communities realize the significance of the change. At the same time, it tried through military demonstrations to intimidate the Africans into accepting British rule. As early as 1900, Ralph Moor, a high commissioner in the service of the Southern Nigerian government, warned the Colonial Office in London that the entire territory between Benin City and the Niger was "still in an unsatisfactory state." He reminded the British government that the whole district beyond Aboh and Asaba had been hostile, and had given a great deal of trouble to the Royal Niger Company. He therefore suggested that it was "essential that some demonstration of an established government should be made in this direction." With such a demonstration, he continued, "practically all the territories in the protectorate to the right or west of the Niger will be brought fairly under Government control."[8] Official consent for military "demonstration" (or more accurately, invasion of these territories) was soon received but troops were not immediately sent into Western Igboland. Rather, they were employed against the people of Esan and Aro, who at that moment, seemed to pose the greatest threat to British authority in Southern Nigeria.

The postponement of the military demonstration notwithstanding, the people of Western Igboland were worried about renewed British activities in the territory. While the agents of the Royal Niger Company had confined their activities to the banks of the river, the new colonial government officials penetrated further inland, roamed about the countryside with bands of armed soldiers, gave orders to chiefs there, and terrorized the entire population. Following the defeat of the Otu Ochichi in 1898, the Christian missionaries began to spread their activities into the neighboring towns and, at the same time, intensified their interference with local customs. In 1901, for example, a party of CMS agents, led by Rev. G. T. Basden, came over from Onitsha and toured nineteen towns in Western Igboland, preaching the gospel. When the party arrived at Onicha-Olona, its members called at the home of an important man "who had decided to give up idolatry." The news of this visit caused a large crowd to gather around the man's house. Suddenly, "ten local adherents" and the visitors began to collect various objects of worship—medicine pots, hunting gods, and the blacksmith's gods—all belonging to the man. They piled them in front of his house, which was situated by the main road leading into the town, and set them on fire. They also destroyed the man's shrine. While the burning and destruction were going on, the large crowd that gathered "watched in awe and half terror wondering what vengeance the gods would take." And as soon as Basden and his men left Onicha-Olona, the townspeople retaliated by plundering and pulling down the homes of two Christians.[9]

An atmosphere that was already charged with suspicion and hate was worsened when the Catholic fathers denounced in clear terms all aspects of the traditional customs and religion of the Western Igbo people. Their zeal easily surpassed that of the Anglican priests and, on a number of occasions, the fathers took it upon themselves personally to destroy the objects of worship belonging to the local people. In one instance, Reverend Father Voigt, while on his way to Illah, set fire to a shrine, and the local community, baffled by this unprovoked behavior, "decided to revenge this desecration of their shrine."[10] Even colonial government officials were appalled by the activities of the priests. They attributed the outbreak of the 1898 uprising to "Fathers mixing in politics,"[11] and Sir Ralph Moor, the high commissioner, insisted on abstention from politics as a necessary condition for allowing Christian missionaries to establish themselves in these territories. At the same time he ordered the Catholics to leave Issele-Ukwu and Illah entirely.[12]

By 1902 most Western Igbo had become convinced that another war with the British was both inevitable and desirable. At the time, however, the district lacked effective leaders because some of the chiefs who initiated the formation of the Otu Ochichi society in the 1890s had been killed or imprisoned by the officials of the Royal Niger Company. Some were still in hiding, many were weary of war, and some had embraced Christianity and been baptized.

On the other hand, the restless young men and some young chiefs, who were dissatisfied with the apparent withdrawal of their fathers from this struggle, prevailed, reviving the Otu Ochichi society from a dormancy that had begun in December 1898. Most of the chiefs who had originally formed the society were excluded from this new phase of the society. Although the youths had acquired a great deal of experience from the previous battles, they were totally unfamiliar with the military capability of the newly formed West African Frontier Force. They were aware, though, that the communities had become significantly infiltrated by a large number of European sympathizers and collaborators. In addition, slaves were once again pushing for freedom and were prepared to act as spies for the administration. Thus realizing that their obstacles had changed dramatically, the resisters went underground. They adopted silence and guerrilla tactics as their primary war strategy, which earned for them the nickname "the League of the Silent Ones" or *"Otu Ekwunokwu"* which, as we have seen, the British mispronounced as "Ekumeku."

The meetings of the society were held at night and in secret places. Only those who had taken the oath of secrecy were admitted. No one, except its members, knew how the society organized its activities or where its headquarters were. It was now thrown open to all able-bodied young men who wished to demonstrate their prowess and local patriotism.[13] The town clubs which had formed the nucleus of the movement were also excluded even though the activities of the society were still organized around some prominent men like Dunkwu, Elumelu, Obiora, Idegwu, and Chiejina of Onich-Olona; Elikwu, Ofogu, Umejei, and Uwechua of Igbuzo; Nzekwe and Nwabuzo Iyogolo of Ogwashi-Ukwu; Awuno Ugbo, the Obi of Akumazi; the Obi of Ubulu-Ukwu; Nkwo and Modi, also of Ubulu-Ukwu; and Onwuadiaju of Issele-Azagba.

Contacts were mostly between these prominent men, through the use of emissaries. Neither the leaders nor their followers were seen in action during the day. The mode of summoning meetings was kept secret, and it included the shaking of bullet containers around private homes in a carefree manner to announce the time of meetings without actually saying a word, or the use of trumpet notes intelligible only to initiated members, or seemingly ordinary finger counting and gesticulations.[14] By 1902 the society had become a secret war cult.

The initial objective of the Ekumeku was to halt the spread of Christianity, which its members regarded as having a very corrupting influence on the communities. By 1902 missionary settlements had sprung up in virtually every town in the Asaba district. These establishments attracted not only slaves and commoners, but also some prominent local men. If the Ekumeku warriors frowned upon slaves and the ordinary folks who embraced Christianity, they were bitter with chiefs who received the water of baptism, not only because these very chiefs had spearheaded the launching of the resistance movement in the 1890s, but also because their conversion was having a most destabilizing effect on local customs and religion. In the traditional context, a titled chief was not only a political leader; he was also a ritual figure, the head of an extended family and a living representative of the departed founding fathers of the clan. To take a title was to receive the gift of immortality, which transformed the recipient from the status of an ordinary human to that of a god. As immortality could not be inherited, so could a title not be passed from father to son; it had to be achieved or acquired through a process of title taking called *ichi-echichi,* that is to secure the breath of life, to attain immortality or godship.[15] It is significant that the Igbo word *chi* represents invisible forces, spirits, and personal gods; it is the root of such words as *Chineke,* the Creator, *Chukwu,* the Great God, *ichie,* a titled man, and *ndichie,* titled men.

The teachings of the Christians contradicted these Igbo notions of status achievement, however. To become a Christian was to forsake one's ancestors. An *ichie* who embraced Christianity was expected to give up his idols, among which was his *ofo,* a ritual object which indicated that at some time in the past, the ancestors he represented took a title.[16] A convert's newfound religion—Christianity— also required him to shun all forms of animal sacrifices, which denied the ancestors their fair share of the bounty harvests they had helped to instigate. The starving and irate ancestors might then descend upon the community with their vengeance, placing it in a state of ritual siege; plants, animals, and human beings might die, an epidemic might sweep through the community, and the land might be scorched by drought. Thus a society that believed strongly in ancestor worship would consider all chiefs who embraced the Christian faith as good as dead, having consciously thrown away their right to exist and lead.

Further, most Western Igbo chiefs were polygamists and, upon conversion to Christianity, were required to cast away all their wives except the first one in order to qualify for baptism. All chiefs (and commoners) who refused to divorce their extra wives were denied baptism even though their wives were baptized. A Miss Warner, an agent of the Church Missionary Society, reported in 1901 on a chief of Akwukwu who attended devotional services in the company of all his household, but "he had many wives on account of which he was refused baptism even though some of his wives had been baptized." Warner also told of another Akwukwu man, a commoner, who had only two wives. The man and his wives had embraced the Christian faith, but he was denied baptism even though his wives had been baptized. To remove his disqualification and be baptized, this man sent away one of his wives who, sadly enough, was nursing a baby. But the wife who was sent away "took kindly to her disgrace" and when her suckling baby was to be baptized, "instead of angry feeling, she asked the first wife to stand as godmother to her baby."[17]

The Christian missionaries' insistence on monogamy had other repercussions within Igbo society. For example, the war of 1898 against the Royal Niger Company had resulted in the death of many men; a society that was already saddled with large numbers of orphans and widows was now faced with the prospect of caring for a growing population of divorced and unmarried women as Christianity spread.

The members of the Ekumeku movement therefore regarded all those who embraced Christianity as traitors who deserved to be punished. Mention has already been made of an Akwukwu chief who was visited by the members of the Ekumeku and warned that if he failed to wash from his head the water he was supposed to have received in baptism, he would be shot.[18] Likewise, at Igbuzo, Obi Ajufo, a chief with twelve wives, was threatened, not only by the Ekumeku warriors, but also by his own children and wives, after his conversion to Catholicism. Obi Ajufo was a wealthy and influential man who had taken an active part in launching the Ekumeku movement in the 1890s. His conversion in 1901 was most disturbing, not just because he was the first chief of Igbuzo to join the Christians, but also because of the influence which his conversion would have on other chiefs and the community at large. Obi Ajufo described his opposition:

> Petitions, insults, curses, the most biting gibes — my ears heard all these. My children declared they would no longer cultivate my farms, the eldest threatened me, axe in hand. My wives swore they would all sleep on the public way, outside my gate, so that I might be put to shame. The chiefs of the town have excluded me from the great council because my mouth no longer speaks the language of our fathers.[19]

Many Christian converts and European sympathizers were punished outright. Some were visited and shot. Others had their crops destroyed, their livestock killed or stolen, and their houses burned. The foreign missionaries and government officials could not explain the cause of these killings. Father Strub described them as "cowardly and sordid,"[20] and Ralph Moor, the high commissioner, concluded that the perpetrators were brigands engaged in nocturnal activities, including robbery, seizures, and other criminal acts, which provoked disorder and lawlessness. Moor was convinced that only a strong demonstration of an established government would restore law and order.[21]

These events illustrate what Frantz Fanon would term "collective auto-destruction."[22] This is a case in which the indigenous communities, when confronted with the dangers and humiliations of colonial subjugation, or when "trapped in the tight links of the chains of colonialism" adopt "a suicidal behavior " in their attempt to find an outlet for their anger. At the individual level, each man reaches for his knife at the slightest provocation in a bid "to defend his personality vis-à-vis his brother." At the communal level, they let out their "muscular tension" in "tribal warfare, in feuds between septs, and in quarrels between individuals." Ironically, the oppressor interprets this "collective autodestruction" as conclusive evidence that the "natives are not reasonable human beings," and therefore intensifies his repression of them.[23]

News about the revival of the Western Igbo resistance movement under a new name reached the ears of British colonial officers and in mid-October 1902 Ralph Moor notified headquarters about it, explaining that in its old form, when it was under the control of chiefs of the area, the movement had been broken by the Royal Niger Company.[24] A few weeks later Moor sent a memorandum of instructions for dealing with what he called "difficulties in the Asaba hinterland and the Agbor district." He suggested that a force of about two hundred men under Captain Moorhouse should be assembled. The object of the patrol, he declared, was "to persuade the natives, if possible, to give up the Ekumeku or Otuochichi society." If time permitted, troops should visit the Agbor District to deal with the Ika people.[25]

On December 1, 1902, the Ekumeku warriors, who had made adequate preparations for war, struck simultaneously in the towns of Onicha-Olona, Ezi, and Ogwashi-Ukwu. There was panic within colonial and missionary circles, and government officials could no longer delay. Troops were at once assembled at Asaba. Their first objective was to march on Onicha-Olona, which was chosen as the first target for three reasons. First was the fear that the Church Missionary Society's establishment in that town would be destroyed by the insurgents. Second, the Royal Niger Company's factory and the Catholic church at Illah had been attacked by the insurgents in 1898, and since Onicha-Olona was only a short distance from Illah, the administration feared that the Ekumeku would attack those targets again.[26] Third, after the destruction of Igbuzo in 1898, Ogwashi-Ukwu and Onicha-Olona emerged as the most powerful outposts of the Ekumeku and, in British reckoning, these towns had to be punished immediately.[27] Widenham Fosbery, the commissioner of the Central Division, took it upon himself to visit Illah, where he learned from the agent of the Niger Company that "the natives were on the verge of an outbreak,"[28] and that the Roman Catholic missionaries were very frightened and were preparing to move to Asaba.

The colonial troops sent out from Asaba, commanded by Fosbery, first stopped at Okpanam, where he summoned the chiefs of the town. They were asked to provide thirty carriers for the force's use, but they managed to provide only twelve; Fosbery warned that if they failed to provide the workers, young chiefs would be made to serve as carriers instead. The young chiefs fled, but the British troops quickly seized five elderly chiefs and marched them to Issele-Azagba. The townspeople were told that the five elderly chiefs would be released when the exact number of carriers was provided.

The incident was an act of provocation that had the potential of arousing even a peaceful community into open hostility. Okpanam, like Asaba, had been intimidated by the presence of the constabulary forces of the Royal Niger Company and had remained subdued during the Ekumeku war of 1898. The populace of Okpanam was therefore unprepared for the white man's forcible abduction of five of its elderly chiefs; the people did not know how to respond to such overt domination. That evening the people of Okpanam sent eighteen carriers to Issele-Azagba; the elderly chiefs were sent back to their town to inform the residents that the matter would be pursued when Fosbery returned to Asaba.

The colonial troops marched on, and at Issele-Azagba, they had free rein. They took from adjoining farms whatever they considered necessary for their sustenance. They arrested three chiefs, bringing them before the divisional commissioner and charging them with opposing the head chief, especially in regard to carrying out government orders. These chiefs, Odiaka, Ugbo, and Odiachi, were given a trial *in camera,* found guilty on all the charges, and sentenced to a jail term of six months in nearby Asaba.

The colonial force soon arrived at Akwukwu and from there messengers were sent to Onicha-Olona, the major target, to inform the chiefs that the troops were coming and to advise them to prepare food and water. The messengers were sent back with the message that the people of Onicha-Olona did not want to see the white men or their soldiers; neither water nor yams would be collected. This response was nothing short of defiance, a declaration of war.

An agent of John Holt and Company trading in Onicha-Olona and an agent of the Church Missionary Society later arrived at Akwukwu to inform the divisional commissioner that the warriors of Onicha-Olona were arranging themselves in companies in preparation for war. Fosbery was also told that Dunkwu, leader of the Ekumeku, and his men were marching to Akwukwu to attack the British, a piece of misinformation, since Dunkwu and his forces never actually appeared.

The next morning, December 3, the British troops marched into Onicha-Olona and found the town virtually deserted. They pitched their camp in an open space called Agbanu. Soon representatives from three quarters—Ishiekpe, Idumuoji, and Ogbekenu—came in with a few yams and gourds of water and pledged their support to the government. These representatives stated that the men of the remaining three quarters, Ogbeobi, Umuolo, and Agba, were waiting in the bush to fight under the leadership of Dunkwu.

The British troops could observe armed warriors of Onicha-Olona "continually crossing a broad avenue" leading from the camp through the Umuolo quarter. All during this period no shot was fired. Later in the day the commanding officer of the British troops, Major Moorhouse, marched a column to the Ogbeobi quarter of the town. As the column approached, the warriors of Onicha-Olona, who had observed these movements from the bush around Dunkwu's house, opened fire. After a brief skirmish the troops managed to dislodge Dunkwu's men and set the village on fire. This column then marched to the Umuolo quarter, where they found the enemy occupying a strong position. Again there was a brisk gun battle. The Ekumeku forces retreated into the bush and the troops entered the Umuolo quarter and set it ablaze, then returned to camp. Later in the evening the warriors of Umuolo made a sudden attack on the British camp but were driven back.

The next day, divisional commander Fosbery accompanied a column to nearby Ezi, but the troops were strongly opposed. First, the soldiers discovered that the town had been deserted and the houses were "absolutely empty, not even a fowl to be seen." As the troops advanced through the bush opposite the head chief's house, the men of Ezi opened fire on them, retreating afterward into the bush. The troops gave vent to their anger by setting the town on fire and hurried back to their camp at Onicha-Olona. As they retreated, however, the men of Ezi gave chase, firing at the rear guard. When eventually the troops reached the outskirts of Onicha-Olona, Dunkwu and his men emerged and joined the warriors of Ezi in the attack. Ekumeku reinforcements from the neighboring towns also joined the fray.

During the next few days, British soldiers continued to destroy houses in the hostile quarters. At the same time, they entered into a dialogue with the chiefs of the so-called friendly quarters. The divisional commissioner seized this opportunity to explain "the folly of resisting the power of the Government," arguments that appeared to work, as the friendly chiefs asked for permission to bring their women and children back from the bush. The request was granted and, as Fosbery reported, "the next day their quarters presented their normal appearance."

Having achieved this success, the British tried their hand at further diplomacy. They pressed the friendly chiefs to intervene and persuade the citizens of the hostile quarters to abandon their leaders and to use their influence to bring the conflict to an end. Fearing that this move in itself might not achieve the desired objective, the British added that they would continue to destroy houses until the Ekumeku leaders, especially Dunkwu, Elumelu, and Ebora were brought in.

The friendly chiefs, who were frightened by this threat, consulted among themselves and asked the British for a cease-fire to permit contact with the hostile warriors. The colonials consented but during the next few days it began to appear that the friendly chiefs were not fulfilling their promise. The British applied great pressure, threatening further damage to houses and farms. The friendly chiefs capitulated and sought to negotiate with the men of the hostile quarters, who gave up fighting and sent representatives to talk to the white men. Among these representatives were Elumelu and Ebora, who, before opening discussion, asked for a guarantee for their safety. Because Dunkwu was not present, Fosbery refused to hold discussions, but made no attempt to arrest anyone, another diplomatic tactic that worked. On December 8, a message reached the colonials that Dunkwu was now ready to come but wanted a guarantee that he would not be arrested. Fosbery again refused the request and warned that if Dunkwu, Elumelu, and Ebora failed to come in within half an hour the demolition of houses would recommence. To the surprise of the British, all the leaders of the Onicha-Olona branch of the Ekumeku appeared by the deadline. The divisional commissioner at once instituted a tribunal composed of members of the Asaba Native Council with chiefs from the friendly quarters of Onicha-Olona. Elumelu, Ebora, and Dunkwu were tried and all found guilty. Their sentence was exile, but as Dunkwu's sentence was being pronounced, he made a sudden dash for freedom. In the confusion that was caused by this bold maneuver, Dunkwu succeeded in escaping the throng of soldiers and police. He slipped into the bush while Awudu Doki, a lance corporal of the "C" Company, made "a very plucky but unsuccessful attempt to catch Dunkwu"; his plucky move earned him a machete wound.[29]

The escape of Dunkwu brought to naught the diplomatic gains of the preceding days and the British were infuriated by the fact and the implications of this loss. Elumelu and Ebora were at once seized and removed to Asaba to serve various terms of imprisonment. The British allowed the people of Umuolo to return to their homes because their head chiefs had been removed. The divisional commissioner made the people of Ogbeobi understand, however, that the government still regarded them as hostile; they would not be allowed to rebuild their homes until Dunkwu was brought in or gave himself up. Fosbery also reminded them that "Dunkwu was not regarded as any worse than them" and reaffirmed that the Ekumeku leader's sentence was only six months imprisonment at Asaba.[30] The divisional commissioner ordered six chiefs arrested and sent to Asaba as hostages pending the surrender of Dunkwu.

Meanwhile, as Fosbery was battling the Ekumeku at Onicha-olona,

Ezi, and Akwukwu, other colonial troops were fighting the resisters in several other locations. The details of these encounters are not so important as the very fact that they were happening; suffice it to mention that the district commissioner, Chichester, marched with an escort commanded by Captain Caree to Ugbodu and the surrounding settlements, attacking them with heavy armaments. The troops also fought the Ekumeku at Idumuje-Ugboko, Onicha-Ugbo, and Issele-Ukwu, before returning to their headquarters at Asaba. A widespread uprising was in effect.

Another British contingent marched via Issele-Mkpitima, Issele-Ukwu, and Ubulu-Ukwu to Ogwashi-Ukwu, attacking the inhabitants en route. The towns of Ogwashi-Uno and Akpoma were visited and burned down. A company marched under Major Mackenzie to Ogwashi-Azagba with the intention of attacking it but the town's people surrendered just in time "to prevent their houses being burnt." Ani-Udalla was found deserted and, as its inhabitants refused to come in and meet with the government representatives, their houses were destroyed.

Having effectively punished Ogwashi-Ukwu and the outlying districts, the troops proceeded to Igbuzo, where they met with "a cordial reception." The troops passed on to their headquarters at Asaba but a few days later a strong column, under the command of Captain Caree and accompanied by Fosbery and Chichester, marched back to Igbuzo to arrest some chiefs. Predictably, Igbuzo became the scene of arrests and the burning and destruction of houses. The most wanted men of Igbuzo were Chidi, Uwechua, Ofogu, Umejei, and Elikwu. Troops returned on January 7, 1903 to deal with the people of Oko, who were charged with acts of violence against a Native Court policeman and others. Like Igbuzo, Oko was left in ruins by the time troops returned to headquarters. Some chiefs of Oko were removed to be tried by the Native Court of Asaba.[31] The whole uprising lasted six months.

By April 1903, the major events in the Ekumeku rising of 1902-03 had been concluded. The towns most affected were Onicha-Olona, Ezi, Ogwashi-Ukwu, and Akpoma, although nearly all the Western Igbo settlements in the Asaba district suffered in one way or the other. Many titled chiefs were removed from their home areas. Sir Ralph Moor defined this form of exile somewhat differently, saying that he was "personally taking some of them to Old Calabar for a period where they will have an opportunity of seeing a more advanced state of civilization than exists in their own country which on their return they may introduce among their own people."³²

Concluding his report, Widenham Fosbery, commissioner of the Central Division, noted that his main object in dealing with these people had been "to allay the evident feelings of distrust shown towards the Government and to inspire that confidence which is so essential if law and order are to be maintained by pacific measures." He observed that for several years previous the inhabitants of various large towns had "been accustomed to view each other with feelings of enmity and to regard their guns and machetes as the best means for settling their disputes." He asserted that the Ekumeku and other secret societies had been completely broken and the power of the government had been fully demonstrated.³³

The degree to which a "feeling of distrust" could be allayed by a process of destruction cannot be easily determined. Perhaps more "specific measures" would have guaranteed a more lasting peace. As we have seen, on many occasions the actions of the missionaries and British agents were clearly provocative. Despite Fosbery's assurances otherwise, "distrust" remained plentiful and "confidence" in the government rare. And far from being "completely broken," the Ekumeku movement had merely gone underground.

As the Royal Niger Company had been dragged into a war that was provoked largely by the Christian missionaries in 1898, so was the British colonial administration compelled to defend the Christian preachers who burned *juju* shrines, incited slaves to rebel against their masters, and persuaded converts to cast away their wives. Although the British eventually crushed the uprising of 1902-03, the conflict created a deep feeling of distrust for the colonial government and slowed down the spread of Christianity. Reverend Julius Spencer recalled grimly the events of that period:

> During the months of January and February [1903] all the outstations, with two exceptions, presented a sorrowful spectacle. Mission-houses and churches were either razed to the ground or burnt down. The houses of converts were destroyed and the converts themselves had fled. During these months it seemed as if the labour of years had been brought to naught.³⁴

What was not yet apparent to the British was that several years of "labour" against the Ekumeku lay ahead.

NOTES TO CHAPTER FIVE

1. For the various British forces in Nigeria, see Anthony H. M. Kirk-Greene, "A Preliminary Note on New Sources of Nigerian Military History," *Journal of the Historical Society of Nigeria,* 3, no. 1 (1964): 129-47.
2. Collin W. Newbury, *British Policy Toward West Africa, Select Documents, 1875-1914,* (Oxford, 1971), 2:405-18.
3. For the conditions of the soldiers of the RNC see the military notes of Maj. Claude McDonald, chap. 10 (PRO, F084/2019). See also John Flint, *George Goldie and the Making of Nigeria* (Oxford, 1960), 129-55.
4. Charles Orr, *The Making of Northern Nigeria* (London, 1964), 203.
5. Quoted in Newbury, *British Policy,* 405.
6. Samson C. Ukpabi, "The Origins of the West African Frontier Force," *Journal of the Historical Society of Nigeria,* 3, no. 3 (1966): 500.
7. PRO, C0520/115/17924, confidential enclosure, Lord Lugard to Secretary of State for the Colonies, December 11, 1913; PRO, C0520/128/44624 of December 29, 1913, the Government of Southern Nigeria to Colonial Office, December 1, 1913.
8. PRO, C0520/3/320/2519, Ralph Moor to Colonial Office, December 29, 1900.
9. *Church Missionary Intelligencer,* 1901, 306.
10. SMA, 14/80404/15794, Strub, "Le Vicariat Apostolique de la Nigerie Occidentale depuis sa Fondation jusqua a nos jours," Folio 14.
11. SMA, 14/8032, 16005, Zappa to Superior, September 14, 1899.
12. PRO, C0520/15/338, Ralph Moor to Colonial Office, August 22, 1902.
13. Philip Igbafe, "Western Ibo Society and Its Resistance to British Rule: The Ekumeku Movement 1898-1911, *Journal of Africa History,* 12, no. 3 (1971): 444.
14. Ibid.
15. NAI, Kwale Dis 10/8, Taking of the Ozo Title in the Awka Division.
16. Ibid.
17. *Church Missionary Intelligencer,* 1901, 388.
18. PRO, 20520/24/20839, W. E. B. Coupland-Crawford, divisional commissioner, Central Division to the government of Southern Nigeria; June 13, 1904.
19. SMA, Annals of the Propagation of Faith (1902), 70, letters from Father Zappa.
20. SMA, Strub, Folio 13.

21. PRO, C0520/15/338, Ralph Moor to Colonial Offices, August 22, 1902.

22. Frantz Fanon, *The Wretched of the Earth*, trans. Constance Farrington (New York, 1977), 54.

23. Ibid.

24. C0520/16/501, Ralph Moor to Colonial Office, September 22, 1902.

25. Enclosure in ibid.

26. C0520/18/7937 of February 29, 1903, Widenham Fosbery, District Commissioner, Central Division, to the High Commissioner, Southern Nigeria, January 2, 1903.

27. Enclosure in ibid., Maj. M. C. Moorhouse, report on operations in Asaba Hinterland, December 1902.

28. For this and the entire account of the incident, see PRO, C0520/18/7937 of February 29, 1903, Widenham Fosbery to High Commissioner.

29. Maj. H. C. Moorhouse, report on Operations in Asaba Hinterlands, December 1902. Enclosure No. 2 in ibid.

30. PRO, C0520/10/7937 of February 29, 1903. Widenham Fosbery to High Commissioner.

31. For the entire account of the incident, see ibid.

32. Ralph Moor to Secretary of State for the colonies in ibid.

33. Widenham Fosbery, to High Commissioner, Southern Nigeria, in ibid.

34. *Church Missionary Intelligencer,* 1908, 767.

CHAPTER SIX

The Ekumeku War, 1904-1905

THE ELDERLY CHIEFS of the Asaba district did not mastermind the eruptions of 1902-03, but once the struggle started, many could not dissociate themselves from it. The battle ended in defeat and humiliation and, after the conclusion of peace, the rest of the chiefs who managed to escape imprisonment or execution retired once more to their homes, perhaps inclined to let matters lie. Such resignation was short-lived, for barely one year later, they were constrained to rise again to protest the dismantling of their political and economic institutions.

One of the major problems that the new colonial government had to grapple with was a scarcity of labor. In Western Igboland the chiefs still controlled the local labor supply; certainly there was no assurance under the prevailing hostile conditions that they would be willing to release their slaves and other dependents to supply labor to the colonial economy. The colonial administration required workers to build roads and bridges, to produce and deliver commodities to the European buying stations, and to build government houses and military barracks. The intelligence reports of the Royal Niger Company had accurately reported that Western Igboland was rich in agricultural products, especially rubber, cotton, timber, and palm products. In addition, the results of the mineral surveys of the early twentieth century confirmed the existence of lignite and possibly coal deposits.[1] To displace the amount of labor the colonial economy required, the colonial administration adopted a policy which officials described as the suppression of slavery and the establishment of a free-labor market.[2] Between 1900 and 1904, colonial government officials, under the guise of setting free all slaves and rendering illegal all future transactions in human beings, passed several laws which in effect would transfer the control of labor from the hands of indigenous chiefs into those of officials. For example, under the Master and Servant Proclamation No. 12 of 1903, slaves were now to be called "apprentices," and both they and their masters were to be bound by contracts laying down terms of service.[3] The law made it illegal for any slave to leave his master's house and prescribed a term of imprisonment for any person wandering abroad or having no apparent means of subsistence. Another law authorized officials to call on chiefs or heads of houses to provide forced labor; it stipulated that "every chief may require all able-bodied men between the ages of 15 and 50, and all able-bodied women between the ages of 15 and 40 residing within his jurisdiction . . . to work in accordance with his direction on any river, creek, or road."[4] Anyone who refused to carry out the orders of his chief or house head was to be punished by fine, imprisonment, or flogging. Of course, the chiefs who would be giving orders to these workers were themselves under the control of the colonial government.

To enforce these laws the government established Native Courts in eight Aniocha towns and appointed warrant chiefs to sit in them and try cases coming before them.[5] In the event of a dispute arising between a slave and his master, the final decision in the matter rested with the Native Courts; a detachment of the Southern Nigeria Regiment stationed in Asaba had policing powers. Since the warrant chiefs were government appointees, they were required to advance British interests rather than those of the indigenous communities they were supposed to represent. Although some warrant chiefs were "accredited" members of the community, many were "upstarts" who earned their certificates of warrant by virtue of the fact that they were prepared to act as agents of British colonialism.[6] Officials sometimes referred to them as "friendly chiefs," while the local people sometimes called them "government chiefs."

With the creation of the Native Courts came the transfer of effective political control from the traditional ruling elite to a new ruling class composed mainly of warrant chiefs, district officers, and British merchants. In fact, Native Courts, as Philip Igbafe has rightly pointed out, were merely an extension of the process of the consolidation of British rule, whose principal ingredients were patrols, escorts, and military expeditions. They were both the props of the British judicial system and the bases of the administrative and executive aspects of British control.[7]

The Christian missionaries and converts, the warrant chiefs, and other government functionaries drew the attention of slaves to the declining power of the local chiefs. The government, fearing that the new laws might lead to social unrest, tried to restrict slaves from immediately deserting, but in fact thousands of them did flee. For instance, more than half the population of Abala town simply moved away in a body and established another settlement a few miles away.[8] In most towns slaves who did remain converted their slave villages into autonomous settlements and farmed for themselves rather than for their masters. Other slaves who feared persecution took refuge in the Christian missionary establishments.

Mass Revolt

By 1904 the traditional chiefs had been brought face-to-face with what they had most feared, namely, that the white man had displaced them as the dominant class in their own society. The idea that both slave and master would now submit themselves to the white man's law was very disturbing. There was no provision for the compensation of masters for the loss of their slaves. Moreover, many customary laws and practices were now threatened with extinction by the new British laws. The atmosphere grew very tense; any misunderstanding, however small, was sufficient to instigate a fight. The inevitable occurred in 1904 when disturbances broke out in Ubulu-Ukwu and Onicha-Olona, leading to a mass uprising.

The Obi of Ubulu-Ukwu was one of the most influential paramount chiefs of Western Igboland in the late nineteenth century. He was the acknowledged overlord of the Ubulu-Ukwu, Ubulu-Uno, Ubulu-Okiti, and Ashama clans. He was a wealthy man and the master of hundreds of slaves, some of who looked after the royal graves.[9] Rev.

Julius Spencer observed during his 1878 visit to Ubulu-Ukwu that the Obi's court was run like that of the Oba of Benin. The Obi, he said, was attended by twelve eunuchs, some of them carrying the scepter and other insignia of royalty. When the Obi made a public appearance, he was "flanked and followed by a large body of his nobility and gentry."[10] The Obi had welcomed the prospects of a Christian mission and had invited the representatives of the Church Missionary Society to visit his chiefdom in 1878. When Rev. Spencer arrived, the Obi offered him many gifts and praised him for the trouble he took to travel so far inland, saying: "As long as ages and traditions last, it shall ever be remembered that in my reign an *oyibo* penetrated thus far."[11] The agents of the Church Missionary Society eventually built a church and a school at Ubulu-Ukwu and during the disturbances of 1898 and 1902-03, the Obi protected the small Christian community there.

In addition, when the representatives of the British government came to Ubulu-Ukwu the Obi concluded with them a treaty of trade and friendship. For some years after the signing of this treaty the Obi remained friendly toward the British. But when the colonial administrators passed the anti-slavery laws of 1901-03, established a Native Court in Ubulu-Ukwu in 1903, and appointed warrant chiefs to sit in this court and try cases coming before them, the Obi was alarmed. First, the anti-slavery proclamations threatened to strip him of his slaves and undermine his source of wealth and influence. Second, the Native Court stripped him of his position as the ultimate court of appeal in Ubulu-Ukwu. Third, barely one year after the Native Court was established its officials were found to be very corrupt in the discharge of their duties.

The Obi and his people protested the unjust practices of the court and as no action was taken by government officials to remedy the situation, they decided to boycott its proceedings. Thenceforth, the people of Ubulu-Ukwu refused to answer its summonses; court messengers and policemen who carried summonses were beaten up by irate crowds. W. E. B. Coupland-Crawford, the divisional commissioner, later argued that sufficient supervision was not given to this and similar courts in the district and that "abuses as were inevitable to some extent crept into their conduct." He admitted that heavy fines were in some cases inflicted for minor offenses, bribes frequently accepted, and favoritism shown in the decisions given.[12]

In January 1904, Coupland-Crawford requested a Mr. Boyle to proceed to Ubulu-Ukwu "to enquire into the matter," but he was turned back by messengers from the chiefs who insisted that "they would not allow Government representatives to enter their town." Coupland-Crawford made several more attempts "to settle the matter by peaceable means and to enquire into the grievance," but the chiefs would not rescind their decision.[13] Coupland-Crawford viewed this refusal as an act of rebellion and contemplated a punitive expedition, but while he was making preparations for the military invasion of Ubulu-Ukwu, he learned of a more serious conflict between the traditional chiefs and the warrant chiefs of Onicha-Olona, which hastened his action against Onicha-Olona and Ubulu-Ukwu.

The conflict started in April 1904, when Chike of Onicha-Olona, a wealthy slave-owning chief, died. As a titled chief, custom demanded that he should be accompanied to the land of his ancestors by at least one attendant. Ogbolu, the brother of Chike, bought a female slave, Ubomi, from a man called Nwabudike, and as arrangements were being made to perform the final rituals that would usher Chike into the world beyond, the warrant chiefs of Onicha-Olona arrived with police and tried to arrest Ogbolu and Nwabudike for breaking the law against slave dealing. To the titled chiefs of Onicha-Olona, the action of the warrant chiefs was outrageous; they at once seized the intruders and brought the warrant chiefs before their own court. Before going into action, a leading chief of Onicha-Olona declared, "As the white man has come suddenly upon us, as if it were from the skies, so have we equally suddenly, and now people will have to carry water for us instead, for the white man and those people friendly to him are to be driven into the sea."[14] The warrant chiefs were described as enemies of the people and were tried for helping the white men spoil the country. They were found guilty as charged and sentenced to death.

The reports that some warrant chiefs were awaiting execution at Onicha-Olona spurred officials into a hasty rescue operation which they successfully accomplished. But this unexpected entry of government soldiers into Onicha-Olona infuriated the populations of that and surrounding communities, and simultaneously attacks were made on churches and courthouses in Ezi, Akwukwu, Ubulu-Ukwu, and Issele-Ukwu, among others.[15] Angry warriors also attacked Christian converts, warrant chiefs, and government officials. Some members of the Church Missionary Society were cut off in Idumuje-Ugboko, while others there, like Rev. Edward Dennis, were fortunate enough to be warned by some local converts early enough to allow their escape.

This popular uprising instigated the revival of the Ekumeku movement, which had gone underground since the previous year. Even though the sudden anger expressed over the unexpected entry of troops into Onicha-Olona quickly cooled off, the Ekumeku arose as the only organization likely to unify the population against possible British retaliation. A large number of chiefs declared for the Ekumeku. Others like Dunkwu, who had gone into hiding since the previous year, reemerged and proceeded to organize their followers for the inevitable battle. Most importantly, the Obi of Ubulu-Ukwu, who had so far adopted a very cautious attitude toward British intervention, declared openly for the Ekumeku society.

The leaders of the resistance movement then proceeded to adopt a war strategy that was to make the engagements of 1904-05 the most violent yet. First, they fortified Onicha-Olona and Ubulu-Ukwu, transforming them into their war capitals. Then under the leadership of Dunkwu the Ekumeku warriors gathered at Onicha-Olona to fight the British, agreeing to retire to Ubulu-Ukwu should Onicha-Olona fall into enemy hands. The Ekumeku also fortified Ukwunzu, a town fifteen miles away from Onicha-Olona.

When Coupland-Crawford, the divisional commissioner, and a Mr. Davidson, the assistant district commissioner, heard of the reemergence of the Ekumeku movement, they immediate assembled troops, and after garrisoning Asaba, marched to Issele-Ukwu, which they occupied to save the Roman Catholic Mission building from destruction. Another government official, Widenham Fosbery, led a large force through the district, passing through Atuma, Akwukwu, Onicha-Olona, Ezi, Onicha-Ukwu, and Idumuje-Ugboko; he observed that the local populace had closed all the roads, attacked and destroyed the stations belonging to the Church Missionary Society and the native courthouses, and released all those awaiting trial.

It was not until January 1905, however, that actual fighting began. On the night of January 18, an Ekumeku force passed through Issele-Mkpitima on its way to Akwukwu to intercept a column of British troops returning from the Kwale country. The officer commanding the Asaba Hinterland Expeditionary force learned of the movement and decided to pursue. Leaving guards at the Catholic mission at Issele-Ukwu, he moved out early the next morning and encountered the rear guard of the Ekumeku near Atuma. The Ekumeku opened fire, but because of the unexpected arrival of colonial troops, the Ekumeku fighters could not put up a determined resistance. Instead they retreated into the neighboring forests, from which they could use guerrilla tactics to drive the colonials back. Leaving some of his troops at Atuma, the commanding officer moved to Onicha-Olona, where he met heavy opposition in the streets of the town. From Onicha-Olona, the colonials advanced to Ezi, which also became the scene of a bitter encounter with many deaths.

After a week of fighting at Onicha-Olona and Ezi, the Ekumeku abandoned this area entirely as had been planned and retreated toward Ukwunzu via the Ezi road. The colonial troops followed the Ekumeku, hardly perceiving the trap that awaited them. There were many engagements with the British suffering some casualties as they fell into ambushes at Obomkpa, Onicha-Ukwu, and Ugbodu. It was at Ukwunzu that the colonials suffered their greatest losses as they tried to enter the town. Militarily Ukwunzu occupied a strong strategic position as it was situated on a small hill which could only be reached by a path leading through a narrow gorge and surrounded by thick forest. The Ekumeku had lured the British troops in that direction and had assembled in ambush to await their arrival. When the colonial troops appeared, a fierce battle broke out, with both sides suffering some casualties. The colonial troops soon realized they could not take Ukwunzu by assault; their losses were increasing, and in the end they decided to withdraw. The British had relied on their superiority of arms and the Ekumeku on their knowledge of the country; this time the guerrilla tactics worked. The success at Ukwunzu has been attributed to the leadership of an Ukwunzu warrior nicknamed *Nwa ngwele amane,* a good hunter and a ruthless fighter who lured the colonial troops to their destruction.[16]

The retreating colonials now turned to Ugbodu, which had been deserted, and occupied it with a view to using it as a convenient center from which to operate more effectively against Ukwunzu and Onicha-Ukwu. After more than a week of waiting, however, the British leaders realized there was no one in that area to fight; most of the Ekumeku in the eastern section had moved to the western headquarters centered at Ubulu-Ukwu.

Captain Wallis, who was wasting his time and troops at Ugbodu, was instructed to attack Idumuje-Ugboko. To reach that town the troops would have to go through or near Idumuje-Uno, where the danger of ambush was great. Captain Wallis was forced to make his way by a circuitous route, passing through Ani-Ofu before arriving at Idumuje-Ugboko, where he met with the expected "stiff resistance" but nonetheless succeeded in taking the town.[17]

Between February 4 and 11, 1905, colonial troops were sent out from the town daily to destroy farms, bush camps, and crops. Messages were sent to neighboring towns considered friendly "to impress on the inhabitants the necessity of co-operating with the Government in their own interest" and to warn them against sheltering "fugitives." Many of the towns that previously had been damaged were again visited and destroyed. By mid-February, the town of Idumuje-Ugboko and the surrounding settlements seemed to be subdued, so that government troops were instructed to march on Ubulu-Ukwu, which official reports described as "the last and most important center remaining to be dealt with."[18]

Meanwhile, the colonial administration was becoming increasingly alarmed by news of the war, especially by the fact that hostilities were spreading over a wide area. Acting High Commissioner Coupland-Crawford and Captain H. P. Gordon called in reinforcements from the Ifon district. The commanding officer of the Asaba Hinterland Expeditionary force was recalled to Asaba to meet Coupland-Crawford personally in council with the divisional commissioner of the Central Provinces. The primary object of the discussion was the final assault on Ubulu-Ukwu.

The British leaders considered the battle of Ubulu-Ukwu particularly crucial to the entire war against the Ekumeku; they knew they were facing a major struggle. In the first place, they feared that the Ekumeku fighters would put up determined resistance there because most of their leaders had retreated to that town. In addition, Ubulu-Ukwu had never been drawn into battle with either the Royal Niger Company or His Majesty's Imperial Government, and so, argued the British, "It considered itself more than a match for the government forces."[19] Finally, reliable information from Europeans who had visited

Ubulu-Ukwu indicated that the town was a geographically unfavorable town to attack. Based on these rationales, the British made elaborate preparations before launching their attack on the town.

The Ekumeku warriors assembled at Ubulu-Ukwu also began to make war preparations. They were dismayed by reports that when the British overran Issele-Azagba they succeeded in enlisting the assistance of Onwuadiaju, a prominent Issele-Azagba resident who had personally helped organize the Ekumeku movement there.[20] The information reaching Ubulu-Ukwu confirmed that Onwuadiaju was actually showing the colonial troops a secret route leading to Ubulu-Ukwu. The Ekumeku warriors who knew this secret route acted quickly, setting up an ambush for Onwuadiaju and the British soldiers, and an Ubulu-Ukwu marksman, Nwaniaboh, was specifically asked to shoot Onwuadiaju. Nwaniaboh's gunshot would be the signal setting off the battle.

As expected, the vanguard of the colonial troops approached the ambush prepared for them. The Ekumeku warriors were poised silently as Nwaniaboh aimed his rifle and waited for the intruders to move into range. The unsuspecting British, led by Onwuadiaju, came closer. Nwaniaboh pulled the trigger and Onwuadiaju fell, mortally wounded. With the sound of the gunshot, the Ekumeku forces rose from their hiding places, opening fire on the colonials and driving them back.[21]

The colonials regrouped. From Issele-Azagba Captain Ian Hogg sent out scouts to locate the positions of the Ekumeku, a precautionary exercise that proved helpful, for, as Captain Hogg testified, the colonial troops would have been destroyed if the scouts did not disclose the Ekumeku ambushes. On February 14, backed by reinforcements from Old Calabar and Ifon, the colonial troops advanced toward Ubulu-Ukwu.

There were hot engagements on all the fronts as the soldiers fought to gain entrance into the town. Ekumeku riflemen occupied the natural and artificial trenches they had dug on the eastern approaches of Ubulu-Ukwu, from where they kept up a brisk fire and were able to move rapidly through the bush from one point to another. The Ekumeku fighters had also cut small paths in the bush, linking the trenches with sunken avenues which in turn led to the various compounds in the town. The whole "architecture," wrote Captain Ian Hogg in his report, was well planned and designed in such a way that all the paths, compounds, avenues, and trenches were connected to the Obi's palace.[22]

The colonial forces were strained to their limit not only because of the skill of the military operations of the Ekumeku, but also because of logistics. First, the colonial troops, taking advantage of their superiority in fire-power, were able to dislodge the Ekumeku from their first line of trenches, but were disappointed to find that the Ekumeku had retired to a second line of pits, from where "they kept up a desultory fire," killing and wounding some soldiers. Second, the colonial troops were disturbed by the fact that they fought an enemy they could not see. The more sophisticated weapons of the colonial troops enabled them to continue the battle, however, even though they suffered heavy casualties. Their prime target was to capture the palace of the Obi of Ubulu-Ukwu.

The day following the initial assault, the colonial forces managed to fight their way to a clearing close to the center of the town. From this point footpaths led to the various quarters of Ubulu-Ukwu. Bushes and tall trees were on all sides, and just to the east of the clearing was a very large pond which the people of Ubulu-Ukwu called *ogodo alum*.[23] From near this pond one could see any moving object in the immediate vicinity. The Ekumeku knew that their cause was hopeless if the British seized this ground; hence they were determined to hold it.

Since the enemy would have to cross this area to gain access to the Obi's palace, the Ekumeku dug a narrow hole and placed a trumpeter (*onye akpela*) in it; he was covered with earth up to his shoulders and his head protected with a metal pot (*ite igwe*).[24] From this location the trumpeter observed the movements of the colonial troops, which he described perfectly through a coded language on his trumpet, giving exact information about enemy movements to the Ekumeku who were silently hiding in nearby pits and trenches. Each time the colonial troops advanced toward an Ekumeku fortification, the trumpeter sent the necessary coded message to his compatriots, who emerged and shot down the enemy at close range. Local lore has it that some confused colonial troops shot indiscriminately while others fired in the direction from where they thought the sound of the trumpet was coming. Despite heavy losses, however, the British managed to hold to their position, and the trumpeter's strategic contribution was undermined.

The colonial troops next made one swift push and succeeded in displacing the Ekumeku from their second line of pits. Moving quickly, the British forces seized the main path leading to the king's palace. Sensing their danger, the Ekumeku struggled desperately and regained their second line of pits, from where they fought bravely, and almost succeeded in driving back the troops, who now began to use shrapnel and their maxim guns.[25] The last mile or so to the king's palace witnessed some of the fiercest fighting of the entire Ekumeku war.

At this point Captain Hogg despatched his advance guard to clear what he called "the most obstinate Ekumeku." To achieve this, the troops resorted to successive rushes and flanking movements supported by heavy gunfire, finally driving the Ekumeku from their last trenches flanking the road that lead to the palace. Eventually, the colonial troops reached their target and pitched a camp in the Obi's compound. The battle was over. It would be the last of the major struggles by the Ekumeku to keep the British out of Western Igboland.

On February 16, 1905, several chiefs sent peace parties to mediate between the colonial government and the Ekumeku. The government first demanded the unconditional surrender of the resisters, a demand contrary to the Ekumeku conception of what peace negotiations involved, and they responded by resuming their resistance. The next week saw a continuation of hostilities. Various neighboring towns were visited by the troops and attacked for supporting the Ekumeku. Captain Gordon was sent back with four sections to Onicha-Olona with instructions "to go round the Eastern area and to endeavor to effect the capture or surrender of the various ringleaders." Captain Hogg himself led five sections to the western side, while Captain Gordon and Captain Wallis planned to operate against the outlying districts and eventually to meet at Ugbodu. Meanwhile, Ubulu-Ukwu continued to be occupied by Coupland-Crawford and the rest of the British troops.

For all intents the Ekumeku insurrection of 1904-05 was at an end, though for several more months British troops continued to patrol the various towns in Western Igboland, tracking down fugitives, imposing heavy fines on "several nominally friendly towns" that were believed to have sheltered fugitives, and attacking others that refused to pay fines. One such place was Esan, where a large number of men described as fugitives from Idumuje-Ugboko were captured. The colonial administration justified the attacks and the arrests by claiming they were necessary to avoid an annual recurrence of these disturbances and to ensure a permanent pacification of the hinterland. Many towns were punished "with sufficient severity to make a lasting impression on the inhabitants of the power of the government and its intention to establish law and order in the hinterland."[26] Several Ekumeku leaders were also removed from Western Igboland to serve various terms of imprisonment elsewhere, while others were executed outright. Among the latter was Dunkwu of Onicha-Olona, who was put to death by government troops in his home town.[27]

By March 12, 1905, the whole area inhabited by what was described as "the Asaba speaking people" had been subdued. Officials claimed that over 250 leaders of the Ekumeku society had been captured and were awaiting trial at Asaba, leaving some 15 prominent men still at large. All the towns that took part in the uprising were made to pay heavy fines and to surrender their guns. Many were compelled to rebuild the mission and government houses that had been destroyed during the war.

On the other hand, the government forces also suffered severe casualties. According to the medical officer in charge of the expedition, "The number of casualties was high; the proportion of killed to wounded and of severe to slight wounds was also large." He attributed this to "the very close ranges at which the wounds were inflicted and also to the nature of the projectiles which, in all cases, were large, more or less irregular shaped pieces of hammered iron or brass."[28] No casualty figures were recorded, however.

The British reports of casualties were accompanied by other reports that distorted the facts concerning the war and served to justify British aims and tactics. For example, one report claimed that the object of the Ekumeku was to drive the white man back to the sea and to kill all the indigenous people who were favorably disposed toward him. The report further stated that the Ekumeku "desired the continuance of their old barbaric customs and the expulsion of the white man and civilization from their midst."[29] Such reports were intended to deceive the British public, which was demonstrating concern about British military activities in the colonies.[30]

What the reports did not say was that the Ekumeku uprising of 1904-05 was a reaction to official insensitivity to the dislocation and disturbance that colonial policies had caused in local communities. In their desire to introduce what they called a "more just and civilized method of government," the British agents decided to overthrow indigenous institutions. Although some officials tried to work through and with the assistance of the chiefs, in some cases they appointed the wrong persons to sensitive positions, completely disregarding the social and class structures within which the native Africans were operating. "Upstarts" and even men of doubtful birth and integrity were made members of the Native Courts. Determined to exploit their new stations, these individuals demanded bribes and imposed heavy fines on those who challenged their authority. Also, under the guise of implementing the provisions of the Roads and Creeks Proclamation of 1903, warrant chiefs compelled youths to render forced and unpaid labor on their private farms, and flogged or imprisoned all those who refused to work for them.

These "government chiefs" soon became so powerful and overbearing that they were dreaded more than the white men whose instruments they were. The authority which the warrant chiefs commanded was strange, points out Obaro Ikime, in that it transformed "mere delegates into effective rulers," concentrating vast amounts of power "in individual hands to an extent unknown in traditional usage."[31] The Western Igbo people were further appalled by the manner in which the business of the Native Courts was conducted. The Igbo had used a variety of judicial techniques to settle their disputes. The nature of the dispute, points out Simon Ottenberg, determined which judicial agent to be sought; sometimes the disputants and their relatives decided where to present their case — before patrilineal elders, village elders, clan elders, famous oracles, or simply by swearing innocence to a spirit which they believed would kill those who lied to it.[32] The Igbo had no prison or jail houses, and no matter a man's offense, he remained a free man, carrying out his daily activities, until his guilt was established. The idea of locking up people, depriving them of their freedom and livelihood even before their guilt was established, was most disgusting to the traditional Igbo mind.

Furthermore, the district officers who presided over the Native Courts were ignorant of native laws and customs and, even though they were supposed to work with the warrant chiefs, the decisions reached were mostly at variance with what the Igbo regarded as justice.

Most of the district officers were young army officers or administrators who, as Philip Igbafe has pointed out, "found themselves invested with wide judicial powers which made them the arbiters of the fate of many indigenous people whose own judicial system had been disorganized and driven underground."[33] Further, the Native Courts were controlled by the Supreme Court, meaning that the idea of English law and procedure were used to decide issues that had local origins. Appeals reaching the Supreme Court were in turn reviewed by judges who were learned in European laws but had little or no knowledge of native law and custom.[34]

It is no wonder therefore that barely three years after the introduction of the Native Court and Warrant Chief systems, the Western Igbo people rebelled against them. It should be pointed out that opposition to the Native Courts and warrant chiefs continued throughout southeastern Nigeria, culminating in the anti-tax riots of 1927-28 in Western Igboland and the Western Delta, and the famous Aba women's riots of 1929, which compelled the colonial administration to reorganize the native authority government in the 1930s and 1940s. Indeed, as Terence Ranger and A. B. Davidson have observed, not all African resistances were in vain; many of them not only wrung concessions and preserved pride, they also left their mark on the most important internal processes of development of the Africans.[35]

To this day many elders of Ubulu-Ukwu remember a song that was popular during the Ekumeku wars:

> Iyele bu omu egbe [A gun is a stone that produces sparks]
> Iyele by omu egbe [A gun is a stone that produces sparks]
> Iyele bu omu egbe [A gun is a stone that produces sparks]
> Iyele bu omu egbe [A gun is a stone that produces sparks]
> Onye ga fu ndi anyali ogbura [Who would not kill an albino
>   (a whiteman) on sight]
> Iyele bu omu egbe. [A gun is a stone that produces sparks]

The comparison of Europeans with albinos, who were used for ritual sacrifices, illustrates the mistrust which the Igbo developed for the Europeans during this period of resistance, and which lasted throughout the colonial period (1900-60). As anyone familiar with the history of Nigerian nationalist movements would testify, the Igbo were one of the most militant anti-imperialist groups in Africa. And even though they were receptive to culture change and were most willing to accept western ways, as Simon Ottenberg has observed, they believed that they could "become westernized more rapidly if freed from British rule."[36] Their violent agitations for freedom in the 1940s and 1950s were a continuation of the primary resistance movements of the 1890s and the early twentieth century.

NOTES TO CHAPTER SIX

1. PRO, CO520/101/6586, enclosure in Confidential Dispatch, Governor of Southern Nigeria to Colonial Office, January 30, 1911.
2. PRO, C0520/13/83, Ralph Moor to Colonial Office, February 26, 1902.
3. PRO, C0588/1, The Master and Servant Proclamation No. 12, 1903.
4. PRO, C0588/1, The Roads and Creeks Proclamation No. 15, 1903.
5. PRO, C0520/18/7937, Widenham Fosbery to High Commissioner, January 2, 1903.
6. See Obaro Ikime, "The Anti-Tax Riots in Warri Province, 1927-1928," *Journal of the Historical Society of Nigeria* 3, no. 3 (1966): 560. See also A. E. Afigbo, *The Warrant Chiefs: Indirect Rule in Southern Nigeria, 1891-1929* (Ibadan, 1972), 7.
7. Phillip A. Igbafe, *Benin Under British Administration: The Impact of Colonial Rule on an African Kingdom, 1897-1939* (London, 1979), 182-83.
8. NAI, CS026/10, 26769, E. A. Miller, Intelligence Report on Aboh-Benin Clans, 1930-31.
9. Sylverus Onochie, interview at Ubulu-Ukwu, March 23, 1978.
10. *Church Missionary Intelligencer*, 1879, 239.
11. Ibid., 239.
12. PRO, C0520/24/20839 W. E. B. Coupland-Crawford, Divisional Commissioner, Central Division to the Government of Southern Nigeria, June 13, 1904.
13. Ibid.
14. Ibid.
15. For a complete account of the uprising, see PRO, C0520/24 of March 14, 1904. Capt. Ian Hogg, Officer Commanding Southern Nigeria Regiment, Asaba.
16. According to information gathered at Onich-Olonam, however, *Nwa ngwele amane* was the nickname of a British soldier who fought the Ekumeku at Ukwunzu. But according to information gathered at Ukwunzu, *Nwa ngwele amane* was the nickname of the leader of the Ekumeku of Ukwunzu who drove away the British. Such contradictions exemplify one of the prob-

lems of relying upon oral history to reconstruct past events. For an account of the battle see His Royal Highness, Obi Ogoh I of Ukwunzu, interview at Ukwunzu, December 20, 1982.

17. PRO, C0520/24 of March 14, 1904, Capt. Ian Hogg to the Officer Commanding Southern Nigeria Regiment, Asaba.

18. Ibid.

19. Ibid.

20. Vincent C. Modi, interview at Ubulu-Ukwu, December 10, 1982.

21. Ibid.

22. CO520/24 of March 14, 1904, Capt. Ian Hogg to Officer Commanding Southern Nigeria Regiment.

23. J. O. Adinpu, interview at Ubulu-Ukwu, December 19, 1982.

24. Henry N. Abili-Mordi, interview at Ubulu-Ukwu, December 20, 1982.

25. CO520/24 of March 14, 1905, Capt. Ian Hogg to the Officer Commanding Southern Regiment.

26. Ibid.

27. SMA, from Father Zappa's diary, in *The Missionary Endeavours in the Diocese of Benin City,* p. 34.

28. CO520/24 of March 14, 1904, enclosed in Captain Hogg's despatch, "Medical Report on the Asaba Hinterland Expedition."

29. PRO, CO520/24/20839 of June 13, 1904, W. E. B. Coupland-Crawford, Divisional Commissioner, Central Division, to the Government of Southern Nigeria.

30. The most notable anti-imperialist association in Britain at this time was the British Anti-Slavery and Aborigines Protection Society. It was a humanitarian organization to which some members of the British Parliament belonged.

31. Obaro Ikime, "The Anti-Tax Riots in Warri Province, 1927-1928" *Journal of the Historical Society of Nigeria,* 3, no. 3 (1966):560.

32. Simon Ottenberg, "Ibo Receptivity to Change" in *Continuity and Change in African Cultures,* ed. William Bascom and Melville J. Herskovits (Chicago, 1959), 138.

33. Igbafe, *Benin Under British Administration,* 190.

34. Ibid., 192.

35. Terence O. Ranger, "Connections Between Primary Resistance Movements and Modern Mass Nationalism in East and Central Africa," *Journal of African History,* 9 (1968): 441; A. B. Davidson, "African Resistance and Rebellion Against the Imposition," (Dar es Salam, 1968), 178.

36. Ottenberg, "Igbo Receptivity," 130.

CHAPTER SEVEN

The Last of the Ekumeku

APART FROM A NUMBER of sporadic outbursts in the area, it appeared that Western Igboland was about to enjoy a period of peace. In 1909, however, a new outburst erupted in Ogwashi Ukwu, and with it arose speculation that hostilities, as had previously been the case, would spread to other parts of the hinterland of Asaba. The cause of the current rising was not immediately apparent, but it soon became evident that the conflict started as a succession dispute between two prominent Ogwashi-Ukwu families.

In Western Igboland the notion of hereditary succession was foreign. Thus, all the communities that did recognize hereditary monarchies must have adopted the idea from Benin or Idah. In Benin, succession followed the rules of primogeniture, but in those regions of Western Igboland where the institution of Obiship existed, each candidate was chosen from among the members of certain families in rotation, and the choice of each candidate ultimately rested on the community at large. During selection, every member of the affected *umunna* showed particular interest in the selection processes.

During the late nineteenth and early twentieth centuries it appears that the obiship of Ogwashi-Ukwu rotated between two lineages, namely, the families of Nzekwe and Okonjor. Nkekwe was the Obi of Ogwashi-Ukwu; following the tradition of the clan, he would have been succeeded by Okonjor, but Okonjor died before Nzekwe. Meanwhile the Obiship of Ogwashi Ukwu was undisputed as Nzekwe continued to rule, and no arrangements were made as to what would happen in the event of Nzekwe's death. When in 1907 Nzekwe died, two candidates emerged aspiring to the Ogwashi-Ukwu throne. These were the sons of Nzekwe and of Okonjor, respectively, both with equal claims to the throne. Nevertheless, the son of Nzwkwe was accepted by "a large majority of the town" as their new Obi. It is said that during a meeting at Ogwahi-Ukwu at which the district commissioner was present, the townspeople expressed their wish that Nzekwe, son of the deceased Obi (hereafter referred to simply as Nzekwe) should be the Obi; the government thus recognized him as such.

Okonjor the son (hereafter referred to as Okonjor) and a section of the Ogwashi-Ukwu community were dissatisfied with the decision. They pointed out that if the elder Okonjor had lived, he would have succeeded on the elder Nzekwe's death. Okonjor insisted that "as his father would have succeeded Nzekwe's father he had a right to be considered as the Head Chief." The issue was raised several times and the various district commissioners upheld Nzekwe's claim.

Okonjor nursed his grievance and in 1909 contacted an Asaba chief who introduced him to one Mr. Dove, a Sierra Leonean lawyer, living in Onitasha. Okonjor paid the sum of £127, out of which Dove received £80, the rest going to a John Bright, who, apparently, was a commissioned agent. Dove wrote a petition to the commissioner on Okonjor's behalf, backing up his petition with an assurance to Okonjor that he would do all in his power to persuade the authorities to depose Nzekwe and install him in his place.[1]

The details of this arrangement were soon known to Nzekwe, who probably would have remained undisturbed if the district commissioner had not, at this critical moment, summoned him to appear at Igbuzo. The summons was not in any way connected with the succession dispute at Ogwashi-Ukwu, but involved the case of an Igbuzo man who had been killed at Ogwashi-Ukwu under suspicious circumstances, a man regarded as a spy who disclosed to the colonial government the activities of the Ekumeku. A number of arrests were made and fines imposed on some Ogwahi-Ukwu quarters. Some of these quarters collected their own share of the fines and at the time Nzekwe was summoned to Igbuzo, he already had in his possession £100 contribution from his lineage.[2] Nzekwe mistakenly attributed his summons to Igbuzo to the activities of his rival and, afraid that he would be arrested and stripped of his obiship, refused to go.

The colonial government had a different view, however. It saw Nzekwe's refusal to comply with the wish of the government as "a boast of his power." As the quarrel between Nzekwe and Okonjor deepened, so also did Nzekwe's hostility toward the government, and he used his considerable influence to stir up general dissension, not only in Ogwashi-Ukwu, but also in the neighboring towns, including, curiously enough, Igbuzo, the home town of the murdered man.[3] When the British became convinced that Nzekwe was bent on starting off a general rising, R. A. Roberts, a political officer in the Asaba District, was sent to Ogwashi-Ukwu to see Nzekwe and if possible, defuse the tension. On October 30, 1909, Roberts left Asaba "with a final ultimatum to Nzekwe to come in and discuss the government's demands within forty-eight hours." Nzekwe was warned that failure to comply would result in an immediate invasion of his town.[4]

An ultimatum was hardly the best way to ease tensions, and, as might have been expected, the ultimatum was ignored. On November 3, a British column was despatched, arriving at Ubulu-Ukwu two days later. From Ubulu-Ukwu messengers were sent to Nzekwe; by 4 p.m. the messengers returned with a very distressing reply. Nzekwe had received the messengers outside his house, where he was surrounded by several armed people, including his sons. He had told the messengers that he did not know who reported him to the government and that he would not come in to see the white men. If the white men came to his town, he said, he would fight them. Such a response only made the British more resolute to strip Nzekwe of his power and, if necessary, destroy Ogwasi-Ukwu. The order was given for Captain G. Nelson Sheffield to occupy the town.

Troops left Ubulu-Ukwu on November 7, and by 7:30 that morning Ogwashi-Ukwu was occupied; a minor encounter had left one government soldier mortally wounded. Nzekwe and his men, in accordance with the usual Ekumeku guerrilla tactics, had withdrawn to one of their war camps, reportedly located toward the south.

The uprising, far from being scotched at the very outset, was only just beginning. In fact, before Nzekwe and his men withdrew to their war camp they had seen to it that the native courthouse, which symbolized to them the instrument of British oppression, was destroyed.

They also destroyed the Church Missionary Society building.

The Roman Catholic Mission center faced a similar fate. Father Carlo Zappa's role in the events leading up to the confict had been significant, and Nzekwe had ordered the Roman Catholic mission to be destroyed in retaliation. Throughout his stay in Western Igboland, Zappa, like most Roman Catholic priests, had acted as an informal, unpaid agent for the colonial administrators. For example, in 1894 Zappa personally took the agents of the Royal Niger Company to Okpanam, "to show them the way" at a time when the company was at war with the people there.[5] No wonder, then, that when the company's forces menaced Okpanam in 1897 and Zappa tried to intervene, the people of Okpanam rebuffed him, pointing out that soldiers had been in the mission house and that a Catholic priest had been seen with them.[6] Some months before the expedition entered Ogwashi-Ukwu the district commissioner at Onitasha had requested Father Zappa to inform him in writing, if possible, of what the priest knew of the general state of the surrounding towns. In a reply dated August 28, 1909, Father Zappa had told the commissioner:

> All I know about the general state of the surrounding towns is that up to this date only Akpuma, Igbede, part of Olo and two other villages S.W. of Ogwashi have declared themselves ready to stand by the king. Ogwashi-Azagba and Edo have refused to join, it is the same with Uburu-Uno. In Ogwashi town itself the quarter named Ogbe-Akwu has not joined the movement. This is very lucky for it is this part of the town one reaches first when coming from Ibusa or from Ogwashi- Azagba. Nearly all the other entrances are strongly barricaded and flanked by thick bush.[7]

In the same letter Zappa had also disclosed that during the preceding days the paramount chief had been sending messages about the town to recruit Ekumeku warriors. Zappa had gotten the information from townspeople who came to him secretly to ask whether they should refuse or accept. He had further claimed that at Idumje-Uno he was told that the old members of the Ekumeku group were following with great interest and eagerness all news coming from Ogwashi-Ukwu.

Father Zappa had continued his role of informant by sending word of the preparations for resistance that the people of Ogwashi-Ukwu were making. He told of "a young ju-ju man from Agba" who was selling to the people of Ogwashi-Ukwu "a special medicine" which was supposed to make them invulnerable, and of a "stout ju-ju woman" from Nsukwa who was "burying in several spots of the town some *malefices* [charms] intended to kill the soldiers when they pass upon them." Father Zappa had declared that as a priest he still wished matters could be settled peacefully, "but to put it very mildly, the situation seems hopeless." Finally, he pleaded, "In case the Government were to decide for an expedition, you would kindly give me information of the movement of the troops before they get ready at Onitsha. . . . You may rely on me as regards the prudence with which I may make use of the information."[8] The district commissioner, grateful for such valuable intelligence information, informed Zappa that he had forwarded his letter to headquarters, hoping that the government would shortly take action. He had further told Zappa that he would be informed when the necessary action would be ordered.

The colonial administrators lived up to their word. On October 22 they told Zappa about plans for an armed force to leave Asaba on October 28 or 29 under the political guidance of R. A. Roberts, senior district commissioner. They requested Father Zappa to warn his followers that during the operations their lives would be at risk if they remained in the town.

Father Zappa seemed to have known well in advance about troop movements. In his reply to the district commissioner's letter he disclosed that the Ogwashi people knew on October 21 that carriers had been asked for at Onicha-Olona, and, Zappa added:

> Herewith I send a copy of the plan of Ogwashi-Ukwu which might be of some use to the officers in case they meet with opposition, in which case also it would be useful to us by sparing us the visit of an unlooked for shell. The plan had been taken with prismatic compass, and gives the principal streets as well as some paths with the dotted lines.[9]

He concluded his letter by warning that although opinion among the Ogwashi people was divided, the expedition, however peaceful, should be ready to meet stiff opposition.

It is no wonder, therefore, that Nzekwe, who knew about the agreement between the Catholic father and the soldiers, should have reason to act against the mission when hostilities broke out. But colonial forces entered the city before he could carry out his threat; they found that Zappa and some 150 followers had barricaded themselves inside the mission against possible attack by Nzekwe, who had already fled. The soldiers freed Zappa and his group and proceeded to encamp in the mission compound.[10]

Infuriated by Nzekwe's escape, the commander of the British troops daily dispatched men to destroy all the areas of Ogwashi-Ukwu that he considered hostile to the British. Messengers were sent to the various villages and to all the people living in the bush summoning them to come and meet with the government. The colonials declared Nzekwe and a number of others "wanted men" and urged local residents to find them and turn them over to the authorities. The district commissioner of Agbor was asked "to warn all chiefs of towns bordering on the Asaba District to keep a look out for Nzekwe or any Ogwashi-Ukwu people whom they should immediately arrest and bring in to him."[11]

The quarters of Ogwashi-Ukwu that gave the greatest trouble to the British troops were those collectively known as *Azungwwu*, that is the quarters behind the big tree called *Ngwu*. Anger and frustration over colonial losses mounted, especially after November 10; in skirmishes that day, four British soldiers were wounded and one sergeant killed. In retaliation Captain Sheffield, acting on the instructions of the political officer, had the old *Ngwu* tree felled.[12]

In course of time, the British realized that the situation was getting worse, as disaffection was spreading, not only to the various quarters of Ogwashi-Ukwu, but also to many of the neighboring settlements. Towns and villages that had chafed under the British yoke saw Nzekwe's rebellion as an opportunity to give vent to their own dissatisfaction. During the ensuing weeks, violence spread; out of thirty-three settlements, eleven were reported to be friendly to the government, sixteen hostile, and the inhabitants of another six, whose disposition could not be determined, merely ran away into the bush.

In the eyes of the British the most notorious among the hostile villages was Ogwashi-Uno, situated four miles south of Ogwashi-Ukwu. The British strongly believed that an assault on Ogwashi-Uno would result in two important breakthroughs. First, it was thought that since the kinship ties between Ogwashi-Uno and Ogwashi-Ukwu were very strong, Nzekwe and his men could be using the village as a base for Ekumeku operations. Second, the British thought that if they moved troops to Ogwashi-Uno they would be able to collect useful information about Nzekwe.

On November 19, 1909, Captain Sheffield with a column of his soldiers set out for Ogwashi-Uno. As the direct route was blocked, the force marched via the Igbuzo road, through the town of Abo-Ogwashi, and occupied Ogwashi-Uno without opposition. This easy entry into Ogwashi-Uno soon proved illusory, as the troops found themselves in "a considerable amount of fighting" in which they suffered some casualties. In their bid to retain Ogwashi-Uno the British had to carry out two night attacks on the combined forces of Ogwashi-Ukwu and Ogwashi-Uno. In spite of these full-scale operations the British could not capture a single enemy prisoner. According to the commanding officer, "No prisoners were captured and no information was received about the whereabouts of Nzekwe and the other ring-leaders." Their objectives in launching the assault were frustrated.

Toward the end of November 1909 the British realized that both capturing Nzekwe and crushing the Ogwashi-Ukwu resistance were more than the forces at their disposal could achieve. Consequently, Captain Sheffield sent a telegram to Agbor requesting reinforcements. Captain Purcell was ordered to join Sheffield at Ogwashi-Ukwu on November 25, 1909. On the appointed day, Sheffield, in utter frustration, abandoned his Ogwashi-Uno location and returned to his "original camp" at Ogwashi-Ukwu to meet Purcell and the troops from Agbor. Acting on information from Chief Elumelu of Abo-Ogwashi to the effect that Nzekwe and his followers were living in the Umudei quarter of Ogwashi-Ukwu, Sheffield staged an early-morning raid on November 29. The only thing accomplished was the acquisition of "some evidence that the houses had been occupied within a few hours."

The British decided to retain their camp at Ogwashi-Ukwu with Sheffield in charge, while Purcell roamed with a sub-column, descending upon and intimidating those settlements believed to be hostile to the government. Purcell and his troops were very active; during this mission they burned down what they described as "bush-camps" and destroyed houses and farms. In a night attack at Akpoma, two Ekumeku warriors were captured. These prisoners-of-war were hastily dispatched to Ogwashi-Ukwu, where a "certain amount of information was extracted from them as to the camps of the ring leaders." What the British learned was only that Nzekwe's base of operations was within a two mile radius of Akpoma.

On December 10, 1909, Captain Purcell and his troops embarked on one final operation. His mission was to lead a sub-column to Akpoma, from where he would range about in the vicinity, with the usual purpose of trying to flush out Nzekwe. The force spent eight days "discovering and destroying bush camps and farms," but having failed to capture the "ring-leaders," Purcell returned to Ogwashi-Ukwu a week later. The British had operated in Ogwashi-Ukwu and neighboring districts for over a month without achieving their objectives. Neither was the resistance crushed, nor Nzekwe captured. Reinforcements had been sent but despite a determined effort, the British could not achieve any appreciable military success.

On the other hand, and for reasons that were not immediately known, there occurred what R. A. Roberts, the political officer who reported on the events, described as "a marked improvement in the political aspect generally," as the people of certain quarters of Ogwashi-Ukwu came in and declared for the government. This development was completely unexpected. To determine the Africans' sincerity in the matter Roberts asked them to bring in their chiefs and the rest of their people from the bush. The locals dispersed and a few days later various chiefs and representatives of Ogwashi-Ukwu and Ogwashi-Uno appeared, some even arriving with the fines they had refused to pay following the murder of the Igbuzo man. Roberts later explained this surrender by suggesting that the majority of the enemy had had enough of the war, and that the only reason that had prevented them from coming to sue for peace was that they were afraid of the soldiers.

Following this surprise surrender, the political officer arranged to hold a meeting of all the friendly groups on December 16. During the meeting, he explained at some length the series of events that had led through the past six months to the present state of affairs. He told the populace that as they now wished for peace the government was prepared to withdraw the soldiers. He asked them to let this information reach every district, and to tell all those who were either still afraid or hostile to return to their homes and submit to the government's authority. He said that troops would be withdrawn entirely from the district for three weeks to give all parties time to consider the matter.

Roberts ended his long address by imposing fines on Ogwashi-Ukwu and the outlying settlements and naming Igbuzo as the place where all the fines should be paid. Interestingly, the three quarters that took the most active part in the hostilities were not fined. Instead, Roberts gave them three weeks to carry out the government's demands; after the expiration of this period, troops would visit them again to deal very severely with those who had not fully complied. Colonial officials assured those quarters that had already surrendered that "nothing was to be feared by them in the event of the troops returning."

After a thorough rehearsal of warnings and assurances, the British withdrew. Purcell left for Agbor accompanied by his men while Roberts, Sheffield, and the rest of the troops proceeded to Igbuzo and eventually to Asaba. They took with them items seized, including "some three hundred guns, some thirty five heads of cattle . . . besides a large number of yams." Despite the seeming calm of the area they left behind, Roberts still had his doubts over what would happen once the troops were withdrawn. He was almost certain, he later reported, that it might be necessary to bring troops back to Ogwashi-Ukwu.

Indeed, barely two days after the withdrawal of troops, the warriors of the Ogbe-Nta and Umudei quarters of Ogwashi-Ukwu struck again, attacking and destroying the Roman Catholic church and a number of houses, all belonging to the Catholics.[13] This distressing news caused the colonial administrators to reconsider the wisdom of withdrawing, which, they later said, was merely done to allow the inspector general to inspect the troops.[14] After the renewed violence confirmed that a tactical error had been made, colonial troops once again marched back to Ogwashi-Ukwu.

Nzekwe and his men had not been deceived by the assurances and guarantees. The insurgents knew that the British would return and consequently had adopted a method of resistance that the British themselves described as "scientific."[15] The Ekumeku erected stockades and dug trenches at various points in the area. More important, they succeeded in inciting a large section of the inhabitants in the adjoining districts to join the resistance movement. The Ekumeku in the northern and western districts of the Asaba hinterland rallied round and declared for Nzekwe, so that when the British returned to

Ogwashi-Ukwu, they were alarmed to discover they were fighting enemies drawn from a wide area. Worse still, the conflict dragged into months, and, as Major G. E. Bruce observed, by now it was apparent that "the war has long ceased to be an affair of one town, and is now an Ekumeku rising."[16] The situation was indeed disturbing; the British had hoped that this would be a short, sharp operation intended to capture a particular "rebel," but it had now turned into a full-fledged war. In their bid to solve this puzzle, the British began to inquire into a number of events. They discovered, for example, that the behavior of Okonjor, Nzekwe's opponent in the Obiship dispute that had precipitated British intervention in the first place, served to prolong the war. From the day Nzekwe and his supporters retreated into the bush six months earlier, Okonjor had labeled himself "the great chief who can call the white man in to defeat his enemies." It was widely rumored that the lawyer Dove, Okonjor's "friend," had sent the government soldiers to help the chief. Okonjor reportedly discredited and implicated all chiefs and important persons who appeared to be friendly with the government by trumping up charges against them. The report added that Okonjor aimed at keeping contact between the local people and the government strictly in his own hands. Okonjor himself was, however, arrested on a trumped-up charge of treasonable felony. He was "found in possession of a government .303 Carbine and ammunition and was sentenced on various charges to 10 months imprisonment and a fine of £10."[17]

After the arrest and imprisonment of this instigator, the general atmosphere in the area seemed to turn rapidly in favor of the British. Colonial forces continued to attack and destroy towns and villages supporting Nzekwe; eventually, following a betrayal, the Ekumeku leader's war camp was discovered. On May 11, 1910, it came under heavy attack; after fierce fighting the camp was destroyed but once again Nzekwe managed to escape. The British acted swiftly, fearing that he might yet reassemble his men and move his headquarters to a new location. They assembled the chiefs of the defeated towns and warned that if enemy forces ranged unreported in their immediate neighborhood again, they would be held responsible.

The inability of the troops to capture Nzekwe increased the authorities' concern. More disturbing still was the fear of a mass Ekumeku rising. Intelligence reports indicated that throughout the area preparations were being made for an outbreak in October. Gunpowder and iron bars for bullets were being freely distributed. A report further stated that "the amount of yams and other foodstuffs under cultivation far exceeded the needs of the country and the talk has been fairly open that the white man was now going to be driven back into the sea immediately the yams were in about October next."[18] Lt. Col. Norton Harper, the political officer accompanying the Ogwashi-Ukwu patrol, affirmed that there was no such thing as "a friendly town within or around the hostile area." According to Harper, even towns that professed friendship had also indicated fear of reprisal if they failed to obey and aid the Ekumeku.[19]

At this juncture, the governor of Southern Nigeria, Sir Walter Egerton, instructed the provincial commissioner of the Central Province to visit the area and address the chiefs of the principal towns. The provincial commissioner carried out this instruction and confirmed that certain towns were passively, if not actively, assisting Nzekwe and his men by harboring refugees, and feeding and supplying them with powder; the men of Igbuzo and Ubulu-Ukwu were particularly active in such support.

Addressing himself to the governor of Southern Nigeria, H. C. Moorhouse regretted to report that "the whole of the Asaba District was in a very restless state, the Ekumeku society which had been dormant was again becoming active." He warned that "the people were swearing juju not to attend court or obey summonses and were showing a determination to throw off government authority." He expressed the feeling that Captain Sheffield, with the force at his disposal (three sections and a maxim gun) was not in a position to take effective action against Nzekwe and his fighting men "in a country of dense bush and against an enemy who in the past as in the present operations has shown himself capable of making a determined resistance without incurring the risk of reverse, or at all events a retirement which would have the most far-reaching and disastrous effects on the whole of the Asaba District." If a repetition of the rising of 1904-05 was to be avoided, the commissioner finally warned, a rapid and successful action against Nzekwe was most desired. This was to be followed by what he described as a "strong and repressive action against the Ekumeku," failing which, he feared, there would be further trouble sometime in October, when the crops were gathered.[20]

THE SURRENDER OF NZEKWE

While the lack of improvement in the general military situation disturbed the colonial agents, Nzekwe was also suffering from serious reverses. With his war camp destroyed and many of his followers killed or wounded, Nzekwe found himself more and more in danger of encirclement by his enemies. He continued to carry out hit-and-run raids, but as time passed, he and his forces became more and more weary of the war. The British were proving too strong and too stubborn, and continuing the uprising would only mean greater loss of life. On May 27, 1910, Nzekwe and two hundred of his fighting men surrendered, followed by the dispersal and surrender of the Ekumeku.[21]

This unexpected turn surprised the British, and, as if to ensure that the mass surrender was real, they quickly seized the guns of the Ekumeku warriors. A few days later the government announced the imposition of heavy fines—a penalty that would prove as ruinous as the war itself. The chiefs of Ogwashi-Ukwu were so overburdened by the fines, levied on top of the expenses of war, that they asked to be allowed to sell their women to raise money.[22] As in the past, the British used failure to pay promptly as the pretext for further punitive actions. An "Unlawful Societies Ordinance" was invoked and many of the Ekumeku resisters were punished under it.[23] Some were executed outright while others were deported to Calabar.

On hearing that hostilities had finally been brought to a close, Father Carlo Zappa promptly petitioned the government to compensate his mission for property destroyed or stolen. In its reply, the administration disclosed that, as part of their punishment, the "natives" had been asked to rebuild and replace the damaged and stolen property. Father Zappa objected to this decision:

> There is something odious in having the church rebuilt directly by people mostly opposed to our religion, who, besides doing it in a compulsory way and as if by punishment will certainly not feel inclined to perform it in that careful way which becomes of a building of that nature, but more probably with hatred and contempt.

He insisted that compensation should be paid in cash:

> I respectfully beg that we be granted an indemnity to compensate for the destruction of the said mission, for loss of property for which the rebels are responsible, as well as for damages caused to the plantation and resulting to us by the occupation of the land by the troops.[24]

The colonial administrators responded that according to their information, he had been found barricaded at Ogwashi-Ukwu on the arrival of the troops, he had been fired at by Ekumeku before the arrival of troops, and in view of the nature of those hostilities, there was every reason to believe that had the troops not been sent, the missionaries would have been expelled from Ogwashi-Ukwu and their property destroyed.

The reappearance of Father Zappa in these proceedings once again highlights his significant role in the events leading up to the Ekumeku War of 1909-10. Had Zappa been a mediator rather than an agitator, had he explained to Nzekwe that the summons to Igbuzo had nothing to do with the succession dispute, perhaps Nzekwe might have gone to see the government and the war might have been avoided. Colonial government officials and a large number of residents of Ogwashi-Ukwu disapproved of Zappa's actions both during and after the war, and in consequence, the government officials wrote to Zappa ordering that his contemplated visit to the people of Ogwashi-Ukwu should be postponed until the country was more settled. The provincial commissioner felt compelled to take this step, he wrote, in view of the fact that there appeared to be a certain feeling of hostility in the town against the Roman Catholic mission. Further, on July 27, 1910, Zappa was informed that until further notice the government did not consider it advisable that the Catholic mission should be reestablished in the Ogwashi-Ukwu district.[25] Following this directive, the Ogwashi-Ukwu mission remained unoccupied until 1915 despite all attempts by the priests to overturn the government's decision.

The closure of the Ogwashi-Ukwu mission not only caused the priests great pain, but it also resulted in a considerable loss of prestige in the surrounding districts. As soon as the uprisings of 1909-10 were over, many communities protested to the government against the continued existence of the Roman Catholic missions in their midst. For example, "at the request of the chiefs and people" of Issele-Azagba, the Roman Catholic mission in their town was ordered closed and the entire mission property removed.[26]

The remaining principal in the conflict was Nzekwe. During his trial his lawyer contended that Nzekwe had no wish or intention of fighting the government; he had been driven to violence by the activities of his rival, Okonjor, and Okonjor's lawyer, who gave the impression that the government wished to depose Nzekwe and install Okonjor in his place. There is sufficient evidence to confirm that in some respects the colonial administration had some sympathy for Nzekwe's position. Usually, any "native" who took up arms against the British government ran a terrible risk. But rather than punish Nzekwe, Lt. Col. Norton Harper argued in his favor. He wrote persuasively:

> Nzekwe is a man of very great power in the district, everyone kneels to him with the salute AGU (Lion). He is supreme throughout the South of the Asaba District and his word is Law. He has always been friendly to the Government and was undoubtedly driven into the war by Okonjor and the Lawyers. His surrender immediately brought the war to a finish. If I may venture to suggest, it would be the most satisfactory solution of the difficulty if Nzekwe is re-instated by the Government as Head-Chief of Ogwashi-Uku. He has already sent messengers throughout the country stating that peace has been declared and that the Government is to be obeyed; the result of this message has been extraordinary. It is in my opinion absolutely safe for anyone to travel wherever he wishes throughout the disturbed area.[27]

Most colonial officers shared this opinion. Writing strongly on the matter, Widenham Fosbery, the acting high commissioner of Southern Nigeria observed:

> I am strongly inclined to agree with Mr. Norton Harper in the opinion that Nzekwe was more sinned against than sinning and that he drifted into active conflict with the government owing to the mischievous interference of lawyers in political matters which engendered the erroneous belief that he was fighting his rival, Okonjor.[28]

The acting governor further stated that Nzekwe's influence was very great and that his removal could lead to fresh unrest. In the end, he recommended that Nzekwe be reinstated, and the recommendation was accepted. Nzekwe regained his freedom and his stature. The reinstatement of Nzekwe was followed by another great event for Ogwashi-Ukwu. The town was selected as the new headquarter of the Asaba district, which had hitherto been administered from Onitsha.[29] Lt. Col. Norton Harper was rewarded for successfully bringing the Ogwashi-Ukwu uprising to a close by being appointed the acting district commissioner of the Asaba District.[30] The choice of Ogwashi-Ukwu as the new district headquarters was influenced by the colonial government's desire to clamp down on the Western Igbo people by keeping a strong military force in their midst. According to the administration:

> The inhabitants of this district have given trouble for many years. In 1898 a large force of the Royal Niger Constabulary troops was operating in this country, and many expeditions have been through since, without apparently any lasting effect. The people are splendid bush fighters and if the government decides to station a force in the center of disaffection it should be sufficiently strong to hold its own in the event of further trouble. Natives appreciate the strength of troops they can see, but have not as a rule sufficient imagination to understand the military strength which government has in reserve. Onitsha is too far away to impress them.[31]

Be that is it may, with the closure of the Ogwashi-Ukwu hostilities in 1910, all parts of Western Igboland remained relatively quiet until 1914, when war broke out again in the Kwale district as the spirit of resistance was rekindled.[32]

NOTES TO CHAPTER SEVEN

1. PRO, C0520/93/17110 of June 6, 1910, Lt. Col. H. C. Moorhouse to the Governor of Southern Nigeria, April 24, 1910.
2. Enclosure in ibid. Sworn statement by Iwedike of Agidiehe Compound of Ogwashi-Ukwu, taken by A. Norton Harper, A.D.C., April 19, 1910.
3. PRO, C0520/91, confidential dispatch of December 23, 1902, R. A. Roberts to the Governor of Southern Nigeria.
4. See ibid. for details on the entire incident.
5. SMA, The Arti-Gex Document in *Journals of Some Early Fathers of the Diocese of Benin City* trans. from the French by Father J. J. Hillard, SMA Catholic Mission, Ogwashi-Ukwu, September 6, 1962.
6. SMA 15912, May 18, 1807, Zappa to Superior.
7. SMA Ref. SMA 3 B 45, 44.
8. Ibid., 46.
9. Ibid., 47-48.
10. PRO, C0520/91, confidential enclosure in the Provincial commissioner's dispatch of January 29, 1910, Capt. G. Nelson Sheffield reporting on the Ogwashi-Ukwu outbreak.
11. C0520/91, confidential dispatch of December 23, 1909, R. A. Roberts to the Governor of Southern Nigeria.
12. The Roberts report is the source for the entire account of Ogwashi-Ukwu clash.
13. SMA, from the diary of Father Zappa in the *Journals of Some Early Fathers*.
14. PRO, C0520/91, confidential dispatch of September 19, 1910, draft comment (signed) C.S.
15. Walter Egerton to Colonial Office in ibid.
16. PRO, C0520/93/18685 of June 18, 1910, enclosure in Governor's dispatch to Colonial Office.
17. Ibid.
18. Enclosure no. 2 in Ibid, "Interim Report," A. Norton Harper, A.D.C. Political Officer, Ogwashi-Ukwu Patrol, May 18, 1910.
19. Ibid.
20. PRO, C0520/93/1700 of June 6, 1910, Lt. Col. H. C. Moorhouse to Walter Egerton, April 24, 1910.
21. PRO, C0520/93/18685 of June 18, 1910, confidential dispatch, Egerton to Colonial Office, May 28, 1910.
22. PRO, C0520/24, W. Fosbery, Acting High Commissioner of Southern Nigeria, to the Divisional Commissioner, Central Division, on the Ekumeku Uprising, March 12, 1904.
23. PRO, C0520/107/41287, confidential dispatch of December 26, 1911, Egerton to Colonial Office.
24. SMA Ref. SMA 3 B 45, 52, 53-54.

25. Ibid., 53-54.

26. Ibid., 24.

27. GCD71/10, CSE 14/2/1 Enugu Archives, quoted in S. N. Nwabara, *Iboland: A Century of Contact with Britain, 1860-1960* (London, 1977), 137.

28. C0520/94/375 of January 13, 1911, confidential dispatch of June 16, 1910, Acting Governor, Southern Nigeria to Secretary of State for the Colonies.

29. The seat of government was removed from Asaba to Onitsha in 1904. See H. Vaux, "Intelligence Report on the Asaba Clan," Asaba Division, CS026/430927, National Archives, Ibadan. The request for the removal of the seat of government from Asaba to Onitsha is contained in PRO, C0520/3/266 of September 29, 1900, "Report of Sanitary Board formed under instruction from Acting High Commissioner . . . on the relative merits of Asaba and Onitsha as sites for a Government House," (signed) E. J. Moore, D.M.O., Capt. R. L. Cumberland, and P. V. Young, A.D.C., September 11, 1900.

30. PRO, C0520/94/375 of January 13, 1911, confidential dispatch of June 16, 1910, Acting Governor, Southern Nigeria to Secretary of State for the Colonies.

31. PRO, C0520/93/18685 of June 18, 1910, draft comment (signed) R.S.W. to Mr. Strachey, Colonial Office.

32. The wars of resistance in the Agbor and Kwale districts were not part of the Ekumeku movement.

CHAPTER EIGHT

The Ika and Ukwuani Resistance Movements

AS INDICATED IN the introduction, Western Igboland was divided into three cultural districts—Aniocha or Asaba, Ika or Agbor, and Ukwuani or Kwale—and the residents of each of these districts resisted British rule separately, confirming the assertion that one of the weaknesses of African resistance movements derived from their inability to forge a wider coalition against the European invaders. Although this book is concerned primarily with the Ekumeku movement, it is necessary to devote some discussion to the resistances of the Ika and Ukwuani in order to create a larger context for certain features of British colonialism and Igbo responses to them. Two such features were British administrative irresponsibility and insensitivity, and the excessive use of forced labor, which sparked off violent armed uprisings.

Clearly, the Owa war was not an extension of the Ekumeku wars. Although the Owa war was nearly as widespread and fierce as the Ekumeku wars, the former was neither planned nor joined by the members of the Ekumeku. All available evidence points to the fact that the Owa uprising was precipitated by the desire of the Ika people to curb the excesses of British colonial agents, especially those of S. O. Crewe-Read, who compelled them to give free labor on road works, and who flogged chiefs, elders, and youths, asked for free food, and allowed the Benin chiefs to override Owa decisions.

Another characteristic common to the Ika and Ukwani risings was the fact that neither the Christian missionaries nor British traders played any part in provoking the armed conflicts. British administrative high-handedness, together with the excessive demand for forced labor, were clearly the overwhelming causes of discontent. It is important to note that, unlike the people of Asaba, the Ika and the Ukwuani were not brought into early contact with the British, since their homelands were further removed from the Niger River. They were therefore spared the agitation British imperial policies had caused elsewhere, but by the early twentieth century colonial government officials began to enforce the Crown's authority with some earnestness. As in other districts that had felt Britain's iron hand, unrest led to rebellion; the Ika resisted once (1906) and the Kwale twice (1905 and 1914), and like the Ekumeku uprisings, these clashes, while not inspired by religious beliefs or charismatic figures, were nevertheless strong and widespread.

THE OWA WAR: IKA RESISTANCE TO BRITISH RULE

The Ika uprising could be better described as a protest against fairly specific grievances: the great demands for compulsory labor to which Ika people were subjected, the indiscriminate flogging of traditional chiefs by district officers, and the abuse of the authority given by the government to certain Benin City chiefs resident in the Ika district. The Ika were the most warlike of the Western Igbo-speaking people, and for centuries they had acted as a bulwark against the expansion of Benin rule into Western Igboland. From the fifteenth century to the last decade of the nineteenth century, Ikaland had been the scene of conflicts between Benin and the Western Igbo people as a result of the ambition of the rulers (or Obas) of Benin to expand their empire eastward. While many Western Igbo groups, like the Ezechima clan, grew weary of the intimidation, packed their belongings, and fled east, the Ika remained behind, sometimes revolting against the Benin and at other times living uneasily under their domination.

With the defeat of Benin City by the British in 1897, the Ika people might have hoped finally to consolidate their independence, but it was a futile hope. British colonial officials, partly through ignorance of local history and partly through an inflated conception of the extent of the Benin kingdom, committed a political blunder. They imposed the representatives or nominees of the Oba of Benin as the authority over the Ika peoples of Agbor, Umunede, Owa, and Ute-Okpu.[1] Worse yet, Sir Ralph Moor, the high commissioner, fixed a small tribute tax which the Ika villages were supposed to pay to these chiefs for their services.

To the Ika people the decision by Britain to allow Benin chiefs to overrule their decision rendered nugatory their age-long struggle against Benin. It is, therefore, not surprising that from the days when Moor became the principal colonial agent in the area, Ika people registered their protest against the imposition of both British officials and Benin chiefs. In 1902, the district commissioner of Benin City was fired at while passing through Agbor. In the same year, Chief Aguobasimi, son of Ovonramwen, the exiled king of Benin, resigned his appointment as the paramount chief of Agbor, "being frightened to go near the place,"[2] Following this resignation, another Benin chief was appointed and a British military presence was established there to enforce the appointment.

While the Ika chafed under the yoke of Benin chiefs, they were also made to suffer a number of humiliations at the hands of several British colonial administrators. Most of the labor used for road construction in the Agbor district was forced; on some occasions a village had to send as many as two hundred men, women, and children at a time to work on the road.[3] J. Watt, district commissioner of Agbor in 1906, reported that it was not uncommon to find two thousand peasants at work for considerable periods. He also noted that pressure was put upon the chiefs to supply labor and, as a young man of Owa told him, the youths often said, "This is a bad work that our fathers make us do."[4] It is little wonder, then, that by 1904 Owa and a number of towns in the Agbor district had begun to protest British rule. First they refused to provide British agents with the usual free food, and in due course they fled to avoid conscription.

Of all the officials who served in the Agbor district, S. O. Crewe-Read, the district commissioner of Agbor during 1904-06, was the most dreaded. In 1904 he was made the acting district commissioner of Benin City and on a number of occasions he visited Owa and the neighboring towns. As we shall see presently, he was fond of demanding gifts of yams, livestock, and eggs from Ika people; when these were not supplied in the desired quantities, he flogged their chiefs and burned down whole villages. Crewe-Read was also in the habit of asking the chiefs to supply free labor for road work and when they failed to comply, as in the case of Chief Bingi of Ogan, Crewe-Read ordered them publicly flogged.[5] Ika sources stated that every act of omission or transgression by the chiefs was to Crewe-Read an excuse for corporal punishment. Chief Meri of Agbor-Alesima was beaten because he failed to attend a meeting Crewe-Read presided over. In a sworn statement the chief said: "I was flogged in the Agbor Court in the presence of all the chiefs. . . . The District Commissioner called me up and asked me why I was not present to attend the meeting. . . . My statement was not believed and I was put on the ground and flogged. I also had to pay a fine of £1."[6]

These and other oppressive acts by Crewe-Read filled the people and chiefs of Ika with fear and resentment. His arrival in a town often caused the people to flee into the bush. Crewe-Read's arbitrary and heavy-handed approach set the tone for his administration, and most of those who served under him were equally unjust. The Benin City chief, Ayabaham, whom the British imposed on Umunede, was in the habit of indiscriminately flogging young men in the town.[7] In 1905, a man named Pyke, who was acting district commissioner of Benin City, and a Captain Magerson instructed troops to burn down a large section of Owa, destroying hundreds of homes and storehouses, on the charge that a forestry guard had been beaten by some Owa youths.[8]

THE DEATH OF CREWE-READ

Historian Michael Mason has observed that "each form of oppressed labor sets in motion its own opposition."[9] This concept explains the reaction of the Owa residents, who decided to discard all forms of passive resistance to British rule and to resort to violent protests. On the morning of June 8, 1906, a messenger called on the Obi of Owa to inform him that Crewe-Read would personally come to Owa that afternoon; the commissioner wanted yams, eggs, fowls, and water ready for him. He also wanted two hundred additional men to work at the river. The head chief sent out his town crier with the necessary message, but rather than come to the chief's palace with the required provisions, the entire population disappeared into the bush.[10]

At 4 p.m. Crewe-Read, accompanied by P. C. Gilpin, a Native Court clerk at Agbor, a Sergeant Lawani, six police constables, and twelve carriers, arrived at Owa Oyibu but found the town virtually deserted.[11] The head chief, accompanied by a few old men, walked up to the district commissioner and presented him with some yams, eggs, and water and explained that he was having some difficulties with his people, most of whom were hiding in the bush. Crewe-Read asked the chief personally to go into the bush and bring them in.

At 8 p.m. the chief came to the British camp to report that a man named Ekute would not let his people come in and meet the district commissioner. Later that night, a Bini man named Iwagwe went with a lantern to show the police sergeant and three police constables the house of Ekute, the suspected mastermind of the resistance. Gunfire rang out from the bush when the colonials approached Ekute's house; a brief gunfight ensued in which Sergeant Lawani was badly wounded. He was carried back to the camp by his companions. Frightened by this unexpected attack, Crewe-Read sent a messenger to Agbor with two telegrams, one to the provincial commissioner, Central Provinces, and the other to the officer commanding troops at Asaba, asking for assistance. The messenger was driven back by the Ika resisters, and when Crewe-Read sent two others to take the telegrams the Owa men drove them back, too, so that the telegrams never did reach their destination.

Realizing the grave danger he and his small force faced, Crewe-Read decided to return at once to Agbor. Accompanied by his men he left his camp at 3 a.m. on June 9, but hardly had they covered the distance of one mile when they were welcomed by a volley of gunshots from Ika warriors who were waiting in ambush. The colonials fled toward Owanta and the men of Owa gave chase, firing constantly. The police fired back but Crewe-Read, who was on a bicycle, was wounded in the arm by a bullet, forcing him to dismount. Some moments later, another bullet caught him in the side and he died instantly. With the primary object of their hatred dead, the Ika warriors ceased fire and returned to Owa to deal with those who had collaborated in the colonial oppression.

When the news of Crewe-Read's death finally reached Agbor, the Obi sent his messengers to recover the body. Reaching the stream which formed the boundary between Agbor and Owa, the messengers were stopped by the men of Owa and told that the body of Crewe-Read "belonged to the people who had killed it." The Ika guards also warned that, as the people of Agbor were responsible for bringing the white men to their country, the warriors would come to Agbor to wreak vengeance.[12] As if to back up their boast, a large body of Ika warriors began the next day to march toward Agbor, apparently "in a bid to capture that town."[13] Warriors in the force were from the towns of Owanta, Ute-Okpu, Amuhu, Aniero, and Ibi. The head chief of Owa Oyibu commended the action of his people, having declared, "I have sent all the OEBOS [Owa Oyibu] to do that. We are all tired of the white man's work. . . . I do not want any white or Benin man in my town again, only Lagos traders."[14]

MASSIVE RETALIATION: THE OUTBREAK OF THE OWA WAR

News of Crewe-Read's death reached Asaba the morning of June 9. By that afternoon, Captain Rudkin left Asaba with three army officers, one medical officer, one political officer, and 194 troops.[15] They marched all day and arrived at Umunede the following morning. The Ika warriors, meanwhile, had assembled five miles away on the Agbor road. The British troops camped at Umunede, spending the night there and pressing on toward Agbor early the next morning. But en route they "met with a most determined resistance during the whole day"; the Ika fighters made "stand after stand at close quarters and had to be dislodged with the bayonet." The political officer and Lieutenant Walmsley were seriously wounded. In fact, the British troops were soon in "a very crippled condition owing to casualties, two companies having had 40 per cent killed and wounded."[16] By 6:30 p.m., however, the British troops had managed to fight their way to a small river, which was only three miles from Agbor.

In view of the heavy fighting and the large number of casualties, the British requested and received reinforcements of three officers and 111 troops from Awka in the eastern provinces, and heavy arms were sent from Calabar. Between June 19 and July 2, skirmishes continued, with the most serious fighting taking place south and southeast of Agbor. On July 2, the British received further reinforcements of three officers and 130 troops. It was only with the arrival of these reinforcements that they were able to move on to Owa, which they eventually captured. The fall of Owa was a severe blow to the Ikas, disheartening them and reducing their will to continue the resistance. The fighting dragged on for a few more days as outlying towns like Idumuesa continued to resist the British.

On July 10 information was extracted from an Owa prisoner-of-war as to the whereabouts of Crewe-Read's body. The prisoner said that the district commissioner's body was "carefully buried close to the Owa, Offion and Owanta cross-roads. It was unmutilated and his uniform had not been removed."[17] The information was correct; the British hastened to the site and exhumed the body, which was sent to Benin City for final burial.

On July 12, the leading chiefs of Owa surrendered, followed by many of the Owa warriors. During the next few days Ute-Okpu and most of the Ika towns sent in messengers to say that they, too, wished to cease fighting. Other chiefs who did not immediately give themselves up later did so. All resisters were tried for bearing arms against His Majesty's government and for murder. Many people, including Ekute, the supposed leader of the resistance, were sentenced to death and subsequently hanged. Many more were sentenced to various terms of imprisonment, some of the convicted being removed to Benin and others to Asaba. All the towns participating in the uprising were collectively fined, and several thousand guns were seized. It was a period of widespread mourning, both for the large number of fighters who died on the battlefields and those who were hanged or imprisoned.

What became clear during the trials following the cessation of hostilities was a realization that the Ika people had long planned to attack the British, and that the arrival of Crewe-Read at Owa was merely the trigger that fired off the first volley of the war. Reports emerged of elaborate preparations to attack any troops that might be moved from Asaba to Agbor, preparations, commented a colonial agent, that "were kept so secret that no one appeared to have the slightest idea of the intention of Owa natives to kill Mr. Crewe-Read."[18] Not even Crewe-Read himself could have sensed the impending danger. P. C. Gilpin testified that the ambush was well-orchestrated; the troops found Owanowa "deserted, with the exception of Binobi, Obi of Owanowa, who stated that his people had run away."[19] Of course, this was a ruse; the people had only gone into the bush to make final preparation for war.

One reason the Owa conflict has sometimes been linked with the Ekumeku movement is that while the Owa war was still being fought rumor circulated that the Ekumeku, with their base at Ubulu-Ukwu, were planning a general uprising. On the basis of such fears the British ordered a military patrol under the command of Chichester, acting divisional commissioner of Onitsha, to go to Issele-Ukwu; there the colonials learned that the rumor was groundless. They found that all parts of the Asaba district were quiet without "any likelihood of any towns in that hinterland giving trouble," an observation chiefs of Ute-Okpu confirmed, saying they had never heard that the Ekumeku society was active in the towns around Agbor. "We have heard of this society being around Asaba," they said. "We do not think the Ekumeku killed the District Commissioner—it was the Owa people." Both Widenham Fosbery, acting governor of Southern Nigeria, and acting provisional commissioner at Benin, shared the view that the recent rising had no connection with the Ekumeku society.[20]

H. C. Moorhouse, the commanding officer of British troops involved in the conflict, later stated that the Owa war witnessed some of the severest fighting ever experienced by the British in Southern Nigeria. Government troops, Moorhouse said, were operating "against a bold and well-trained enemy always fighting on the defensive with every advantage in his favor in the way of cover and prepared positions." He further reported that he "could not help admiring their tenacity and the stout resistance they showed. Also, once they saw the hopelessness of their cause they did not unduly prolong the operations by refusing to surrender when offered terms."[21]

Although the people of Ika had fought a major war and lost, their resistance led in the long run to a number of important reforms. For example, the fighting drew the attention of the Colonial Office to a number of administrative abuses and irregularities in the colonies. It also drew the attention of the British public to such shameful practices as flogging and forced labor. Finally, it confirmed that the appointment of Benin chiefs to oversee the Ika towns was an administrative error, which was immediately corrected.

THE FIRST KWALE UPRISING

The people of the Kwale district, who had been subjected to the harassment of the agents of the Royal Niger Company and the soldiers of the Southern Nigeria Regiment, decided in 1903 to rid themselves of such oppression by driving away all foreigners from their midst. In July, the Ukwuani people of Amebu, without any apparent reason, raided their own market, seizing the goods of all the Itsekiri and Bini traders whom they regarded as foreigners, and drove them out of the town. They also threatened to kill any government official who might come into their town. The colonial administration considered this an "outrage" and, fearing that the other towns in the district might do likewise, decided to subdue Amebu and a number of Ukwuani towns which had rebelled against British imperial presence during the previous years. Troops were drafted from Asaba, Owerri, and Old Calabar and were instructed to proceed into the Kwale district.[22] The Commanding Officer was to remain at Amebu while the political officer "communicated with the towns of Umutu, Umukwata, Ebedu, Ebedite, Ogume and Amai, all of which have persisted in spite of many warnings in inter-tribal warfare and in closing the country to trade." These towns, and, in fact, all the towns in the area, were to be ordered to explain "the reason of their continual resistance to the Government."[23] In particular, the town of Amai was "to be called upon to explain the reason for the reported killing of a number of people in their town about a year ago."[24]

The arrangements for the invasion of the Kwale district had been concluded when news reached the provisional headquarters that the Ekumeku in the Asaba district had struck again. Because of the urgent need to deal with the Ekumeku menace, the proposed invasion of Kwale was postponed, but colonial officials nonetheless considered it necessary to send a patrol into the Kwale district. Surprisingly, the patrol entered unopposed by the Ukwuani; there was no fighting, and during the remainder of the year, a number of political officers visited various towns in the area and were "received with some measure of friendliness."[25] Thus the authorities assumed that all was well in the district.

However, on September 8, 1905, J. Davidson, the assistant district commissioner of Kwale, reported a disturbance "of such a serious nature" that he was compelled to withdraw from Amai to Abraka. The unrest had been precipitated by events beginning September 2, when Davidson had sent a messenger to Ezionum, a small town about three miles from Amai, to inform the townspeople of the government's decision to establish a Native Court in their town. The people of Ezionum were also supposed to be asked to send the names of those they might wish to represent them in the court. The messenger was accompanied by two policemen and an interpreter, who was to explain to the chiefs the messenger's mission. When the party arrived at Ezionum, the townspeople gathered to hear the message, but realizing that the proposed Native Court would undermine their cherished customs and traditional judicial system at the same time it established an effective British imperial presence, they dismissed the messenger, asking him to inform the assistant district commissioner that they would have nothing to do either with the proposed native court or with the white man. Rather than depart immediately, the messenger tried, with an arrogance characteristic of the first generation of native-born colonial government appointees, to outline the benefits of European rule together with the risks of flouting the whitemen's orders. Halfway through the discussion that arose from the messenger's unsolicited treatise, however, the Ezionum residents seized him, flogged him severely, and drove him and his companions out of town.

Still enraged by the colonial government's plan to establish a native court in their town, the men of Ezionum armed themselves, and on the following morning, charged into Amai, the seat of the assistant district commissioner, and threatened to drive him and all government officials out of the district. Davidson, realizing that he could not defend Amai with his ten policemen, withdrew to Sapele, where he reported the matter to the authorities.[26] To quell the uprising, F. S. James, deputy high commissioner of the Southern Provinces, sent seventy soldiers to deal with the rising at Ezionum and to make a show of force in Amai and at Kokori in the Urhobo country, which was also restive. James reportedly told his troops that "it must be understood that this is not in the nature of patrol work" but an attempt "to enable the authority of the political officer to be reinstated."[27] He trusted that no punitive measures would be undertaken except, perhaps, against the towns of Ezionum and Kokori, which in particular were to deliver up their guns and rifles.[28]

Thus, basing their operations on incorrect intelligence and filled with false confidence, seventy black soldiers and three white officers left for Ezionum on the morning of October 11, 1905. On reaching the farms near the town, the force was fired upon, but it stubbornly pressed on, "as the ground was open." The men of Ezionum persisted in their attack, determined not to allow the invaders to enter their town. The resistance against the government troops was so fierce that the commanding officer, Captain Vassal, was forced to retreat. The men of Ezionum then intensified the offensive and rushed the colonials' only maxim gun, which they nearly succeeded in capturing. The British fighting force was crippled. All three white officers were wounded.

These events were very disturbing to the colonial administration. Davidson later commented that since his arrival in Nigeria he had not seen such stubborn resistance to troops, and suggested that several towns had joined together to fight.[29] When James heard of the setback he proceeded at once to Sapele with the intention of taking the soldiers back to the area of fighting, to protect the "friendly towns from being raided by the Sobos and Kwales till the arrival of reinforcements."[30] Lieutenant Colonel Moorhouse reported that this appeared "to be one of those cases which were frequently cropping up, where it is impossible to estimate accurately the amount of opposition that is likely to be dealt with; the previous performance of the people concerned being the only guide." Along with these military reverses came strong rumors that most of the settlements in the district were planning a general rising. L. Probyn, the high commissioner, was particularly disturbed by "the reverses, their moral effect on the natives, and the strong presumption that the resistance was not confined to the inhabitants of the two towns it was proposed to punish in the first instance."[31]

To avoid another mistake a more powerful force was sent into the Kwale district. Acting High Commissioner Fosbery despatched Captain Haywood with twenty gunners, four maxim guns, and ample ammunition for small and larger arms alike. Lieutenant Colonel

Moorhouse and his troops were also sent to the scene of operations. With such a strong force at their disposal the British expected to have no difficulty in taking control of the area quickly.

Indeed, the show of force and the determination to assert authority enabled the British to break the backs of the resistance. After their defeat, the various Ukwuani towns were subjected to the usual ruinous fines and their guns and rifles seized. District Commissioner Davidson was ordered to reoccupy the station from which he had fled in September.[32] The people of Ezionum and Amai might have been more severely punished had not the death of Crewe-Read some months later at Owa drawn British attention to the Agbor district; the ensuing rumors of a general Ekumeku rising also kept the colonial administrators occupied. After the Ezionum hostilities there were no disturbances in the Kwale district for nearly eight years. It was only in 1914 that the Kwale again rose in arms.

THE FIRST WORLD WAR AND THE SECOND KWALE WAR

On October 17, 1914, the commissioner for the Warri Province reported that "there had been a serious rising in the Kwale District at the towns of Abbi and Oweh which resulted in the murder of two Native Court clerks, some court messengers and Yoruba Traders."[33] By that date the British had become familiar enough with armed resistance against their rule in Southern Nigeria, but this outbreak was particularly troublesome in view of its timing and its wider implications. It occurred soon after the outbreak of the First World War, and there was a strong feeling within British circles that the rising:

> If not directly instigated by Germans on parole, was directly due to the impression made on the native mind that the fact that the Germans were again allowed to trade implied that we had been defeated, and that this impression was fostered by the Germans who had resumed trading.[34]

These reports were confirmed by both F. James, the provincial commissioner, and Lieutenant Colonel Moorhouse. Both men were strong in their belief that the rising was due to the false rumors which the agents of some German firms were spreading in Nigeria regarding the war in Europe.³⁵ More alarming than these rumors was the real possibility that the uprisings, which started in the Kwale district, would spread to other parts of the country. The British feared that the disturbances "in the Kwale country were likely to have a far reaching effect amongst the other tribes, as reports were made . . . as to the attitude not only of the Sobos [Urhobo] but also the Ika and Ibo people in the Agbor and Ogwashi-Ukwu districts."³⁶

To crush the Kwale outbreak and suppress the rumor that had sparked it off, the governor general, Sir Frederick Lugard, instructed that all German and Austrian firms in the Warri, Sapele, and Benin districts should cease trading, and that all subjects of the hostile nations be sent to Lagos. Lugard also sent the acting lieutenant governor, Southern Provinces, from Lagos to Warri and on to the Kwale district "to endeavor to prevent the spread of the rising and to inquire into the report and the causes that led up to it." Lugard ordered that two sections of infantry and fifty police, in addition to the police force already available locally, be sent to the scene of the disturbances. Finally, he ordered that a company of the Nigerian Regiment should proceed at once from Calabar.

On October 24, 1914, Captain D. E. Wilson, the officer who was placed in charge of the Kwale patrol, arrived at Arogun, a town within easy reach of Abbi, where he was met by Raikes, the commissioner of the Warri province. The following day the commanding officer and the commissioner, accompanied by troops and one maxim gun, made for Abbi, the center of the uprising.³⁷

As the patrol approached the town, they discovered that a large trench had been dug across the road. In front of the trench were spikes which the men of Abbi had driven into the ground. Halted by this obstacle, the troops hesitated, whereupon they were heavily fired upon from all directions. Some soldiers were hit and a few others cut by the spikes. For the next hour or so, there was a heated exchange of gunshots, but eventually the troops managed to get around the trench, outflank the men of Abbi, and occupy the town. Wilson garrisoned Abbi and then headed toward Arogun, leaving behind a sizeable number of officers and men.³⁸

At Oweh the troops met with stubborn resistance, but a number of the Oweh fighters were killed and in a short time their town was captured.³⁹ Leaving some soldiers at Oweh, Wilson marched with the rest to Ogume, which was quickly subdued, and then to Utagba, where the inhabitants had burned down some houses belonging to the government. Leaving Utagba, the troops made for Ossissa, where the colonials attacked and burned the entire Umueze quarter and took the head chief captive.

Having overpowered these towns, the British imposed heavy fines on their inhabitants. Abbi was fined five hundred guns and £250. This sum represented a surety for good behavior for the next three years. In addition, Abbi was required to hand over the leaders of the uprising. As part of their retributions, the citizens of Abbi were ordered to construct a direct road to Oweh. They were further informed that they would not be allowed to reoccupy their town until they had complied with all these terms. The terms of surrender of Oweh were identical with those of Abbi. The Emu towns of Umana, Obiogo, Obodetti, and Emu Bendo were collectively fined 250 guns and the sum of £280 as a guarantee for good behavior for three years. They were also asked to construct a road along the Asseh River to Igbuku.

By the end of November the Kwale uprising had been crushed and Acting Lieutenant Governor James personally traveled through the area, explaining "the present situation as regards the war between Germany and England." He told the Africans that it had been necessary to withdraw soldiers for the purpose of defending Nigeria against the Germans in Cameroon. Unfortunately, he went on, certain portions of the country had used the occasion to show disloyalty to the government. In spite of this, he concluded, he had come to show the people that the government was strong enough to carry on war against the Germans and yet see that order and authority were maintained.

In fact, during the operations carried out against the Kwale it was confirmed "from information received from day to day" that the disturbances at Abbi, Oweh, Umannah, Ike-Onicha, and Utagba were precipitated by the knowledge that Great Britain had, in fact, withdrawn some troops from Nigeria; the native population saw the withdrawal as proof that the white man finally was leaving the territory. "This idea that the white man was going to leave the country," commented the officer commanding the Kwale patrol, "was undoubtedly fostered by the knowledge that European Officers would not in future sit in the Native Courts but that the chiefs would try their own cases."[40] Certainly, the Kwales had hoped to return to the traditional judicial system which the British rule had overturned, and were anxious to hasten the dismantling of the obnoxious rule.

For their part, the British were very much alarmed by the fear that such disturbances would spread to other parts of the country. Should this have happened at a time when nearly all the available troops of the Nigeria Regiment were employed with the Overseas Expeditionary Force operating in Cameroon and East Africa, the consequences would have been disastrous. Fortunately for the colonial administration, the numerous resistance movements which occurred in Nigeria during this period remained localized and sporadic. Had they been organized and coordinated, the government might have been overthrown entirely. Akinjide Osuntokun has made it clear that most of these protest movements were not caused by World War I itself. Rather, they represented the people's opposition to certain aspects of British colonial policy and the hardships caused by the war. Some of the hardships took the form of an increased demand for taxes, declining trade, the forced requisitioning of food required for war supplies, the forced conscription of indigenous people either as carriers or soldiers, and the continued use of compulsory unpaid labor even after the introduction of direct taxation.[41]

At any rate, the British colonial forces were able to quell the outbreak and prevent it from spreading into other areas. Indeed, this war marked the final stage of the wars of pacification in Western Igboland. After the demonstration of naked force, and perhaps because of British propaganda urging unity against the horrors of the German threat, many residents of Western Igboland decided to cooperate with Britain.

Still, many Nigerian communities tried to exploit the war situation to express their disaffection with certain government policies. As Osuntokun has put it:

> The war provided the occasion by visibly weakening the military presence of the British, while at the same time creating administrative control and lessened the amount of hard information the British could command on the state of local and regional feelings and opinion.[42]

For instance, the Iseyin-Okeiho rising of 1916 resulted from that people's opposition to certain changes the new British administration introduced into their society, which, points out J. A. Atanda, were in conflict with the existing political and social systems of the Yoruba people in Iseyin-Okeiho area.[43] The protest was in no way directed against the introduction of direct taxation, as taxation was introduced into the area two years after the rising, but against, for example, the native courts, the subjugation of the Iseyin to the Alafin of Oyo's control, and a judicial system which made divorce easier for African women.[44]

Even in Northern Nigeria, where the British managed to rely on the continued loyalty of the ruling Hausa-Fulani class, the common people found contemporary conditions ripe for the demonstration of their opposition to British rule. As in Southern Nigeria some of the causes of the protests can be traced to British policies and the administrative system. Most of the movements in the north were led by commoners, with a few members of the Hausa-Fulani ruling class who had been deprived of their positions of authority in the new colonial system. Others were led by religious leaders.[45]

While these protests may have been minor, the brutality with which they were crushed was not. In the case of the Okeiho uprising, government troops killed many war chiefs and about two hundred of their supporters. In Udi 252 protesters were killed. In Iseyin, the paramount chief and others were publicly hanged, while during the second Egba rising about a thousand people were shot dead.[46] Colonial officials argued that their actions were warranted because such uprisings had to be quashed with sufficient severity to convince all colonial subjects that the government was strong enough to maintain law and order in Nigeria and still carry out war against Germany.[47] Lugard maintained that he regretted no loss of life among the rebels and that the only way to prevent a recurrence of the outbreak was to make resisters realize that they would be severely dealt with.[48]

In any case, although some communities continued to show their disaffection with British rule, many gave up their opposition and cooperated with the government. Some made cash and food contributions toward the war efforts while others enlisted in the army. By 1918 the Great War had come to an end. But there was little joy in Nigeria; that same year an epidemic of influenza killed over half a million people—more people than did all the wars of resistance put together.[49] This deadly disease was brought from Britain by passengers and crews who travelled in European ocean ships. Certainly, the last two decades of the nineteenth century and the first two of the twentieth were a period of great hardships for Nigerians. They were a period of dislocations, of wars of survival, of widespread deaths and epidemics, and of mass withdrawal of labor from food production, with its attendant starvation.[50] Indeed, these were bleak moments in Nigerian history.

NOTES TO CHAPTER EIGHT

1. PRO, CO520/38, confidential enclosure, "Agbor District Rising," F. S. James, Provincial Commissioner, Central Province, Warri to Colonial Office, December 12, 1906.
2. Ibid. The district commissioner's name was Johnson; no further information is available.
3. *West Africa,* August 14, 1906.
4. PRO, CO520/37, J. Watt to Acting Provincial Commissioner, Central Province, September 8, 1906.
5. PRO, CO520/38, confidential enclosure, Acting District Commissioner, Agbor to Walter Egerton, sworn statement by Afidi, Native Court Messenger, taken at Abavo on November 23, 1906 by S. W. Sproston.
6. Confidential enclosure in ibid., sworn statement by Chief Meri of Agbor Alesima, taken at Abavo on November 23, 1906, by S. W. Sproston.
7. PRO, CO520/37/402/2 of October 13, 1906, sworn statement by P. C. Gilpin, taken on July 13, 1906, at Agbor by Reginald A. Roberts. Also CO52/28, confidential enclosure of December 29, 1906, sworn statement by Chief Niago of Umunede.
8. PRO, CO520/38, confidential enclosure 2 of December 29, 1906, to the High Commissioner, prepared by R. A. Roberts, Acting Provincial Commissioner, Central Province, June 20, 1906.
9. Michael Mason, "Working on the Railway: Forced Labour in Northern Nigeria, 1907-1912," in *African Labour History,* ed. Peter C. W. Gutkind, Robin Cohen, and Jean Copans (London, 1978), 56.
10. PRO, CO5210/36 of August 18, 1906, statement by the head chief of Owa Oyibu.
11. The Official British account of the entire incident is from PRO, CO520/36 of July 21, 1906, statement by P. C. Gilpin, Native Court Clerk taken on June 12, 1906.
12. PRO, CO520/36 of July 21, 1906, sworn statement of Egbinoba, the Obi of Agbor, taken on June 16, 1906, at Agbor.
13. PRO, CO520/36 of August 28, 1906, W. Fosbery to Colonial Office, July 28, 1906.

14. Ibid., statement by Omorege, a Benin man sent by the king of Abavo.

15. The official British account of the ensuing events is found in PRO, CO520/45/25, enclosure in dispatch relating to field operations, Walter Egerton to Colonial Office, May 13, 1907, prepared by H. C. Moorhouse, officer in charge, Southern Nigeria Regiment, March 25, 1907.

16. PRO, CO520/54, confidential enclosure, "Report on the Operations in the Agbor District," June-August 1906.

17. Ibid.

18. PRO, CO520/36 of August 18, 1906, W. Fosbery to Colonial Office, July 18, 1906.

19. Enclosures in ibid., statement by P. C. Gilpin, taken on June 12, 1906.

20. PRO, CO520/36 of August 18, 1906, W. Fosbery to Colonial Office, July 18, 1906.

21. PRO, CO520/54, confidential enclosure, "Report on the Operations in the Agbor District."

22. PRO, CO520/21/44970 of December 15, 1903, L. Probyn, Acting High Commissioner, to the Officer Commanding the Kwale Expedition, November 7, 1905.

23. Enclosure in ibid., memorandum on Kwale patrol prepared by F. S. James, Divisional Commissioner, November 22, 1905.

24. PRO, CO520/32/38260 of October 27, 1905. Enclosure 1, to Acting High Commissioner's dispatch, confidential, October 7, 1905, prepared by F. S. James.

25. Enclosure no. 3 in ibid., J. Davidson, Assistant District Commissioner, Kwale District to Divisional Commissioner, Western Division, August 8, 1905.

26. Enclosure no. 3 in ibid., J. Davidson, report on Disturbance in Kwale Country, dated September 8, 1905.

27. PRO, CO520/32/38260 of October 27, 1905. F. S. James, Deputy High Commissioner, to Officer Commanding Asaba Detachment, September 26, 1905.

28. PRO, CO520/32/40884, W. Fosbery, Acting High Commissioner of Southern Nigeria, to Colonial Office, October 20, 1905.

29. Ibid.

30. PRO, CO520/35, confidential dispatch of February 20, 1906, minutes by Lieutenant Colonel Moorhouse, Southern Nigeria Regiment.

31. CO520/32/40448, confidential enclosure, Acting High Commissioner to Colonial Office, October 20, 1905.

32. Ibid.

33. PRO, CO583/21/50715, confidential report by F. Lugard to Lewis Harcourt, Colonial Office, December 1, 1914.

34. Ibid.

35. PRO, CO583/30/4960, confidential report by F. S. James to Lord Lugard, November 30, 1914.

36. PRO, CO583/21/50715 of December 9, 1914, confidential dispatch, Lugard to Colonial Office.

37. Confidential enclosure in ibid., Capt. D. E. Wilson, report on the Kwale Patrol, December 22, 1914.

38. Confidential enclosure in ibid., Capt. D. E. Wilson, report on the Kwale Patrol, December 22, 1914.

39. The official account of the incident is found in PRO, CO583/30/4960 enclosure of February 1, 1915, Capt. D. E. Wilson to the Commandant, Nigeria Regiment, Lagos, November 18, 1914. Ensuing descriptions of the event are from this source.

40. Confidential enclosure in ibid., F. J. Conliff, Acting Commandant, Nigeria Regiment, "Comment on the Kwale Patrol," dated December 15, 1916.

41. Akinjide Osuntokun, *Nigeria in the First World War* (London, 1979), 116.

42. Ibid., 132-33.

43. J. A. Atanda, "The Iseyin-Okeiho Rising of 1916: An Example of Socio-Political Conflict in Colonial Nigeria," *Journal of the Historical Society of Nigeria* 5, no. 4 (June 1969): 97-98.

44. Osuntokun, *Nigeria in the First World War,* 121.

45. Ibid., 144.

46. Ibid., 100-133.

47. CO583/30/4960, F. S. James to Lord Lugard, November 30, 1914.

48. PRO, CO583/33/28160, Lugard to Colonial Office, May 29, 1915.

49. PRO, CO583/77 of September 5, 1919, "Pandemic of Influenza: Experience in the Northern Provinces of Nigeria," and "The Influenza Epidemic of 1918 in the Southern Provinces of Nigeria."

50. Don C. Ohadike, "The Influenza Pandemic of 1918-19 and the Spread of Cassava Cultivation on the Lower Niger: A Study in Historical Linkages." *Journal of African History* 22, no. 3 (1981): 379-91.

CONCLUSION

THE CHIEFS AND people of Western Igboland resisted British pressure for thirty-one years (1883-1914), longer and, perhaps, in a more determined fashion than any other Nigerian community. Their resistance was crushed, however, not because the societies were small in scale, but because they fought with less sophisticated weapons. More devastating than military defeat was the shattering blow which the new colonial regime dealt the Africans' institutions. The policies of the early colonial period were designed to destroy traditional values and pave the way for an effective appropriation of labor needed to take advantage of available resources and build the concomitant infrastructure. Government officials proscribed domestic slavery but introduced forced labor. They outlawed "ritual murder" but shot and killed protesting peasants.

The Ekumeku movement was an organization whose prime objectives were to halt British designs to destroy the accumulated values of the community and to guarantee that the British did not bring to a sudden stop those developments which had been in motion for a thousand years or more. Long before Portuguese ships first sailed down the west coast of Africa in the fifteenth century, Western Igbo people had evolved highly complex institutions. Although the various communities chose to remain autonomous and in conditions approximating so-called "stateless" societies, their affairs were regulated by highly sophisticated, cross-cutting rules, hierarchies, beliefs, and traditions. Each community took definite steps to ensure that individual rights and freedom were not unduly trampled upon. Age was regarded as a symbol of respect and authority, but the elders who ruled over the different communities were not allowed to exercise despotic powers over their people. There was room for initiative. A young man who was wealthy enough and who had satisfied a number of prescribed requirements was allowed to purchase the highest titles in the land and sit among the elders in the grand council of the community. Thus, from infancy through manhood and old age, each individual was preoccupied with the noble task of accumulating wealth and the exhibition of that stature through the purchase of expensive titles.

From very ancient times, too, western Igbo people had been linked in economic interdependence with their neighbors. In particular, they were involved in a long-distance trade in which their yams and other vegetable products were exchanged for salt, fish, cloth, metal ware, and other goods coming from distant lands. From the sixteenth century onward much of Western Igbo trade became largely oriented eastward, toward the Igbo heartland, and southward, toward the Niger delta. The new direction was in response to the development of European trade. Between the seventeenth century and the mid-nineteenth century, the Western Igbo people participated vigorously in the lower Niger trade, their major contribution being yams, which helped sustain both the Niger delta people who could not grow all their food requirements and the European slave ships anchored on the Atlantic coast.

The desire to meet this great demand for yams further encouraged the development of very complex relations of production. There was a rapid expansion of domestic slavery as extra hands were needed to produce the yams that had become a vital source of foreign income. Furthermore, as the society grew generally more affluent, it became more differentiated. At the top level of the social strata were chiefs and at the other were men and women of servile and foreign origins. In between were the untitled free-born who hoped, sooner or later, to climb up the social ladder.

Somewhat paradoxically, the economic prosperity which Western Igbo people enjoyed as a result of their participation in the provisions and slave trades was curtailed by the rise of the palm-oil trade. There is no denying that Western Igbo people were in some ways adversely affected by the Atlantic slave trade; nevertheless, it was the palm-oil trade rather than the slave trade that generated the first serious crisis among them. The fact is, there was a great difference between the conduct of the slave trade and the palm-oil trade. In the first place, the new trade robbed some communities of their middleman's role when British traders ascended the Niger and established trading posts at strategic points on the river. In the second place, in the new competition that ensued, British traders were assisted by the government of their home country. Thus, even before colonial rule was actually established, many Western Igbo polities had suffered economic, military, and political decline as a result of the combined activities of British traders, imperial representatives, and Christian missionary agents.

The Ekumeku movement was launched to resist this decline. Thus, like the Mau Mau and Maji Maji, the Ekumeku wars were not a sudden eruption, but the culmination of a long period of political disturbances touched off by British cultural, commercial, and political ambitions on the lower Niger. The Ekumeku movement, like the Maji Maji, achieved "a far-flung coalition" against British military pressure, demonstrating that small-scale societies were not static but dynamic, capable of responding effectively to external threats. However, unlike the Maji Maji, the Ekumeku warriors were not inspired by any prophetic or magical beliefs, nor was the movement led by charismatic figures. Rather, it was organized under the leadership of a coalition of titled chiefs from many towns. The fighting men were the youthful members of the town clubs and the uncommitted, restless young men. Quick to recognize the advantages of guerrilla warfare, the Western Igbo people did not hesitate to resort to it in their bid to keep the British out of their midst. Considering the fact that they resisted a better-armed and more powerful opponent so stoutly and for so long, it seems clear that they could equally have stood their ground against any indigenous community that might have contemplated the invasion of the region. The members of the Ekumeku movement earned the nickname, the Silent Ones, because of the unique way they silently carried out their activities, but the fierceness of their attacks spoke in loud tones for freedom from oppression.

The resistance movements as a whole had several long-range effects. Among the three social groups into which the precolonial Western Igbo society was divided (i.e., slaves, commoners, and chiefs), the slaves benefitted most from the political disturbances of the period. First, slaves took advantage of the British military presence to desert their masters. Some went into the urban centers or the mines, the timber concessions, and the cotton, rubber, or cocoa plantations in search of paid jobs. Some wandered off in search of their natal homes. Others decided to establish independent settlements nearby. A sizeable number remained in their host communities and worked for themselves as farmers, palm oil producers, canoe men, or porters, rather than work for their former masters. The ex-slaves who did not go away continued to suffer some degree of social discrimination from the members of their host communities in the sense that they were still not allowed to intermarry with the free-born, or to purchase titles. However, these restrictions were relaxed with the rapid spread of "western values," the growth of the concept of Nigerian nationhood, and the rise of large urban centers.

The chiefs, on the other hand, suffered great political and economic reversals as a result of the resistance movements. European traders, missionaries, and British officials regarded the chiefs as impediments to the establishment of commerce, Christianity, and "good government" and so worked toward the elimination of their power. As the organizers of the political uprisings, the chiefs were usually singled out for severe punishment. Many were shot, captured, hanged outright, or sent to prison, thereby causing a dramatic decline in the number of titled chiefs.

Those who survived the wars were made to endure a long period of economic devastation. The emancipation of slaves without compensation robbed the chiefs of their valuable investment. The policy which Ralph Moor and the other officials in Southern Nigeria adopted toward slave-owning chiefs was hasty, violent, and oppressive, and desertion was an inevitable result. In Northern Nigeria, on the other hand, Frederick Lugard collaborated with slave owners and made it possible for slaves to purchase their freedom over a long period of time.[1] They could raise the money necessary for their own manumission either by working for their masters or by working for other employers and making periodic payments. Thus, while Lugard tried to win the favor of slave owners by adopting a cautious approach to the emancipation, officials in Southern Nigeria tried to bring about the abolition with haste, vigor, and violence. In Benin, for example, officials used the attempt to abolish domestic slavery to facilitate the occupation and consolidation of British rule. They also attacked domestic slavery immediately after "the very first entry of British troops into Benin" in 1897.[2]

The foregoing observations should not be construed as meaning that slave owners in Northern Nigeria did not experience a major economic decline after the imposition of legal emancipation. In fact, the vast majority of masters were pauperized or "equalized with the peasantry."[3] Many slave owners were constrained to work their own fields for the first time, using the short-handled hoes they had once furnished their slaves to break the soil.

Having lost their slaves, some Western Igbo chiefs made one more desperate attempt to improve their economic conditions; they resorted to the use of tenant labor to produce palm oil.[4] These tenants were generally slaves or former slaves who had just deserted their masters elsewhere following the British conquest, for during the period 1897-1920 there was a large floating slave populace throughout Nigeria. Many were prepared to process oil, sell it in the marketplace or to the agents of the European trading firms, and surrender a specific ransom to the local chiefs. But the scheme soon broke down, partly because of inadequate control and supervision and partly because, as the price of oil continued to fall, the industry became unprofitable. Even before 1922, when the price of palm oil bottomed out, virtually all tenant laborers had deserted once more.

Perhaps the most painful aspect of the colonial conquest was the chiefs' complete loss of political authority. After their defeat, they were compelled to give up their political powers to the warrant chiefs and colonial administrators and were required to submit themselves to the British legal system. Nothing could have been more galling to the pride of a people who had been accustomed to trying their own cases than to allow themselves to be tried by strangers and under strange laws. In order to convince the community at large that the chiefs no longer constituted the ruling class, officials like O. S. Crewe-Read in the Agbor district sometimes publicly flogged chiefs and compelled them to render unpaid labor on road construction sites, side-by-side with their former subjects and slaves.[5]

Despite these great dislocations, the events that took place in Western Igboland during the post-Ekumeku era confirm the view expressed by A. B. Davidson that "in the course of resistance, tendencies to change developed more quickly."[6] When the community finally realized that the British had come to stay and could not be dislodged with force, it decided as a whole to adjust to the new colonial situation.

Residents accepted the intruder's religion, learned his language, and in due course adopted the political discourse developed by the white man himself to overthrow him. After all, the political sentiments of liberty, equality, and freedom from oppression and domination did not appeal to whites alone.

Western Igbo people were quick to realize that "western education" could be a powerful agent of change in the modern world. Through their contacts with Christian missionaries, traders, and colonial officials, they found that formal education was a powerful instrument for the development of a wide range of skills, including simple bookkeeping, printing, service in the colonial administration, and middle management in commerce and industry. Since "western education" and Christianity went hand-in-hand, a great number of Western Igbo people accepted Christianity as a means to that end. The colonial government was generally indifferent and sometimes openly hostile to the education of its colonial subjects, treating the educated "natives" with great contempt and suspicion.[7] Thus Western Igbo parents had to find support elsewhere for their educational goals, and often that help came from the missionaries. Even while the wars of resistance were being waged, some chiefs perceived the inevitable and embraced Christianity, despite great opposition from the community. Among the first Western Igbo chiefs to quickly recognize the usefulness of western ways and try to promote them were Obi Ossai of Aboh, Obi Igweli of Asaba, Obi Egbuna of Issele-Ukwu, and Obi Ajufo of Igbuzo.

Today, the Western Igbo people are among the most literate in Nigeria. Most of them are Christians even though their forebears burned Christian churches and persecuted Christian missionaries. The slave-owning chiefs who resisted the emancipation of slaves and frowned at slaves who gathered at the mission stations to enroll for baptism classes later sent their own children to these same mission schools. They even helped the missionaries to build the schools. If Western Igboland is one of the greatest reservoirs of skilled labor in modern Nigeria, it is so simply because of its long contacts with the Christian missions and because of the chiefs' prompt recognition of the doors that western education could open. On the whole, the period covered by this study was not only one of disruptions but also of transformations and adjustments.

NOTES TO CONCLUSION

1. J. S. Hogendorn and Paul E. Lovejoy, "The Reform of Slavery in Early Colonial Northern Nigeria," in *The End of Slavery in Africa,* ed. Suzanne Miers and Richard Roberts (Madison, 1988), 394-5.
2. Philip A. Igbafe, "Slavery and Emancipation in Benin, 1897-1945," *Journal of African History,* 16, no. 3 (1975): 410.
3. Hogendorn and Lovejoy, "The Reform of Slavery," 399.
4. Obi Nwobi, interview at Igbuzo, December 8, 1982.
5. See chapter 8.
6. A. B. Davidson, "African Resistance and Rebellion Against the Imposition of Colonial Rule," in *Emerging Themes in African History,* ed. T. O. Ranger (Dar es Salam, 1968), 178.
7. E. A. Ayandele, *The Missionary Impact on Modern Nigeria, 1842-1914* (Ibadan, 1966), 248-50.

Appendix One

As part of the effort to replace the African slave trade with another trade based on agricultural and mineral products, the British government authorized its representatives to conclude treaties of "friendship and protection" with African chiefs. In 1841 Henry Dundas Trotter, William Allen, Bird Allen, and William Cook sailed up the Niger and concluded a treaty with Obi Ossai, the paramount chief of Aboh, who agreed to give up the slave trade if a better form of trade was introduced. This treaty notwithstanding, the Aboh merchants continued to buy and sell slaves for another fifty years because the palm-oil trade which the British introduced increased the demand for captives for domestic use. In addition, there was no means to enforce the treaty.

Treaty between the Queen of Great Britain, and Obi Ossai, Chief of Aboh

There shall be peace and friendship between the people of Great Britain and the people of Aboh, and the slave-trade shall be put down forever in the Aboh country, and the people of Great Britain and the people of Aboh shall trade together innocently, justly, kindly and usefully, and Captain Henry Dundas Trotter, Commander William Allen, Commander Bird Allen, and William Cook, Esq., Commissioners on the part of the Queen of Great Britain, and Obi Ossai on his own part, and that of his people as Chief of the Aboh country, do make the following Agreement for these purposes.

1. The Slave-trade shall be utterly abolished in the Aboh country, and from the signing of this Agreement, no persons whatever shall be removed out of the country for the purpose of being treated or dealt with as slaves: nor shall any persons whatever be allowed to be brought through the country or any part thereof, for the purpose of being treated or dealt with as slaves by way of exportation or otherwise: nor shall any persons whatever be imported into the country for the purpose of being dealt with as slaves, and no subject of Aboh country shall be in any way concerned

in the exporting or importing of slaves, or carrying on the Slave-trade, either within or without the limits of the country. The Chief promises to inflict reasonable punishment on all his subjects who may break the law.

2. The officers of the Queen of Great Britain may seize every vessel or boat of Aboh found anywhere carrying on the trade in slaves, and may also seize every vessel or boat of other nations with whom a similar agreement has been made, found carrying on the trade in slaves in the waters belonging to the Chief of Aboh: upon such seizure, and after regular condemnation, according to the provisions of this Agreement, the slaves shall be made free, and the vessels or boats shall be destroyed.

3. That in all cases of the seizure of vessels and boats, with the slaves on board, under the provisions of this Agreement, the said Commissioners, or those of them who may be present, and in their absence the commissioned or commanding officer on board the British vessel making the seizure, or any agent authorized for that purpose, due examination and inquiry into the case, and shall condemn the said vessel or boat with the slaves on board, if satisfied that the provisions of this Agreement have been thus contravened, or otherwise acquit and restore the same.

4. That from and after the signing of this Agreement, no persons whatever coming into the country shall be reduced into slavery, or treated or used as slaves. All white persons whatever, and all British subjects, of whatever colour, at present detained in slavery, shall be immediately set free.

5. British people may freely come into the Aboh country, and may stay in it, or pass through it: and they shall be treated as friends while in it, and they may leave the country with their property when they please.

6. Christians, of whatever nation or country, peaceably conducting themselves in the dominions of the Chief of Aboh, shall be left in the free enjoyment and exercise of the Christian religion, and shall not be hindered or molested in their endeavours to teach the same to all persons whatever willing and desirous to be taught; nor shall any subject of Aboh, who may embrace the Christian faith, be on that account, or on account of the teaching or exercise thereof, molested or troubled in any manner whatsoever.

7. British people may always trade freely with the people of Aboh in every article which they may wish to sell, and neither the British people nor the people of Aboh shall ever be forced to buy or sell any article, nor shall they be prevented from buying or selling any article with whom-

soever they please: and they shall not be compelled to employ an agent, and the customs and dues taken by the Chief of Aboh in British goods sold in the Aboh country shall in no case be more altogether than one twentieth part of the goods so imported, or their ascertained value, and there shall be no duty, toll, or custom levied on goods exported.

8. The paths shall be kept open through the Aboh country to other countries, so that British traders may carry goods of all kinds through the Aboh country to sell them elsewhere, and the traders of other countries may bring their goods through the Aboh country to trade with the British people.

9. British people may buy and sell, or hire lands and houses in the Aboh country, and their houses shall not be entered without their consent, nor shall their goods be seized, nor their persons touched, and if British people are wronged or ill-treated by the people of Aboh, the Chief of Aboh shall punish those doing such wrong.

10. But the British people must not break the laws of the Aboh country, and when they are accused of breaking the laws, the Chief may detain the person charged with committing any grievous crime in safe custody, taking care that he be treated with humanity; and shall send a true account of the matter to the nearest place where there is a British force: and the commander of such British force shall send for the British person, who shall be tried according to British law, and shall be punished, if found guilty, and a report of such punishment shall be forwarded to the Chief for his satisfaction.

11. If the Aboh people should take away the property of a British person, or should not pay their just debts to a British person, the Chief of Aboh shall do all he can to make the Aboh people restore the property and pay the debt: and if British persons should take away the property of the Aboh people, or shall not pay their just debts to the Aboh people, they shall be subject to the laws of the country for the recovery of the same: provided always that no injury be done to their persons. The Chief of Aboh shall make known the fact to the commander of the British force nearest to the Aboh country, or to the resident agent, if there is one, and the British commander or agent, whichever it may be, shall do all he can to make the British persons restore the property, and pay the debt.

12. The Queen of Great Britain may appoint an agent to visit Aboh, or to reside there, in order to watch over the interests of the British people,

and to see that this agreement is fulfilled; and such agent shall always receive honour and protection in the Aboh country: and the Aboh Chief shall pay attention to what the agent says, and the person and property of the agent shall be sacred.

13. It is understood that all British vessels or boats are at liberty to navigate the river Niger, and its branches and tributaries, without the payment of any duties, tolls, or customs whatsoever. The Chief of Aboh promises to use his utmost endeavour to facilitate the conveyance of messengers and dispatches to or from British people.

14. The power of sanctioning or modifying this Treaty is expressly reserved to Her Majesty the Queen of Great Britain.

15. Any infringement of this Treaty will subject the Chief of Aboh to the severe displeasure of the Queen of Great Britain, and the loss of the duties herein stipulated for.

16. The Chief of Aboh shall within forty-eight hours of the date of this agreement, make a law for carrying the whole of it into effect, and shall proclaim that law: and the Chief of Aboh shall put that law in force from that time forever.

17. The Queen of Great Britain, out of friendship for the Chief of Aboh, and because the Chief of Aboh has made this Agreement, gives him the following articles:

1 ornamented velvet cap, 1 double-barrelled gun,
   German silver mounted flint lock.
1 pair of pistols, German silver mounted flint lock
1 gilt mounted sabre
6 yards of cotton velvet
1 piece of Naddapolan
2 pieces of printed Manchester goods
½ piece of caricature handkerchiefs
5 yards of superfine scarlet cloth
5 yards of superfine blue cloth
36 bead necklaces of sorts
100 flints
1 case, containing razors, knife, and scissors
32 small looking-glasses
1 large lustring umbrella
1 telescope 1 sergeant major's dress complete
4 red jackets, baize

4 shirts
4 black jacks
1½ pieces of handkerchiefs
1 pewter basin
4 brass bracelets (bangles)
1 brass snuff-box
2 dozen gilt buttons
6 large pewter spoons
6 small pewter spoons
2 brass lamps
1 padlock
6 pocket knives
1 saw
2 pieces of Pondicherry
1 piece of Naganapots
2 pieces of brawls
1 piece of brown shirting
2 pieces of cotton Bandanas
1 piece of Niccarree
1 piece of chillo
6 tin horns
1 Arabic Bible
1 oil press

And the Chief of Aboh hereby acknowledges he had received those articles.

And so we, Captain Henry Dundas Trotter, Commander William Allen, Commander Bird Allen, William Cook, Esq., and Obi Ossai, Chief of Aboh, have made this Agreement, and have signed it on board Her Majesty's steam-vessel 'Albert', off Aboh, this twenty-eighth day of August, one thousand eight hundred an forty-one: and this Agreement shall stand for ever.

(Signed)   H. D. TROTTER, Commissioner.
           WILLIAM ALLEN, Commissioner
           BIRD ALLEN, Commissioner
           W. COOK, Commissioner
                         his
           OBI OSSAI, X Chief of the Aboh Country
                        mark

Witnesses,
    J. O. MCWILLIAM, M. D., Surgeon
    JAMES FREDERICK SCHON, Missionary
    WILLIAM BOWDEN, Secretary

Witnesses,

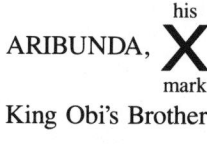

ARIBUNDA, X his mark

King Obi's Brother

AJEH, X his mark

CHIKUMA, X his mark King Obi's eldest Son

ADDITIONAL ARTICLES

The Chief of Aboh declares that no human beings are sacrificed on account of religious or other ceremonies or customs in the Aboh country, and hereby stipulates that he will prevent the introduction of such barbarous and inhuman customs and ceremonies into his country.

And so we, Captain Henry Dundas Trotter, Commander William Allen, Commander Bird Allen, William Cook, Esquire, and Obi Ossai, Chief of Aboh, have made this Agreement, and have signed it on board Her Majesty's steam-vessel, 'Albert', off Aboh, this twenty-eighth day of August, one thousand eight hundred and forty-one, and this Agreement shall stand forever.

(Signed)   H. D. TROTTER, Commissioner
    WILLIAM ALLEN, Commissioner
    W. COOK, Commissioner
    OBI OSSAI, X his mark Chief of the Aboh Country

Witnesses,
    J. O. McWILLIAM, M.D., Surgeon
    JAMES FREDERICK SCHON, Missionary
    WILLIAM BOWDEN, Secretary

APPENDIX ONE

Witnesses,

ARIBUNDA, ✗ (his mark)

King Obi's Brothers

AJEH, ✗ (his mark)

CHIKUMA, ✗ King Obi's eldest son

Appendix Two

The British government granted the Royal Niger Company a wide range of authority over the Lower Niger territories, and the agents of the Company concluded treaties of "protection and trade" with the representatives of the local communities. It is widely speculated, however, that most of these treaties were forged. For example, it is inconceivable that local communities, whose customs forbade even the selling of land, would have voluntarily ceded to the Company forever the whole of their territories. Also, most of the names on the treaties were strange to the local communities which the Company claimed signed them. The treaty printed below is supposed to have been concluded in 1889, when, in fact, the people of Igbuzo and the Company were fighting a war and the road between Asaba and Igbuzo remained closed. (See chapter 5). Some historians have euphemistically described the Niger Company's treaties as X treaties because of the strong feeling that the X marks on them were forged. For the treaties of the Royal Niger Company, see PRO, F02/167.

TREATY MADE ON THE SEVENTEENTH DAY OF MAY 1989 BETWEEN THE KINGS OF IBOUZA [IGBUZO] ON THE ONE HAND AND THE ROYAL NIGER COMPANY CHARTERED AND LIMITED, HEREINAFTER CALLED THE COMPANY ON THE OTHER HAND

1. We the undersigned Kings of Ibouza with the consent of our people and with the view of bettering their condition do this day cede to The Company and to their assigns for ever, the whole of our territory but The Company shall pay private owners a reasonable amount for any portion of land that The Company may require from time to time.

2. We thereby give to The Company and their assigns for ever, jurisdiction of every kind, and we pledge ourselves not to enter into any war with other tribes without the sanction of The Company.

3. We also give to The Company and their assigns for ever, the sole right to mine in our territory.

4. In consideration of the foregoing, The Company bind themselves not to interfere with any of the native laws or customs of the country, except so far as may be necessary for good government and the maintenance of order.

In consideration of the above The Company have this day paid the said Kings of Ibouza goods to the value of Twenty-five measures receipt of which is hereby acknowledged.

This agreement having been interpreted to us, the above mentioned Kings of Ibouza, we hereby approve and accept it for ourselves and for our people with their consent, and in testimony of this, having no knowledge of writing, do affix our marks below it and I, W. A. Earnshaw, for and on behalf of The Company do hereby affix my hand.

X Obi Onyayame
X Obi Ebazoa

We the undersigned witnesses
do hereby solemnly declare
that the Kings whose names
are placed opposite their
respective marks have
in our presence affixed
their marks of their own
free will and consent
and the said W. A. Earnshaw
has in our presence affixed
his signature
(Sgd.) G. W. Molony
    Sub Commander, R.N.
    Constabulary
(Sgd.) N. Robert Taylor
Diplomatic Agent

(Sgd.) W. A. Earnshaw
    Senior Executive Officer
    for Igarra & Anambara
    Districts

X Obi Okudi
X Obi Omoo
X Obi Wanpafari
X Obi Ezuebunem
X Obi Obachi
X Obi Kedi
X Obi Dogar
X Obi Aneyoan
X Obi Atona
X Obi Wanodi
X Obi Eraquay
X Obi Moderi
X Obi Mengen
X Obi Uchaloa
X Obi Aneamanam
X Obi Wanzea
X Obi Tyom
X Obi Chiquay

Declaration by Interpreter

I Nathanial Robert Taylor native of Sierra Leone do hereby solemnly declare that I am well acquainted with the Ibouza language and that on the 17th day of May 1889 I truly and faithfully explained the above agreement to all the native signatories whose marks are affixed to this treaty and that they understood its meaning.

(Sgd.) N. Robert Taylor

Appendix Three

Treaty made on the tenth day of April 1897, between the King and Chiefs of Agbor on the one hand, and The Royal Niger Company, Chartered and Limited, for themselves and their assigns, for ever, hereinafter called "The Company," on the other hand

1. WE, the undersigned king and chiefs of Agbor, with the view of bettering the condition of our country and people, do this day cede to The Company, including as above their assigns, for ever, the whole of our territory, but The Company shall pay private landowners a reasonable amount for any portion of land that The Company may require from time to time.

2. WE thereby give to The Company and their assigns, for ever, full jurisdiction of every kind, and we pledge ourselves not to enter into any war with other tribes without the sanction of The Company.

3. We give to The Company and their assigns, for ever, the sole right to mine in any portion of our territory.

4. We bind ourselves not to have any intercourse as representing our tribe or state, on tribal or state affairs, with any person or persons other than The Company, who are hereby recognized as the authorized Government of our territories; but this provision shall not be interpreted as authorizing any monopoly of trade, direct or indirect, by The Company or others, nor any restriction of private or commercial intercourse with any person or persons, subject, however, to such administrative measures as may be taken by The Company in the interests of commerce and of order.

5. IN consideration of the foregoing, The Company bind themselves not to interfere with any of the native laws or customs of the country, consistently with the maintenance of order and good government, and the progress of civilization.

6. THE Company bind themselves to protect, as far as practicable, the said king and chiefs from the attacks of any neighboring aggressive tribes.

7. IN consideration of the above, The Company have this day paid the said king and chiefs of Agbor a donation, receipt of which is hereby acknowledged.

THIS Treaty having been interpreted to us, the above-mentioned king and chiefs of Agbor, we hereby approve and accept it for ourselves and for our people, and in testimony of this, having no knowledge of writing, do affix our marks below it.

	King Gbenobar	his X mark
WE, the undersigned	Chief Ashima Onisa	his X mark
witnesses, do hereby solemnly	Chief Oriba Isamah	his X mark
declare that the king and	Chief Elunuse Ofijah	his X mark
chiefs whose names are placed	Chief Okobai Ison	his X mark
opposite their respective	Chief Aku Edeh	his X mark
marks, have in our	Chief Oko Azamah	his X mark
presence affixed their marks	Chief Osudeh Owehi	his X mark
of their own free will and	Chief Noka Agbar	his X mark
consent, and that	Chief Tozar	his X mark
JOSEPH FLINT	Chief Osaji Osodeh	his X mark
on behalf of The Company,	Chief Okuboh Ekuagbar	his X mark
has in our presence affixed	Chief Apatta	his X mark
his signature	Chief Okunnuh	his X mark

(SGD.) Frederick Chaplin
      Resident Agent
(SGD.) L. V. Meadows, Resident Agent   JOSEPH FLINT

> for and on behalf of The Company, do hereby approve and accept the above Treaty, and hereby affix my hand.
>   (Sgd.) Joseph Flint—Agent-General

Declaration by Interpreter

I, Isaac Thomas Palmer native of Sierra Leone do hereby solemnly declare that I am well acquainted with the Ibo language, and that on the tenth day of April 1897, I truly and faithfully explained the above Treaty to all the native signatories, and that they understood its meaning.

Signature or mark of interpreter   (Sgd.) Issac T. Palmer

Witnesses to the above
(Sgd.) Frederick Chaplin
(Sgd.) L. V. Meadows

Done in triplicate at Utshi this Seventh day of April, 1897.

Abbreviations

ADC Assistant District Commissioner
ADO Assistant District Officer
CMS Church Missionary Society
CO   Colonial Office (London)
DC   District Commissioner
DMO District Medical Officer
DO   District Officer
NAE National Archives Enugu (Nigeria)
NAI National Archives Ibadan (Nigeria)
PRO Public Record Office (London)
RCM Roman Catholic Mission
RNC Royal Niger Company
SMA Societé de Missions Africaines
         (Society of African Missions Archives, Rome)

BIBLIOGRAPHY

ORAL SOURCES
Interviews were conducted by the author in Nigeria at different times between 1974 and 1985.

ARCHIVAL MATERIALS LOCAL GOVERNMENT ARCHIVES, BENIN CITY
Some intelligence reports can be found at the Ministry of Local Government, Benin City. However, most of these reports are duplicated at the National Archives, Ibadan. Among those I consulted at the Benin City Archives are:

Beeley, J. H. "Intelligence Report on the Illah Village Group." File No. 15346A, March 1938.
"Ezechima Clan Administration: Instructions Concerning." File No. A.D. 632/A, November 13, 1944.
Jull, J. E. "Intelligence Report on the Akwukwu Village Group." File No. 1748C, April 1936.
———. "Intelligence Report on the Ogwashi-Ukwu Clan." File No. 1568C, April 1936.
Keer, R. N. "Intelligence Report on the Ibusa and Okpanam Clans." File No. 13402, April 1937.
Marshall, H. F. "Intelligence Report on the Ute-Okpu Clan of the Agbor District." File No. 13345, July 1936.
Miller, E. A. "Intelligence Report on Abo." File No. 26769, April 1931.
Vaux, H. "Intelligence Report on the Asaba Clan." File No. 188A, November 1934.
Whiting, N. E. "Intelligence Report on the Owa and Idumuase Clans." File No. 13301, April 1936.

NIGERIAN NATIONAL ARCHIVES, IBADAN
This group includes CSO papers relating to the colonial period, especially the Intelligence Reports on the various Western Igbo communities. Not all the files consulted were used in this work, and H. Vaux, "Intelligence Report

on Asaba," is cited again because it contains more information than the duplicated file held at Benin City.

Danton, H. C. B. "Intelligence Report on the Ute Okpu and Ute-Ogbeje of Agbor District, Asaba Division, 1931-4." ASA DIV, 9/1.
Mackey, J. B. Kwale District File 62/1, D. O. Kwale to Resident, 1928.
Shelton, H. "Intelligence Report on the Kwale Ibo Clan, 1933" (with an introduction by Mallison, the Resident). CSO/26 No. 29300.
Simpson, J. M. "Intelligence Report on the Agbor, Oligie and Emuhu clans, Agbor District, 1935." CSO 26/4, No. 3038X.
Vaux, H. "Intelligence Report on the Asaba, 1936." CSO/26, No. 30927.
Williams, G. B. "Intelligence Report on the Ibo-speaking Clans of the Kwale Division, Warri Province, 1931." CSO 26/3, No. 26769, Vol. 1.
Woodhouse, F. M. "Intelligence Report on the Nsukwa Native Court Area, 1936" (with an introduction by Mr. Maddocks). SSO 26/4, No. 30693.

PUBLIC RECORD OFFICE (PRO), LONDON

The relevant Foreign Office and Colonial Office documents consulted include the following:

F.O. 2, volumes 167 and 178
F.O. 84, volumes 1487 and 2019.
F.O. 403, volumes 16-269.
C.O. 520, volumes, 2-131.
C.O. 583, volumes 10-141.
C.O. 588, volumes 1-6.

RHODES HOUSE LIBRARY, OXFORD

MSS. Afr. 701.17 S4/6 Brass Inquiry, 1895.
MSS. Afr. 100.441 S12/1930 (3) Colonial Office. Papers relating to labor conditions in the Colonies, Protectorates and mandated territories.
MSS. Afr. S.544, Butcher H. L. The Ika-Ibo people of the Benin Province, Southern Nigeria.
MSS. Afr. S.1505 (8) Harris (Jack). Ibo Papers, 1938-39, typescript.
MSS. Afr. S.413, Marshall (H. H.). Intelligence Report on the Ika etc.

THE CHURCH MISSIONARY SOCIETY (CMS) ARCHIVES, LONDON

Documents consulted include those in the series G3/A3, CA3, and CA3/04. In addition, useful information was collected from the relevant issues of *The Church Missionary Intelligencer,* and *Niger and Yoruba Notes.*

The Society of African Missions Archives, Rome

In addition to manuscripts, the Society of African Missions Archives holds valuable periodicals, unpublished theses, books, and other relevant printed materials. The following were consulted and used in this work:

14/.80302, letters, mainly from heads of the Mission to the Superior General.
14/80303, letters and reports from the missionary holding the office of visitor to the mission.
14/80404/15794, Strub, "Le Vicariat Apostoloque de la Nigerie Occidentale depuis sa foundation jusqu'a nos jours" (1928).

Journals of Some Early Fathers of the Diocese of Benin City
trans. from the French by Father J. J. Hilliard.

Missionary Endeavor in the Diocese of Benin City from its Foundation to the Present Day. Comp. Father J. J. Hilliard.

Others include:

L'Echo des Missions Africaines de Lyon. The African Missionary, Annals of the Propagation of the Faith, les Missions Cathliques (English version, Illustrated Catholic Mission), *EXIIT.*

UNPUBLISHED THESES, DISSERTATIONS AND RESEARCH PROJECTS

Ekwu, A. "The Establishment of the Catholic Mission in Western Nigeria by the Society of African Missions, 1868-1920." Ph.D. diss., University of Vienna, 1967.
Ifemesia, C. C. "British Enterprise on the Niger, 1830-1869." Ph.D. thesis, University of London, 1959.
Ijoma, J. O. "Igbo-Edo Borderland before 1897." Ph.D. thesis, University of Birmingham, 1978.
Ogedengbe, K. O. "The Aboh Kingdom of the Lower Niger, c. 1650- 1900." Ph.D. diss., University of Wisconsin, 1971.
Ojiakor, N. E. "A Cultural History of Ogbaru Community of the Lower Niger." Research Project, History Department, University of Jos, 1982.
Onianwa, C. N. "The Coming of Christianity to Asaba." Research Project, History Department, University of Jos, 1980.
Walsh, M. J., "Catholic Contribution to Education in West Africa, 1861-1926." Unpublished thesis, S.M.A. Archives, Rome.

BOOKS

Afigbo, A. E. *The Warrant Chiefs: Indirect Rule in Southern Nigeria, 1891-1929.* Ibadan, 1972.
Allen, W. and Thomson, T. R. N. *A Narrative of the Expedition to the River Niger in 1841.* 2 vols. London, 1884.
Anene, J. C. *Southern Nigeria in Transition, 1885-1906.* Cambridge, 1966.
Anstey, R. *The Atlantic Slave Trade and British Abolition, 1760-1810.* London, 1975.
Asiegbu, J. *Nigeria and its British Invaders, 1851-1920.* New York, 1984.
Ayandele, E. A. *The Missionary Impact on Modern Nigeria, 1842-1914.* London, 1968.
Baikie, W. B. *Narrative of an Exploring Voyage up the River Kwora and Benue in 1854.* London, 1856.
Basden, G. T. *Among the Ibos of Nigeria.* London, 1921.
Bernet, D. L., and Njama, K. *Mau Mau from Within: Autobiography and Analysis of Kenya's Peasant Revolt.* New York and London, 1966.
Buijtenhuijs, R. *Essays on Mau Mau: Contributions to Mau Mau Historiography,* Leiden, 1982.
Chinweizu. *The West and the Rest of Us.* New York, 1978.
Cook, A. R. *British Enterprise in Nigeria.* London, 1964.
Crowder, M., ed. *West African Resistance: The Military Response to Colonial Occupation.* London, 1971.
Crowther, S. A. *Journal of an Expedition up the Niger and Tshadda Rivers in 1854.* London, 1970.
⎯⎯⎯⎯ and Taylor, J. C. *The Gospel on the Banks of the Niger.* London, 1868.
Curtin, P. D. *The Image of Africa: British Ideas and Action 1780-1850.* Madison, 1964.
⎯⎯⎯⎯ *The Atlantic Slave Trade: A Census.* Madison, 1969.
Dike, K. O. *Origin of the Niger Mission, 1814-1891.* Ibadan, 1962.
⎯⎯⎯⎯ *Trade and Politics in the Niger Delta, 1830-1885.* Oxford, 1966.
Egharevba, J. *A Short History of Benin.* Ibadan, 1968.
Ekechi, F. K. *Missionary Enterprise and Rivalry in Igboland, 1857-1914.* London, 1971.
Esedebe, P. O. *Pan-Africanism.* Enugu, 1980.
Fage, J. D. *A History of West Africa.* Cambridge, 1969.
Fanon, F. *The Wretched of the Earth.* New York, 1977.
Flint, J. E. *Sir George Goldie and the Making of Nigeria.* Oxford, 1960.
Ford, D., and Jones, G. I. *The Ibo and Ibibio-speaking peoples of South Eastern Nigeria: Ethnographic Survey of Africa.* London, 1950.

Freund, B. *Capital and Labour in the Nigerian Tin Mines.* London, 1981.
Gemery, H. A., and Hogendorn, J. S., eds. *The Uncommon Market: Essays in the Economic History of the Atlantic Slave Trade.* London, 1979.
Grace, J. *Domestic Slavery in West Africa.* London, 1975.
Gutkind, P., and Wallerstein, I. eds. *The Political Economy of Contemporary Africa.* London, 1976.
Gwassa, G. C. K. and Iliffe, J., eds. *Records of the Maji Maji Rising.* Part 1. Nairobi, 1969.
Halet, R., ed. *The Niger Journals of Richard and John Lander.* London, 1965.
Helleiner, G. O. *Peasant Agriculture, Government and Economic Growth in Nigeria.* Homewood, 1966.
Henderson, R. N. *The King in Every Man.* New Haven and London, 1972.
Home, R. *City of Blood Revisited: A New Look at the Benin Expedition of 1897.* London, 1982.
Hopkins, A. G. *An Economic History of West Africa.* London, 1973.
Ifemesia, C. C. *South-eastern Nigeria in the Nineteenth Century: An Introductory Analysis.* New York, 1978.
Igbafe, P. I. *Benin Under British Administration: The Impact of Colonial Rule on an African Kingdom, 1897-1938.* London, 1979.
Ikime, O. *Merchant Prince of the Niger Delta.* Ibadan, 1971.
_____ *The Fall of Nigeria.* London, 1977.
_____, ed. *Groundwork of Nigerian History.* Ibadan, 1980.
Isichei, E. *A History of the Igbo People.* London, 1976.
_____ *The Igbo People and the Europeans.* London, 1973.
_____, ed. *Studies in the History of Plateau State, Nigeria.* London, 1982.
Isaacman, A., and Isaacman, B. *The Tradition of Resistance in Mozambique: The Zambesi Valley, 1850-21.* Berkeley, 1976.
_____ *Mozambique: From Colonialism to Revolution, 1950-1982.* Westview, 1983.
Kaniki, M. H. Y., ed. *Tanzania Under Colonial Rule.* London, 1979.
Kanya-Forstner, A. S. *The Conquest of the Western Sudan, A Study in French Military Imperialism.* Cambridge, 1969.
Kimble, G. M. T. *Esmeraldo do situ orbis.* London, 1973.
Koelle, S. W. *Polyglotta Africana.* London, 1854. Reprinted with a new introduction by P. E. Haire. Graz, Austria, 1963.
Laird, M., and Oldfield, R. A. K. *Narrative of an Expedition into the Interior of Africa by the River Niger.* 2 vols. London, 1837.
Lander, R., and Lander, J. *Journal of an Expedition to Explore the Course and Termination of the Niger.* 2 vols. New York, 1858.

Last, M. *The Sokoto Caliphate.* London, 1967.
Leonard, A. G. *The Lower Niger and Its Tribes.* London, 1968.
Leys, N. *Kenya.* 4th ed. London, 1973.
Lloyd, C. *The Search for the Niger.* London, 1937.
Louis, R., ed. *Imperialism: The Robinson and Gallagher Controversy.* New York, 1976.
Lovejoy, P. E., ed. *The Ideology of Slavery in Africa.* London, 1981.
———— *Transformations in Slavery: A History of Slavery in Africa.* Cambridge, 1983.
Lupton, K. *Mungo Park: The African Traveller.* Oxford, 1979.
McKenzie, P. R. *Inter-Religious Encounters in West Africa.* Leicester, U.K., 1976.
McPhee, A. *The Economic Revolution in British West Africa.* New York, 1926.
Martin, S. M. *Palm Oil and Protest: An Economic History of the Ngwa Region, Southeastern Nigeria, 1880-1980.* Cambridge, 1988.
Mbaeyi, P. M. *British Military and Naval Forces in West African History, 1807-1875.* New York, 1978.
Miers, S. *Britain and the Ending of the Slave Trade.* London, 1875.
———— and Kopytoff, I. *Slavery in Africa.* Madison, 1977.
————, and Robert, R. eds. *The End of Slavery in Africa.* Madison, 1988.
Mockler-Ferryman, A. F. *Up the Niger: Narratives of Major Claude Macdonald's Mission to the Niger and Benue Rivers.* London, 1892.
Newbury, C. W. *British Policy Toward West Africa, Select Documents, 1875-1914.* 2 vols. Oxford, 1971.
Noah, M. E. *Old Calabar: The City States and the Europeans, 1800-1885.* Uyo, 1980.
Northrup, D. *Trade Without Rulers.* Oxford, 1980.
Nwabara, S. N. *Iboland: A Century of Contact with Britain, 1860-1960.* London, 1977.
Nzemeka, A. *One Hundred Years of Roman Catholic Church at Illah.* Benin, Nigeria, 1980.
———— *British Imperialism and African Responses: The Niger Valley, 1851-1905.* Paderborn, 1982.
Nzimiro, Ikeenna. *Studies in Ibo Political Systems.* London, 1972.
Ohadike, D., and Shain, R., eds. *Western Igbo: Jos Oral History and Literature Texts.* Vol. 6. Jos, 1988.
Oliver, R., and Fage, J. D. *A Short History of Africa.* Harmondsworth, 1962.
Orr, C. *The Making of Northern Nigeria.* With a new introduction by A. H. M. Kirk-Greene. London, 1965.
Osuntokun, A. *Nigeria in the First World War.* London, 1979.

Park, M. *Travels in the Interior of Africa*. New York, 1971.
Ranger, T. O. *Emerging Themes in African History*. Dar es Salam, 1968.
Roberts, R. *Warriors, Merchants, and Slaves: The State and the Economy in the Middle Niger Valley, 1700-1914*. Stanford, 1987.
Robinson, C. M. *Hausaland: Fifteen Hundred Miles Through Central Sudan*. London, 1896.
Robinson, R., and Gallagher, J., with Denny, A. *Africa and the Victorians: The Official Mind of Imperialism*. London, 1961.
Rosberg, C. C., and Nottingham, J. *The Myth of Mau Mau Nationalism in Kenya*. New York, 1966.
Rotberg, R. I., and Mazrui, A. A., eds. *Protest and Power in Black Africa*. Oxford, 1970.
Ryder, A. F. C. *Benin and the Europeans*. London, 1969.
Shaw, T. *Igbo-Ukwu: An Account of Archaeological Discoveries in Eastern Nigeria*. 2 vols. Evanston, 1970.
Tasie, G. O. M. *Christian Missionary Enterprise in the Niger Delta, 1864-1918*. Leiden, 1978.
Thomas, N. *Anthropological Report on the Ibo Speaking People of Nigeria; Part IV: Law and Custom of the Ibo of Asaba Districts*. New York, 1914.
Uchendu, V. C. *The Igbo of South Eastern Nigeria*. New York, 1968.
Uzoigwe, G. N. *Britain and the Conquest of Africa*. New York, 1978.
Wiener, L. *Africa and the Discovery of America*. London, 1971.
William, E. *Capitalism and Slavery*. London, 1975.
Wolf, E. *Peasant Wars of the Twentieth Century*. New York, 1969.

ARTICLES

Afigbo, A. E. "On the Threshold of Igbo History: A Review of Thurstan Shaws's Igbo-Ukwu." *The Conch* 3, no. 2 (1971): 152-64.
———. "Patterns of Igbo Resistance to British Conquest." *Tarikh* 4, no. 3 (1973): 14-23.
Alagoa, E. J. "Long-Distance Trade and States in the Niger Delta." *Journal of African History* 11 (1970): 319-29.
Asiwaju, A. I., and Crowder, M., eds. "Protest Against Colonial Rule in West Africa." *Tarikh* 5, no. 3 (1977): 1-56.
Atanda, J. A. "The Iseyin-Okeiho Rising of 1916: An Example of Sociopolitical Conflict in Colonial Nigeria." *Journal of the Historical Society of Nigeria* 4, no. 4 (1960): 497-514.
Ayandele, E. A. "The Missionary Factor in Northern Nigeria, 1870-1914." *Journal of the Historical Society of Nigeria* 3, no. 3 (1966): 503-22.

Baikei, W. B. "Notes of a Journey from Bida in Nupe to Kano in Hausa Performed in 1862." *Journal of the Royal Geographical Society* 37 (1867): 92-107.

Bender, G. J. "The Limits of Counterinsurgency." *Comparative Politics* 4 (1972): 331-60.

Boston, J. S. "Notes on Contact Between the Igala and the Igbo." *Journal of the Historical Society of Nigeria* 2, no. 1 (1960), 52-58.

Davidson, A. B. "African Resistance and Rebellion Against the Imposition of Colonial Rule." In *Emerging Themes of African History.* ed. T. O. Ranger, 177-88. Dar es Salaam, 1968.

Denzer, L. "Sierra Leone – Bai Bureh." In *West African Resistance.* ed. Michael Crowder, 233-67. New York, 1971.

Ekechi, F. "Traders, Missionaries and the Bombardment of Onitsha, 1879-1880." *The Conch* 5, nos. 1 and 2 (1973): 61-81.

Ekejiuba, F. "Omu Okwei, the Merchant Queen of Ossomari. A Biographical Sketch." *Journal of the Historical Society of Nigeria* 3, no. 4 (1967): 633-46.

Hilliard, J. "Father Zappa and His Mission." *EXIIT* 3, (May 1963):

Hogendorn, J. S., and Lovejoy, P. E. "The Reform of Slavery in Early Colonial Northern Nigeria." In *The End of Slavery in Africa,* ed. Suzanne Miers and Richard Roberts, 391-414. Madison, 1988.

Horton, R. "From Fishing Village to City State: A Social History of New Calabar." In *Man in Africa,* ed. Mary Douglas and Phyllis M. Keberry, 37-58. London, 1968.

─────. "Stateless societies in the History of West Africa." In *History of West Africa,* ed. J. F. A. Ade Ajayi and Michael Crowder, 1:72-113. Cambridge, 1971.

Horton, W. R. A. "The Ohu System of Slavery in a Northern Ibo Village-Group." *Africa* 24 (1954): 311-36.

Igbafe, P. A. "Western Ibo Society and Its Resistance to British Rule: The Ekumeku Movement, 1898-1911." *Journal of African History* 12, no. 3 (1971): 441-59.

─────. "Slavery and Emancipation in Benin, 1897-1945." *Journal of African History* 16, no. 3 (1975): 409-29.

Ikime, O. "The Anti-Tax Riots in Warri Province, 1927-1928." *Journal of the Historical Society of Nigeria* 3, no. 3 (1966):559-73.

─────. "Native Administration in Kwale-Aboh, 1928-1950: A Case Study." *Journal of Historical Society of Nigeria* 3, no. 4 (1967): 663-82.

Iliffe, J. "The Organization of the Maji Maji Rebellion." *Journal of African History* 8, no. 3 (1967): 495-512.

Isichei, E. "Historical Change in an Ibo Polity, Asaba to 1885." *Journal of African History* 10, no. 3 (1969): 421-38.

_____. "The Quest for Social Reform in the Religion: A Neglected Theme in West African History." *African Affairs* 77, no. 309 (1978): 463-78.

Jeffreys, M. D. "The Divine Umundri Kings." *African Magazine* 8 (1935): 346-54.

Kirk-Greene, A. H. M. "A Preliminary Note on New Sources for Nigerian Military History." *Journal of the Historical Society of Nigeria* 3, no. 1 (1964): 129-47.

Letham, A. J. H. "Witchcraft Accusations and Economic Tension in Pre-Colonial Old Calabar." *Journal of African History* 12, no. 2 (1972): 249-60.

Lovejoy, P. "The Volume of the Atlantic Slave Trade: A Synthesis." *Journal of African History* 23, no. 4 (1982): 473-501.

Ohadike, D. C. "The Influenza Pandemic of 1918-19 and the Spread of Cassava Cultivation on the Lower Niger: A Study in Historical Linkages." *Journal of African History* 22, no. 3 (1981): 379-91.

_____. "The Rise of Benin Kingdom and the Settlement of Edo- speaking People in the Igbo Culture Area." *Ivie, Nigerian Journal of Arts and Culture* 1, no. 3 (1986): 19-35.

_____. "The Decline of Slavery Among the Igbo People." In *The End of Slavery in Africa*. ed. Suzanne Miers and Richard Roberts, 437-61. Madison, 1988.

Onwuejeogwu, M. O. "Nri Activities and Their Relationship to Igbo Civilization." *The Journal of Odinani Museum* 1, no.1 (March 1972): 9-14.

Oriji, J. N. "A Re-assessment of the Organization and Benefit of the Slave and Palm Produce Trade Amongst the Ngwa-Igbo." *Canadian Journal of African Studies* 16, no. 3 (1982): 523-48.

Ottenberg, S. "Ibo Receptivity to Change." In *Continuity and Change in African Cultures,* ed. William Bascom and Melville J. Herskovits, 130-143. Chicago, 1959.

Person, Y. "Samori and Resistance to the French." In *Protest and Power in Black Africa* ed. R. I. Rotberg and A. A. Mazrui, 80-112. Oxford, 1970.

Ranger, T. O. "Connections Between Primary Resistance Movements and Modern Mass Nationalism in East and Central Africa." Parts 1 and 2. *Journal of African History* 9, nos. 3 and 4 (1968): 437-53 and 631-41.

Robinson, R. "Non-European Foundations of European Imperialism: Sketch for a Theory of Collaboration." In *Imperialism: The Robinson and Gallagher Controversy,* ed. William Roger Louis, 128-51. London, 1976.

Ryder, A. F. C. "The Benin Mission." *EXIIT* 4 (May, 1964):

Temu, A. J. "Tanzanian Society and Colonial Invasion, 1875-1907." In *Tanzania Under Colonial Rule,* ed. M. H. Y. Kaniki, 86-127. London, 1979.

Terray, E. "Long-District Exchange and the State: The Case of the Abron Kingdom of Gyaman." *Economy and Society* 3 (1974): 315-45.

Toner, M. "A Co-operative in Nigeria." *EXIIT* 3 (1963):
Ukpabi, S. C. "The Origins of the West African Frontier Force." *Journal of the Historical Society of Nigeria* 3, no. 3 (1966): 485-501.

INDEX

Abala, 115
Abbi, 158-60
Aboh, 21, 24, 27-29, 33-34, 37, 45, 47, 49-54, 56-57, 63, 66-67, 75, 83, 99, 172, 175-80
Aboh (bombardment of), 52, 56, 58-59, 66
Aboh merchants, 29, 52-54, 56, 175
African Association, 46, 48
Age-grade (associations), 22-23, 30
Aguobasimi [Chief] (son of Ovonramwen, exiled king of Benin), 149
Ani-Udalla, 109
Akpoma, 109, 135-36
Akwukwu, 13, 102-03, 106, 109, 117-18
Alenso, 54, 67
Amai, 155-56, 158
Amebu, 155
Anifekide, 84
Aniocha, 2, 11, 21, 62, 88, 114, 147
Aro, 2
Arogun, 159
Asaba, 14, 16, 21-22, 24, 29, 33, 35, 37-38, 47, 50, 53, 61-62, 64-68, 70-76, 82-85, 87-90, 99, 101, 104-06, 108-09, 113-14, 120, 124, 133-34, 137, 139, 143
Ashama, 115
Atlantic Slave Trade, 23, 25-26, 28, 168
Attah (Igala), 50, 53, 57, 65
Awuno Ugbo (the Obi of Akumazi), 101
Azungwu, 134
Bai Bureh, 81
Baikie, Dr. William Belfour, 49, 51
Basden, A. T., 99-100
Benin, 6-9, 23-25, 83, 99, 116, 129, 147-50, 152-54, 159, 170
Benin Kingdom, 6, 23, 149
Berlin Conference (1884-85), 69
Bida, 34, 95
Bingi of Ogan (Chief), 150
Bonny, 33, 37, 50
Brass, 27, 47, 50-51, 53, 70, 74, 83, 91-92
British abolition, 45-46
British conquest of Asaba, 65-76
British gunboat diplomacy, 45, 50-51
Buck, Rev. John, 64-66
Buxton, Thomas F., 46-47
Captain Burr (of the Warship *Pioneer*), 55

Captain Caree, 109
Captain Haywood, 157
Captain Ian Hogg, 121, 123
Captain Lake (a Liverpool merchant), 47
Captain Purcell, 135-37
Captain Rudkin, 152
Captain Sheffield (officer commanding the Ogwashi-Ukwu expedition), 131, 134-35, 137, 139
Captain Vassal (a commanding officer), 157
Captain Wilson, D. E. (officer in charge of Kwale patrol), 159
Chamberlain (colonial secretary), 93
Chichester (district commissioner), 109, 154
Chidi (mother of Obi of Issele-Ukwu), 84-85
Chidi (of Igbuzo), 109
Chiejina (of Onicha-Olona), 101
Church Missionary Society (CMS), 62-66, 71, 73, 75, 99, 102, 105-06, 116, 118, 132
Clapperton, Hugh, 46
Constabulary Forces (of the Royal Niger Company), 70, 74, 105
Coupland-Crawford, W. E. B. (divisional commissioner), 116-18, 120, 123
Cradle of Igbo people, 21
Dr. Craster (of the Royal Niger Company), 89-91
Crewe-Read, S. O., 147, 149-54, 158
Crewe-Read (death of), 150, 158
Crowther, Bishop Samuel Ajayi, 38, 47, 51-53, 63-67, 73
Dark continent, 49
Davidson, J. (assistant district commissioner, Kwale), 118, 156-58
DunKwu (Isusu), 88, 101, 106-108, 118, 124
DunKwu (death of), 124
Ebrohime, 37, 83
Ebu, 90
Egbas (of southwestern Nigeria), 62
Ekumeku, 2-3, 8-9, 11-17, 21, 30, 35, 39, 45, 57, 61-62, 67, 81, 97, 101, 103-11, 113, 118-24, 126, 129-35, 137-41, 144-45, 147-48, 154-55, 167, 169, 171
Ekute (of Owa Oyibu), 151, 153
Elikwu (of Igbuzo), 82, 101, 109
Elumelu (of Onicha-Olona), 101, 107-108
Emu, 160

201

Epidemic of influenza, 162
Eze, 25, 35-36, 38
Ezeanyanwu (of Asaba), 24
Ezi, 86, 88, 90, 104, 107, 109, 117-19
Ezionum, 156-58
Fernando Po, 63
Festing, Lieutenant, 87
First World War and Resistance Movements, 147-63
Forced Labor, 98, 114, 147-48, 155, 167
Fosbery, Widenham, 105-110, 118, 142, 154, 157
Germans on parole, 158
Guerrilla tactics, 9, 15, 131
Harper, Norton (political officer), 139, 142-43
Idah, 27, 33, 50, 57, 65, 83, 129
Idah (bombardment of), 57, 65, 83
Idumuje-Ugboko, 109, 118, 120, 123
Idumuesa, 153
Igbo kinship systems, 22, 24
Igbo warfare, 9
Igbuzo, 14, 16, 19, 25, 35, 73, 82-83, 86-87, 101, 103, 105, 109, 130-31, 135-37, 139, 141, 172, 183
Ika, 2, 21, 147-55, 159
Ikenga (of Asaba), 24
Ike-Onicha, 160
Ikoro (age-grade), 23
Illah, 62, 86, 88-91, 100, 105
Ilorin, 9, 92, 95, 98
Industrial Revolution, 31, 48
Iseyin-Okeiho Rising, 161
Issele-Asaba, 84
Issele-Mkpitimo, 109, 118
Issele-Ukwu, 62, 83-91, 100, 109, 117-19, 154
Islamic Reform Movements, 34
Isuama, 21-22, 28
Jonas, Simon, 63
Keffi, 95
King Boy (an African trader on the Brass River), 47
Kinjikitile Ngwale, 8, 81
Sir John Kirk (inquiry into the Brass attack), 92
Kokori, 156
Kwale, 2, 16, 21, 118, 143, 147-48, 155-61, 164-65
Kwale Uprising, 155-61
Labor Problem (and supply), 36
Lagos; annexation of, 1
Laird, MacGregor, 27, 34, 47

Lander, Richard and John, 27, 46-47, 49-50
Leonard, Arthur G., 53, 89
Lignite Deposits, 114
Lineages (organization of), 22, 24, 39, 129
Lokoja, 6, 27, 33-34, 47, 49-50, 63, 68, 70, 73, 87
Lugard, Lord Frederick, 6, 97-98, 159, 162, 170
Macaulay, Rev. Hugh S., 73
Magic and warfare, 8-9, 81
Major Mackenzie, 109
Marshall, Sir James, 71-72, 75, 93
Master and Servant Proclamation, 114
Mau Mau, 3, 9, 169
McIntoch, David (general manager, West African Company), 55
Medicine men, 8-9, 73
Meri of Agbor-Alesima (Chief), 150
Modi (of Ubulu-Ukwu), 101
Moor, Sir Ralph (High Commissioner), 72, 99-100, 104, 109, 149, 170
Moorhouse, H. C. (a commanding officer), 104, 106, 139, 154, 157-58
Mozambique, 10-11
Mungo Park, 46, 49
Native Courts, 114-15, 125-26, 160, 162
Ndi Eze, 11
Ngoni (of Tanzania), 10
Niger River, 1, 28, 33, 69, 91, 148
Nkwo (of Asaba), 24
Nkwo (of Ubulu-Ukwu), 101
Nnebisi, 24
Northern Nigeria Regiment, 97
Nteje, 24
Nwabuzo Iyogolo (of Ogwashi-Ukwu), 101
Nzekwe (of Ogwashi-Ukwu), 101, 129-43
Obi Ajufo (of Igbuzo), 103, 172
Oba of Benin, 7, 23, 116, 149
Obi Egbuna (of Issele-Ukwu), 84-87, 172
Obi Igweli, 38, 64, 67, 172
Obi of Owa, 150-52
Obiora [Ebora] (of Onicha-Olona), 101, 107
Obi Ossai, 29, 34, 36, 51-52, 63, 172, 175, 179-80
Obi of Ubulu-Ukwu, 25, 90, 101, 115-18, 122-23, 131, 139, 154
Obomkpa, 119
Obosi, 66
Ode-Itsekiri, 37

INDEX

Odiachi (a chief of Issele-Azagba), 106
Odiaka (a chief of Issele-Azagba), 106
Ofogu (of Igbuzo), 82, 101, 109
Ogbaru people, 28
Ogume, 155, 160
Oguta, 33, 37
Ogwashi-Ukwu, 14-15, 83, 86, 101, 104-05, 109, 129-43, 159
Ogwashi-Ukwu Uprising, 129-43
Ogwashi-Uno, 109, 134-36
Okonjor (of Ogwashi-Ukwu), 129-31, 138, 142
Okpai, 28
Okpanam, 73, 82, 84, 90, 105, 132
Old Calabar, 33, 37, 109, 121, 155
Onicha-Olona, 14, 86, 88, 99-100, 104-108, 115, 117-19, 123-24, 133
Onicha-Ugbo, 109
Onicha-Ukwu, 118-19
Onitsha, 21, 24, 28, 34-35, 47, 49-50, 54-56, 61, 64, 66-67, 72, 83, 99, 133, 143, 154
Onitsha (bombardment of), 55-56, 83
Onwuadiaju (of Issele-Azagba), 101, 121
Opobo, 33, 37, 50
Osamala, 24, 37, 54
Otu Ochichi, 11, 13-14, 83, 86-91, 93-94, 99-100
Oturaza, 22-23
Overseas Expeditionary Force, 161
Owa, 2, 147-54, 158, 163
Owa Oyibu, 151-52, 163
Owanta, 151-53
Oweh, 158-60
Palm-oil Production, 37
Palm-oil Trade, 37
Patani, 29, 95
Pereira, Duarte Pacheco, 26-29
Phillips, Rev. Edward K., 64
Probyn, L. (a high Commissioner), 157
Prophets and resistance, 8-9
Provisioning Trade, 26-28, 34
Rio Real (river), 26, 29
Road and Creeks Proclamation, 125
Roberts, R. A. (political officer and senior district commissioner), 131, 133, 136-37
Romaine, Rev. M., 64
Rousselet, Catholic Father, 85, 87-91
Royal Niger Company, 14, 56, 65, 67-71, 75-76, 82, 87-93, 98-100, 103-105, 110, 113, 120, 132, 155, 183, 187

Salt making (decline of), 27
Schon, James F., 63
Sheffields, G. Nelson (Captain), 131, 134-35, 137, 139
Shona/Ndebele, 3
Sierra Leone, 62-64, 68, 81, 130, 185, 188
Silent Ones (otu ekwunokwu), 2, 13, 15, 101, 169
Slave markets, 34
Slaves (trading), 26, 29-30, 33-34, 36-38, 46, 50-51, 57, 175-76
Slaves (treatment of), 38-39
Slave Villages (ugwule), 38-39, 76, 115
Sokoto Caliphate, 6-8
Southern Nigeria Regiment, 97, 114, 155
Spencer, Rev. Julius, 76, 83-85, 110, 116
Suppression of Slavery, 114
Taubman, George Goldie, 68-69, 92
Taylor, Rev. John Christopher, 61, 64
Theory of collaboration, 4
Title (association), 22, 25, 35-38, 102
Title taking, 35
Turé, Samori, 3, 9
Ubulu-Okiti, 84, 115
Ugbo (a chief of Issele-Azagba), 106, 109
Ubulu-Ukwu, 14, 25, 83, 86, 90, 101, 109, 115-18, 120-23, 126, 131, 139, 154
Ubulu-Ukwu (a visit to—1878), 116
Ubulu-Uno, 115
Ukwuani (Kwale), 2, 21, 147-48, 155, 158
Ukwunzu, 86, 118-19
Umannah, 160
Umejei (of Igbuzo), 82, 101, 109
Umunede, 149-50, 152
Umunri; kingship system, 25
Unlawful Societies Ordinance, 140
Utagba, 160
Ute-Okpu, 149, 152-54
Uwechua (of Igbuzo), 82, 109
Voigt, Rev. Father, 100
Wallace, William, 87
Warrant chiefs, 5, 76, 114-17, 171
Wase, 95
West African Company, 54-55, 68
West African Frontier Force, 70, 76, 97, 100
Whiteman's grave, 47
Yoruba, 23-24, 36, 61-63, 71, 98, 158, 162
Zappa, Father Carlo, 84-87, 89, 91, 132-33, 140-41

About The Author

Don C. Ohadike hails from Igbuzo (Ibusa) in the Aniocha District of Western Igboland of southern Nigeria. After earning his bachelor's degree in History and Archaeology in 1975 from the University of Nigeria, Nsukka, he journeyed to England where he earned a master's degree at the University of Birmingham in 1977. He spent most of 1978 and 1979 in England researching at the Public Record Office and the CMS Archives in London and at the Rhodes House Library in Oxford. He later returned to Nigeria to earn his doctorate at the University of Jos. Don Ohadike has taught at the University of Port Harcourt and later at the University of Jos where he rose to the ranks of Senor Lecturer and Head of History Department. He has also been a visiting scholar at Northwestern and Stanford. Ohadike now teaches courses in African History at Cornell University. His research interests include pre-colonical African History, Contemporary African History and Politics, and African Labor and Economic History.